# Cairo collages

Manchester University Press

# Cairo collages

Everyday life practices after the event

Mona Abaza

Manchester University Press

Published by Manchester University Press
Altrincham Street, Manchester M1 7JA
www.manchesteruniversitypress.co.uk

British Library Cataloguing-in-Publication Data
A catalogue record for this book is available from the British Library

ISBN    978 1 5261 4511 6    hardback

First published 2020

Typeset
by Toppan Best-set Premedia Limited
Printed in Great Britain
by TJ International Ltd, Padstow

# Contents

# Figures

# Acknowledgements

The list of people who contributed to this work is extensive. I would like to begin by thanking the residents of the building of Doqi, in particular Mrs M.'s family, for their unlimited support, the shopkeepers who rent the front space of the Doqi building as stores, the building keeper and his family, the garage keeper, and the rubbish collector, because they are the main characters on the stage of this theatre play. For the sake of intellectual integrity, they must remain anonymous. I would like to dedicate this book, though, to my neighbour, who became a dear friend, the late Ali Sharaawi, who passed away in November 2018. I wish to mention him by name to honour him, and acknowledge his relentless efforts at solving the interminable, unsolvable, hair-raising problems of the building, which we as residents collectively faced. Ali's dedication and patience are truly missed. He was the spiritual pillar that held this edifice together. It was Ali whom I phoned first when the 'little' disasters happened because I knew that I could fully rely on him. Ali had the gift of communicating with everybody. During the year just before his death, Ali did transform the building through a massive upgrading. He consistently complained that this exasperating edifice took so much of his energy, often stating that it dramatically affected him physically. Unfortunately, Ali's health failed him while he was in his mid-sixties. A number of his friends and neighbours thought that he was perhaps slightly exaggerating when he bitterly complained about the fact that the building would eventually kill him. Some neighbours thought that he was perhaps a hypochondriac. However, as it turned out, there was a certain truth in his words ... Although I disagreed once in a while with the way Ali solved the problems, I could hardly ever get angry with him. Ali was the living memory of the place. We talked on the phone for hours to exchange information about the building, while he knew that I was writing notes for the book. He had promised to sit with me so that I could record the history of the departed residents, an idea that unfortunately never materialised.

I wish to thank Michael Burawoy, who with great perseverance tirelessly encouraged me to continue my project. When Michael visited Cairo during the first violent Mohamed Mahmud incidents in November 2011, he was supposed to give a series of public lectures, which were cancelled because they were to take place on the old Tahrir campus, while Tahrir Square was experiencing violent confrontations and killings. We ended up instead going to Tahrir Square together with Samia Mehrez. Michael and I wandered around Downtown every single day he was in Cairo. With Michael, we lived a unique and dreamlike moment of the *dérive* of the city, in an effervescence that I have attempted to convey in the first chapters.

Leila Zaki Chakravarti, a dear friend with whom I share so many affinities and sentiments, enriched me not only with invaluable intellectual discussions, gifts, books, and generous advice on long lists of readings I discovered through her, but she also thoroughly read the entire manuscript. The final outcome of this work is the result of an ongoing dialogue and intensive exchange with her, not only of ideas but of amulets invoking good spirits. Leila's relentless critical eye remains unfailingly present throughout the entire work.

Catherine Farhi (and Jean-Jacques), Gisela Romain (and André), Huda Lutfi, Malak Varichon, Marlis Weissenborn, Samia Mehrez, Samia Mohi Eddin, Heba Yassine, and Christel Faber remain my precious treasure in women's solidarity, who rescued me at various hard moments in my life. Nadim Spiridon gave me so much courage and hope in life.

Far away in the United States, and yet so near to me, are Jennifer Robertson and Celeste Brusati, whose worthy advice in managing my illness, and their moral support, never failed me. Sam and Martha Peterson, my late mother's close friends in the US, have given me tremendous moral support. I thank them for the wonderful time and inspiring discussions we had in Malmö. Galila El Kadi's expertise as an architect, the endless discussions we shared, the ideas I borrowed, and the exchange of notes on our respective prosaic buildings, the failing elevators together with the predictable accidents that followed, the numerous visits to the police stations, and the noisy commercial rentals united us in sardonic comparisons for a number of years. I also dedicate this work to the memorable summer 2018 we spent together in Aix-en-Provence.

Soraya al-Torki and Shahrokh, Magda Baraka, Shukri Fuad, and Rosemary and Hani Thabet were my *fuul* and *ta'miyya* breakfast companions at the Gezira Club. These breakfasts brought me happiness and a cheerful lightness of being in the dark comedy I was living.

In Berlin, a number of friends made my life more enjoyable: Irene and Raman Revri, Daniele and Stephan Nobbe, Peter and Ina Heine, and Claudia Ehle; Noha and Franck Mermier for the elective affinities we share on the urban appreciations of the Middle Eastern cities; Dina al-Khawaga for her sharp observations; and Laila Bahaa Eddin.

Stephan Guth and Elena Chitti are to be thanked for inviting me to present parts of this work at a conference at the Department of Culture Studies and Oriental Languages, Oslo University, in 2016. Anke von Kugelgen and Monica Corrado encouraged me to write for the *Festschrift* of Reinhard Schulze. I would like to thank a number of scholars from the editorial staff of *Theory,*

*Culture and Society* for their patience and guidance in revising the articles and for encouraging me to write a series of articles on Cairo after 2011. A special thanks to Mike Featherstone, Simon Douwes, Roy Boyne, Ryan Bishop, AbdouMaliq Simone's inspiring work and encouragement to write for him, Joshua Synenko, Lars Meiers and Lars Frers, and Lori Marso for the extensive feedback and collaboration.

Mohamed ElShahed published a series of articles in *Cairobserver* about my students describing their neighbourhoods in the course I taught on 'Cairo Collage' in 2016. A special thanks to Doa Keddah and Salwa Yehya Salman; Jim Logan for his brilliant description of the Masakin al-Gamea quarter, which was of great inspiration to the class; and Maria Fernandez Vivancos Marquina, who produced a wonderful work on class, lifestyles, and the history of automobiles in Cairo. Mohamed Shawki Hassan and Omar Omar provided nuanced and intelligent observations on the Sheikh Zayed satellite city. Omar turned out to be an excellent guide for our class in touring Sheikh Zayed and its grandiose shopping centre.

Johanna Baboukis has been extremely patient with my endless alterations of the text. She did a superb job with editing and revising the manuscript. Noha Fikri is thanked for the bibliography. Anne Marie Willis let me use from her collections the photograph of Frank Hurley titled 'Looking over modern residential part of Cairo, El Duqqi, from above English Bridge to the Pyramids [picture]: [Cairo, Egypt, World War II]' created and published between 1938 and 1945; the National Library of Australia granted permission to reproduce the photograph in the book (Figure 15). Finally, I am grateful for the sharp and unrelenting criticism of my daughter, Laura Stauth, who constantly warned me that my repetitions and fixations were a sign of ageing, if not an unconscious somatising that has to be worked out through writing. Laura remains my charming and delightful *garde-fou*; I thank her for her anthropological instinct and wit in redirecting me after derailing. I wish also to thank Robert Byron from Manchester University Press for his support and invaluable efforts in materialising this project and the anonymous reviewers' sharp reports that certainly refocused and improved the text.

Some ideas developed in this book have been published in the following works: 'Public space in Cairo: Dubai contra Tahrir', *Contemporary Political Theory* 15 (2016), 427–35, https://doi.org/10.1057/s41296–016–0012-z, published online 30 June 2016; 'Violence, dramaturgical repertoires and neo-liberal imaginaries', *Theory, Culture and Society* 33:7–8 (2016), 111–35; 'Cairo: Restoration and the limits of street politics', *Space and Culture* (2017), 1–21; 'Cairo after the event: Fiction and everyday life', in F. Zemmin, J. Stephan, M. Corrado, and A. von Kugelgen (eds), *Eine Festschrift für Reinhard Schulze* (Leiden: Brill, 2018); 'Memory expurgation? Cairo: A comment on photographs', *Media Theory*, 7 May 2018. These have all been reworked, as they were the prelude to this larger work on urban Cairo.

# Introduction

Le quotidien, c'est ce qui nous est donné chaque jour (ou nous vient en partage), ce qui nous presse chaque jour, et même nous opprime, car il y a une oppression du présent. Chaque matin, ce que nous reprenons en charge *au réveil*, c'est le poids de la vie, la difficulté de vivre dans telle ou telle condition, avec telle fatigue, tel désir. Le quotidien, *c'est ce qui nous tient intimement, de l'intérieur.* C'est une histoire à mi-chemin de nous-mêmes, presque en retrait, parfois voilée: on ne doit pas oublier ce 'monde mémoire', selon l'expression de Péguy. Pareil monde nous tient à cœur, mémoire olfactive, mémoire des lieux d'enfance, mémoire du corps, des gestes de l'enfance, des plaisirs. Peut-être n'est-il pas inutile de souligner l'importance du domaine de cette histoire 'irrationnelle' ou de cette 'non-histoire', comme le dit encore A. Dupront. Ce qui intéresse l'histoire du quotidien, c'est l'*invisible*. (De Certeau, Giard, and Mayol, 1994: 11)

(The everyday is what is given to us each day (or comes to us as a shared gift), which urges us every day, and even oppresses us, because there is this oppression of the present. Each morning *when we wake up*, we take up again the weight of life, the difficulty of living in this or that condition, with such fatigue, such a desire. The everyday is *what sustains us intimately, from the inside.* It's a story halfway within ourselves, almost withdrawn, sometimes veiled: we must not forget this 'world memory', in the words of Péguy. Such a world holds us close to its heart, the olfactory memory, memory of childhood places, body memory, childhood gestures, pleasures. Perhaps it is worth emphasising the importance of this realm of 'irrational' history or the 'non-history' as A. Dupront called it. The history of everyday life is about the *invisible*.)

## Why write a book?

The original idea of this book started – like the countless citizens who witnessed the January 2011 revolution – with an unrelenting urge to document the fast-unfolding events that were transforming the urban life of Cairo. Alas, coincidentally, the path of this work took on an entirely different and unexpected course. As time went on, publications on Tahrir flooded the market, and my reluctance to write yet another account of the Egyptian revolution grew by the day. Yet what kept me going at the beginning of the events, when adrenaline was high and emotions unsettled, was the instant and quick writing I did in the form of short photojournalism articles that allowed me

**Figure 1**    Police running away from protesters, Cairo, 28 January 2011.

to maintain a chronology of sorts about particular moments and situations experienced in the streets of Cairo.[1] I clearly recall that after January 2011, the velocity of the successive incidents made me feel deeply defenceless, and often even unaware of what sequences of events were a priority, as I was unable to construct any holistic vision of what was to come. This particular temperament, though, allowed me to write in more spontaneous eruptions, which in the final instance hampered me from bringing into being any extensive analytical work on the grand narrative of the revolution.

As time passed, in particular in the run-up to the summer of 2013 when the military seized overt power under General Sisi, I ended up, like many, grieving over what became apparent then, even though I was amongst those who unambiguously opposed the short rule of the Muslim Brotherhood, which differed little in its authoritarianism from the previous regimes. Perhaps, too, some of the people who share my political affiliations have also come to miss, since Morsi's removal, the euphoric collective temperament of dissent, the biting satire against the rule of the Muslim Brotherhood, and the mes- merising explosion of artistic expressions that paradoxically thrived during their short and much contested reign. Nonetheless, many felt powerless in the overwhelming apolitical, traumatic moment after the killings in Rabe'a al-'Adaweyya Square and the military takeover. In retrospect, I believe that the aftermath of 2013 was a watershed moment of descent into the grave for the spirit of Egypt's 2011 revolution, and also into a collective state of mental depression, combined with a devastating sentiment of failure, not to mention disappointment with the politics dominating the scene. Those who stood in the grey zone of neutrality – who supported neither the Muslim Brotherhood nor the military rule – had no place within the dominant rising populism, which was spurred on by the shrill tone of state propaganda.

On a personal level, this stage was followed by a prolonged period of illness when, in December 2016, I was diagnosed with breast cancer. The years between 2011 and 2014, years that marked the lives of millions of Egyptians for life, were highly emotional, volatile, and yes, quite exciting, but certainly emotionally exhausting. Expectations and dreams for a better life, and especially high aspirations for change, arose with the events of 2011, only to be quickly and violently crushed. Evidently, I was not the sole person who suffered after the event from illness or depression, as so many of my friends, acquaintances, and even strangers I have met seemed to have experienced a similar nemesis. This coincided with a certain set of adverse conditions that forced me to move from a flat I had lived in for seventeen years to the residential island of Zamalek.

## Everyday life and resilience after 2013

Consequently, instead of writing about the grand chronicle of Tahrir, not-withstanding the bloody incidents of Mohamed Mahmud Street in November and December 2011 and 2012, which remain insufficiently documented to this day, I ended up, like millions of others, being swallowed by the draining and exhausting daily life of a city caught up in the aftermath of revolt. Draining but triumphant – a daily life that transformed countless people into all-embracing apolitical subjects. A daily life that turned me into an incessant *jongleur* in trying to manoeuvre the chaos, the constant noise, and the air pollution, all of which resulted in extreme exhaustion, recurrent lung infections, prolonged colds, the impossibly long hours wasted in the daily commute to my work, and the encounters with Herculean bureaucracies requiring infinite, useless streams of paperwork in order to obtain vital documents. It should astonish no one that Cairo recently claimed the status of the second most polluted city in the world, after New Delhi. Not only that, it is the second worst city on the planet for noise pollution. *Cairo's Bad Breath* is the title of one of the most recent and alarming UN environment reports, with its bleak perspective on the way the Government refuses to deal with the aggravating air pollution (Cairoscene Team 2018; CEDEJ 2018). It was no coincidence, then, that I found myself caught up in – or, rather, obsessed about – docu-menting and recording the everyday forms of assault of the nasty soundscape of the street as a personal therapy to overcome a growing and exasperating melancholy.

As time went by, I repeatedly asked myself why I ended up writing about the 'little story', narrating the quotidian of an unnoticed, degenerating, middle-class building in Cairo. Why was I keen on documenting tedious and fairly 'boring' and 'uninteresting' details about rubbish collection and sewage pipelines at a time when I was caught in a mental paralysis, when work on the grander narrative of the revolution was more urgent? And why was I overwhelmed for so long by an intense panic of failure, exhaustion, and disappointment, not only with politics but precisely with existential questions of an uncontrolled feeling of precariousness?

Here I would like to express gratitude to my friend, the anthropologist Leila Zaki Chakravarti, who, after thoroughly reading and commenting on the first draft of the manuscript, made me realise the fact that my erratic psychological state of mind finds intellectual resonance in the field of anthropology of ethics. Leila astutely contextualised the meaning of my obsession with the 'little story' as a kind of an instinctive and logical reaction to post-traumatic syndrome, a longing for 'normalcy' and 'routine' precisely after the tumultuous years that followed 2011. Leila offered me an extensive list of readings, amongst them the prominent and inspiring works of Veena Das, followed by the work of Stef Jansen, who both reflect upon the functionality, indeed the instrumentality, of longing for ordinary daily life in the wake of wars and disasters. In the introduction to her work on violence in India after its partition, Das contemplates the multiple meanings of violence in relationship to the 'event and the everyday' as follows:

> But my engagement with the survivors of riots also showed me that life was recovered not through some grand gestures in the realm of the transcendent but through a descent into the ordinary. There was, I argue, a mutual absorption of the violent and the ordinary so that I end up by thinking of the event as always attached to the ordinary as if there were tentacles that reach out from the everyday and anchor the event to it in some specific ways. (Das 2007: 7)

Das's meditation confirms that the process of the 'descent into the ordinary' is exactly what I was experiencing, even if on a smaller scale,[2] by developing an obsession with accumulating details, connected with an urgency to record, as a sort of lifebelt, to survive the feeling of disappointment that overtook me after 2013.

Stef Jansen (2015) bases his theoretical framework largely upon Das's work. His book on the daily life of an apartment complex in Sarajevo was equally enlightening for me in the way he depicted the residents' longing for 'normalcy' and 'routine' during and after the disrupting moments of a prolonged war in the former Yugoslavia. An intriguing section in Jensen's book, titled 'When buses do not arrive', skilfully describes citizens' reactions to the eternal delays of waiting for the bus to make an appearance. Although they complain about the unaccounted and wasted hours waiting for things to happen, the situation reveals not only their daily endurance in commuting, but also the complex relationship which the unsatisfied citizens maintain with the omnipotent but dysfunctional state that fails to deliver goods to its citizens. Jansen's main concern here is to focus on the question of people's governmentality. He first refers to Sartre's reflections on people waiting for a bus in Paris, which Sartre calls '*séries*', meaning an agglomeration of people representing a plurality of solitudes (Jansen 2015: 65). Then, referring to Alain Badiou, Jansen argues that in theory the *séries* could be turned into a positive and more constructive act of political dissent. This would occur when the bus did not arrive and people would almost console each other about the unbearable state of affairs. Eventually, through the exchange of information at the bus station, they would join forces in a collective act of protest. However, Jansen reverses Badiou's argument to further propose one alternative possibility. He argues that under today's crises, endurance and silence seem to be the main resort for citizens. He seems to be arguing that in the end, in Sarajevo, neither the celebration of endurance nor the muttering of complaints while waiting for the bus would generate any rebellious forms of reciprocity. In reality, what counts most is 'the calibration of routines through city transport – the ways in which it orders everyday lives in particular ways' (Jansen 2015: 70). Oddly enough, my own chapter on the commute to the American University in Cairo, which I had already written prior to reading Jansen's book, conveys a similar exasperated state of mind through personal ruminations, even though the long road to Cairo's Eastern Desert landscape bears little resemblance to Sarajevo's post-war reconstruction.

My yearning for trying to institute a kind of normality in my quotidian life, or even the 'semblance of ordinary life' – as Jansen articulated it and juxtaposed to the violent state of 'abnormality' that various societies experienced in wars like in the former Yugoslavia, or the case of the Palestinians under Israeli occupation – made a lot of sense in view of the conditions of everyday life in Cairo after the 'event'. Deriving inspiration from Das and Jansen, I have concluded that the longing for a kind of normalcy in everyday life can itself turn into a survival strategy. Jansen's interpretation of resilience as a quest for normalcy in daily life could perhaps explain why the text culminated in an exercise in the tedious, even in the 'boring' and the 'non-spectacular' (Jansen's words), as a piece of documentation of a daily routine in my building. Perhaps, too, it was a way of trying to keep sane vis-à-vis a Kafkaesque political situation under an overwhelming military presence in civil life.

Strangely enough, it can be argued that accepting the state of collective amnesia might not be the worst-case scenario, as has previously been suggested. Many Egyptians have turned into apolitical beings in the aftermath of the turmoil of 2011. Many have already withdrawn into an 'inner migration', a kind of enforced 'internal exile' that has metamorphosed us into obedient but self-absorbed beings. On the other hand, a sense of desolation and angst has visibly distracted us, as colleagues leave the country with no intention of returning and friends seize any opportunity to find a job overseas and disappear for good and almost without trace. If they can't make it to the United States or Europe, then hopefully Dubai, Bahrain, or Qatar could become their next lifebelt.

Taking to the streets has become a risky enterprise after 2014, in view of the forced disappearances and massive jailings – unspoken subjects. In what way would resilience be different, then? This question leads me to reflect upon the limits of the performative and theatrical euphoric aspect of the revolution, which mesmerised the world precisely because of its innovative satirical element.[3] While this particular moment in history enriched the image of Cairo's creative chaos as if it were a surreal Bruegelian tableau, how long could a revolutionary liminal moment last? For how long could the power of the street have survived? What timeline can we estimate was needed for the power of mass demonstrations to stand a chance against the violent confrontations and the mounting toll of deaths by the day? How long could the oft-repeated slogan heard in the street have helped keep the revolution alive: 'More blood ought to be spilled in the streets and more martyrs are needed to complete the revolution'? These questions are speculations that attempt to challenge, or even provoke, the issue of the longevity attached to the revolution and the precariousness of the modes of resistance of the recent performative 'Occupy' movements on the global scale. However, while they are certainly unique, these movements have proved ephemeral. Therefore, Tahrir will likely not be duplicated, and even if it were, the fear of unleashing violence from the military against any contemplated insurrection can be clearly foreseen.

Sherry B. Ortner's extensive critique of ethnographic 'thinness', as a counterweight to Clifford Geertz's concept of 'thickness' (meaning 'understanding through richness, texture and detail') as applied to the notion of resistance (Ortner 1995: 174), was another helpful work in deciphering the post-2011 Egyptian context. Ortner reflects upon the complexity, subtlety, and various forms of resistance, when reviewing multiple accounts excavated from the long history of anthropology.[4] She focuses on the diverse interpretations of what is defined as the 'political' in various cultures, in particular in colonial, pre-industrial, and peasant societies. Her aim is to critique the inadequate and conflicting readings of individual and collective forms of resistance under colonial subjugation. She also addresses the question of the resilience of the silent subalterns and how a reconceptualisation of the notion of culture and religion in peasant rebellions implies multifaceted readings in the subtle and variegated exercises of resistance. Ortner also identifies political and cultural authenticity as becoming the major elements in Indian subaltern studies, emphasising that this is 'a major part of its effort to recognize the authentic cultural universe of subalterns, from which their acts of resistance grew' (Ortner 1995: 180–1).

Ortner's reflections on resistance inspire speculation that perhaps heroism persists in the enduring banality of daily life under military authoritarianism – an authoritarianism that parallels the grandiose, inflated neo-liberal urban schemes that address solely the interests of the rich and powerful. One might even dare say that after 2013, the militarisation of everyday life became far more tactile than during the previous and highly contested eras of the Sadat and Mubarak regimes. The military takeover has clearly brought a decisive end to the budding, but weak, constituents of civil society and the dreams of possible change. All oppositional forces and activists were violently crushed; many were sentenced to years of imprisonment; countless young activists, writers, and academics have left the country as exiles as a result.[5] The feeling of moral panic mixed with defeat compelled me, along with other Egyptians who experienced 2011 and its aftermath, to voluntarily 'hibernate' and become part of a passive, submissive, apolitical being.

Yet, if for some people exile meant mental depression and ending up working overseas in poorly paid restaurants for sheer survival, there is a reverse side to the story that still needs to be narrated. For quite a number of activists, the aftermath of 2011 has also meant novel ways of recognition through both Western and Arab media that have focused attention on their biographies and activism. Similarly, a number of graffiti artists became 'stars' to be celebrated by both local and international media, showered with invitations to numerous international forums and exhibitions, and invited to paint murals in a number of European cities in prestigious neighbourhoods and institutions (Abaza 2017). One has to admit that, for quite a number of young activists, the theme of the Arab Spring opened new job markets, participation in endless forums and conferences overseas, and publication outlets not only in the Arab world, in particular Lebanon, but mainly in Europe and the United States. This resulted in an unprecedented international recognition of Egyptian 'activists', such as television satirist Bassem Yussef, who now lives in the United States, and the numerous scholarships and residencies in academia that were given to activists such as Wael Ghoneim, who obtained a scholarship to Harvard (Ghoneim 2018). A significant number of Egyptian activists have landed in Berlin as PhD candidates at the Free University of Berlin, while the city has become an emerging important hub for Egyptian emigrés. The 'singer of the revolution', Ramy Essam, was granted a scholarship in Malmö, which transformed his habitus and persona. It is interesting how the status of the 'revolutionary in exile' metamorphosed Essam's physique in Sweden into a mimicry of the 1960s, hippie, long-hair type. Even as the multiplication of writings on the Arab revolutions became the entrance ticket for an academic career, the intriguing question persists: how would those who remained in Egypt (in particular the ones imprisoned, or impeded from leaving the country) feel about those who left? Resentment, or only envy?

## City of exhaustion

Today's urban momentum might perhaps be described as a post-euphoric Bakhtinian collective trauma: Cairo the inferno, Cairo the city of collective exhaustion (Abaza 2011a ). These observations have been expressed since the notorious Maspero massacre in October 2011, and it continues until the

**Figure 2**   An incident on Mohamed Mahmud Street (Street of the Eyes of
Freedom), 23 November 2012.

current moment. This ongoing claustrophobic collective sentiment emerges
once again in Ian Alan Paul's article on the *Jadaliyya* website (Paul 2015) on
the way in which Cairo's street confrontations in January 2015 created a
concrete physical as well as mental state of 'asphyxia', if not a continuous
'endurance'. This *mal de vivre*, or *le spleen*, as a collective depression, translates
into the unspoken phenomenon of suicide. Some human rights organisations
have pointed to the rising suicide rates in 2018, which they seem to attribute
to unprecedented and unbearable economic hardship for the poor (Arab
Network for Human Rights 2018). In 2015, for instance, according to Egypt's
Central Agency for Public Mobilisation and Statistics, the number of suicides
had already reached some half a million ('Metro is not a suicidal destination',
2018). One of the most poignant incidents, which went viral just five days
before the fourth anniversary of the January revolution in 2015, was the circulation in the media of a picture of a driver who hanged himself out of despair
from a large billboard on the Ismailiyya desert highway (Tarek 2015). The
aggressive advertisements of luxurious villas and compounds on billboards
along the highway epitomise the symbols of the dramatic class cleavages in
Cairo today. Obtaining accurate numbers of suicides is practically impossible,
as suicide is condemned in both the Islamic and Christian faiths, so the true
cause of death often goes unreported by the families of the deceased. However,
the phenomenon has recently caught much attention from human rights

organisations as clear evidence of the rapid, material deterioration that is affecting a silent majority (Hashem 2018).

'The Metro is not a suicidal destination; this phenomenon incurs losses after each case of suicide.' This sentence showcases the official statement issued by the Cairo Metro company after several suicide attempts in the system in summer 2018 ('Metro is not a suicidal destination', 2018), involving mostly very young men and women barely in their twenties.[6] It has been extensively commented upon in sardonic tones in the increasingly silenced alternative social media. The public discussions on suicide in the official press have revealed, not by coincidence, that the prioritisation of law and order, and most of all, the Government's main focus on the flow of traffic, outrank the gravity of the loss of human lives, which, to no one's astonishment, remains trivial and 'unimportant'. Is it a coincidence then that earlier this year, the Metro ticket prices were increased for the second time in a year, from two to seven Egyptian pounds, depending on the length of the commute? Just a year earlier, a ticket cost one pound regardless of the length of the trip (Ismail 2018).

On the other hand, this act of enduring seems to produce remarkably inventive forms of solidarity amongst the poor – to survive, circumvent state authoritarianism, and reshape their unbearable daily lives. Endurance itself is becoming a genuine form, if not *an art of resistance* (Paul 2015). It is an idea that merges with the notion of 'assemblages' and the emerging new fluidities and blurring of spatial borders in the cities of the global South, which, as AbdouMaliq Simone argues, address the notion of 'uncertainty' as the core problematique of contemporary urbanism (Simone 2013: 245). It may be noted here that 'endurance' is equally a concept that Simone developed in analysing how Jakartans negotiated their daily lives (Simone 2015). I see more affinities between Cairo and Jakarta when I read the work of Simone on the dilemma of the descending/declining middle classes, marked by ill-defined and poorly remunerated daily informal economic practices that are quite often labelled as 'bizarre'.[7] Cairo and Jakarta are becoming cities of 'assemblages' of collective endurance (Simone 2013), defined by precariousness in habitat (even for the middle classes), and by precarious life histories as a collective trait of the floating masses.

Discovering Jessica Greenberg's *After the Revolution: Youth, Democracy, and the Politics of Disappointment in Serbia* (Greenberg 2011) was one more consolation, as it provided a convincing explanation for what I perceived as a collective depressed mental state in Egypt. Greenberg bases her theoretical framework on the inspiring concept of the 'politics of disappointment', which was developed by the Serbian student activists who were faced with an unmanageable, incoherent set of practices after the event. Greenberg addresses the issue of how chaotic and emotionally exhausting revolutions are, and how the high aspirations for utopia, which are impossible to achieve, lead to what she describes as a kind of 'contingency of action' (Greenberg 2011: 8).

In fact, in the aftermath of the Arab Spring the discussion of the works of Hannah Arendt and Franz Fanon in Egyptian intellectual milieux raised questions and doubts regarding the linearity of revolutions and resistance, since they seem so often to turn unavoidably to violence. It was often proposed that almost all revolutions were doomed to fail, if failure means that those who rebelled failed to reach power. Meanwhile, it usually takes long decades to seriously evaluate any positive transformations that the revolution might have brought about. This sad path justifies and explains the traumatic move from euphoric utopian dreams to the current dystopian reality.

### Failed state housing policies

More than 12 million people live in Egypt's sprawling informal settlements (slums), over half of them in the Greater Cairo region. Driven into these set-tlements by an acute lack of affordable housing in the cities, they find themselves in homes unsuitable for human habitation or at grave risk because of rockslides, floods, fires, railways, high-voltage wires, open sewerage systems and other threats to their lives and health. Despite daily reminders of the perils, most of them remain where they are, waiting for an alternative they can afford or for the authorities to make sure their homes are safe and adequate through slum upgrading projects. Meanwhile, they strive to connect their homes to water, sewerage and electricity networks and to secure their tenure. (Amnesty International 2011: 1)

So why zoom into the microscopic world of a building into which I had just moved in the Doqi neighbourhood in 2016, if it was not a move in accordance with the major urban reshuffles that the city was undergoing, bringing about devastating and violent transformations? Perhaps what caught my attention was that, although Doqi is still regarded as a middle-class quarter, a significant portion of its middle-class residents who did not manage to leave for more affluent areas are clearly still there because they have experienced a descent in status into 'neither middle class nor poor', a status that Simone and Rao have defined as the new 'in betweens'. They were speaking of recent trans-formations in Jakarta, but the phenomenon certainly applies to Cairo as well (Simone and Rao 2011: 4). These descending middle classes have become much more vulnerable to precarity and uncertainty in their daily lives since 2011. Like the residents of Jakarta, they have been under pressure to reinvent ways of generating income through informal activitivies, such as renting out their own spaces as commercial space and furnished flats to foreigners. Unfortunately, however, a large number of foreigners have left the country and prices have fallen.

Perhaps, too, this tale of mine has turned into an exercise in struggling to address the flagrant paradox of the housing problem in Egypt, as a dynamic example of the process of 'accumulation by dispossession' that David Harvey convincingly demonstrates on the global scale (Harvey 2008: 34). Like never

**Figure 3**  Deserted construction opposite my building, Doqi, 23 December 2017.

before, Cairo abounds with surreal landscapes of unfinished ghost satellite cities and endless deserted cement towers as a symptom of frenetic real-estate speculation, while densely populated, nightmarish 'slums' continue to sprawl, housing not only the deprived, but also a large segment of the educated and professional middle classes including medical doctors, engineers, and professionals. The two landscapes are juxtaposed at the heart of the city. And yet, as Simone and Rao argue, the script that reads the juxtaposition of the 'slum' versus the 'superblock' as a simplistic landscaping of the megacities of the global South has provided policy makers, urban planners, and governments, in some way, with a ready-made comparative narrative, either for nationalist agendas, or for the integration of the city into global markets, or for the need to establish order (Simone and Rao 2011: 3, 4).

The label 'informal settlements', obviously preferred by 'experts' on Egypt instead of the negative connotation of the 'slum', is applied mostly to red-brick high-rise constructions on former agricultural land, which today encompass over 65 per cent of Cairo's population. These informal settlements expose the long years of the State's failure to develop an equitable public housing policy (Séjourné 2009). As the research of Salma Shukrallah and Yahia Shawkat on the ongoing uncontrolled commodification of housing shows, there are in today's 'modern' Egypt some 11.7 million empty apartments that could in principle be occupied by some 50 million people, or more than half of Egypt's population, while in 2016 almost half of Egyptian households were unable to purchase what the authors labelled as 'median priced homes' (Shukrallah and Shawkat 2017).

The story of my building, witnessing at that juncture a massive exodus by a number of its original residents, meant that almost half of the flats were deserted; this presents an account that closely follows these grander lines, narrating the flagrant urban inequalities in post-January 2011 Cairo. Farouq Guweida's article in the semi-official newspaper *al-Ahram* (Guweida 2017: 13) points out the fact that the unprecedented wild competition in real-estate speculation seems to be working as a fortunate entente, as this highly lucrative business is shared between the Government and the private sector controlled by a number of established tycoons. This seems to be one main reason why real-estate prices have soared as they have, reaching surreal figures, far surpassing the markets in metropolises like New York, London, and Paris. The happy few would argue that the hyperbole generated by these replicable global 'evil paradises' (Davis and Monk 2007) for the super-rich, which Mike Davis and Daniel Bertrand Monk have focused on, is far from worrying, since the crash that should follow the hyper-inflated real-estate bubble has not yet occurred and perhaps never will, because this non-productive sector has been booming in Egypt for almost three decades now. Still, Egypt has not yet reached the incredible price of US$90 million for a beach house in the Hamptons (Davis and Monk 2007: 13), so one should remain optimistic.

Guweida begins his article by commenting on the circulating news that some villas in the exclusive resorts of the North Coast of the Mediterranean have recently been purchased for the astronomical price of 110 million Egyptian pounds (L.E.) (roughly US$6 million, at the September 2018 exchange rate), while the cheapest variety within the same compound were sold for 37 million L.E. (roughly US$2 million). In dismay, Guweida laments the fact that almost all of these villas, used for just a couple of months a year as secondary summer residences, are already sold out. When the large majority of the middle classes remains unable to purchase the cheapest public housing flats, at prices that begin at 600,000 L.E., one is led to wonder whether housing should not be a human rights concern for the Government under these acutely degenerating circumstances.

Guweida astutely observes the amazing continuity of the identical neo-liberal policies set in motion by the two previous regimes of Sadat and Mubarak, and which continue unchecked under the current military regime. This is because, if one were to decode post-January 2011 Cairo with the lens of David Harvey's reading of the 'right to the city' or impediments to it (Harvey 2008) – i.e. through the capitalist monopoly of private property that appropriates surplus production – and regarding housing as one main urban resource that needs to be reconsidered in transforming the city we live in, it could be argued that the 2011 revolution has had no real impact on transforming the blatant inequalities in Egyptian urban life. It is surprising, for example, that in spite of the political turmoil the country experienced, specifically the escalating violence and instability in the streets, the real-estate market never collapsed. To the contrary, even during the rule of the Muslim Brotherhood from 2012 to 2013, an unprecedented boom in land speculation was observed. After June 2013 and the massacre in Rabe'a al-'Adaweyya Square, advertisements for villas and flats in gated communities and sea resorts flooded the market. Sea resorts continue to multiply wildly all along the North Coast and the Red Sea, in spite of the unprecedented scale of run-down, failed resorts constructed during the 1990s that resemble war ruins. Except that, in contrast to David Harvey, who argues convincingly that bank credits and the expanding mortgage market turned out to be the two key stabilisers of global capitalism, the problem in Egypt is that no established mortgage and credit systems to finance real estate were developed – thus raising the unanswered question of how such an extravagant real-estate explosion has remained sustainable for such a long time.

We are told that, since not all the rich could move their cash abroad, real estate remains the most lucrative, secure, and quick-profit investment in Egypt. With the sharp devaluation of the Egyptian pound against the US dollar in March 2016, the media have repeatedly pointed to the alarming rocketing real-estate investments. The mega-satellite walled cities 'Dreamland' (Mitchell 2002: 272–304) and 'Utopic',[8] noted by several observers over the past three decades (Mitchell 2002; Kuppinger 2004; Denis 2006: 47–72), continue to boom, supported by aggressive advertising, on endless billboards and TV screens, of virtual landscapes yet to come.

Not only that, but some of the forthcoming gated communities and highly luxurious cities have recently been advertised with the subversive symbols and language of January 2011. 'Join the lifestyle of the revolution' is the advertising catchphrase for the desert satellite Taj City, accompanied by a glamorous picture of a rich young couple in a tango pose, in a pseudo-Versailles setting ('Taj City', 2015).

Various urban experts have pointed to the deregulations through privatisation that are to be expected in the neo-liberal city, and which have mainly
disenfranchised the destitute (Davis 2006a ; Harvey 2008; Bayat 2012), and
Cairo is no exception. It is evident that Cairo witnessed an unprecedented
conquest of the streets and public spaces through the rampant 'passive
encroachment' of the destitute classes (Bayat 2012). Since 2011, a pervasive
and unprecedented public visibility of the subaltern poor has been witnessed
in the various neighbourhoods in the centre of the city. The poor, barely
surviving through informal-sector activities such as mobile food carts, stalls
or spaces for selling drinks, car parking, or simply street vending, have
invaded numerous old residential quarters and are to be seen everywhere,
with the exception, of course, of the walled, segregated spaces. But that is
not the only reason why the rich are leaving the centre. The unresolved
antiquated rental laws, the intrusion of offices, businesses, and cafés into
residential spaces, the massive high-rise buildings that mushroomed after
2011 because of unregulated construction, destroying countless classified
historical buildings – all add to the obvious visual chaos that had already
existed for many decades. It would seem that the post-January 2011 urban
reshaping of Cairo translates today into an unparalleled massive exodus of
the well-to-do to the desert cities, intensifying the process of 'de-densification
of the urban center' (Denis 2006). The heart of the city of Cairo (with the
exception of the project of renovating the *Belle Epoque* Downtown) is falling
into a rapid and unmanageable state of decay.

**Figure 4**    Panorama of Mohamed Mahmud Street, 22 February 2013.

In the end, the exercise of focussing on the microcosmic world of my building became an involuntary step to shield myself from an alienating everyday life.[9] Perhaps, too, right after the eighteen days of occupying Tahrir Square, there was a momentum, or more precisely a popular sentiment, that correlated with the images that travelled around the world: images of the protesters sweeping and cleaning Tahrir Square, the Kasr Al Nil Bridge, and the streets around the square. The public act of cleaning the streets was powerful symbolically. It succeeded in conveying collective dreams of genuine change by starting with small-scale local interventions.

It is important to recall the intense public discussions and meetings after Mubarak was ousted. A number of lively committees were created to focus on activism and collective work on the micro level of neighbourhoods and local communities. The obvious retreat of the State from welfare responsibilities dates back several decades and is not new. It triggered in its wake an unbridled informal sector, clearly observable on all levels of life. 'What is to be done?' was the basic challenge of the activists during the period of the post-January momentum. A number of those who participated in Tahrir struggled to find answers to the failing and impotent role of the State. It paradoxically produced a parallel collective sentiment of empowerment on the local and communal level in the early days of 2011 and 2012, exemplified in the innumerable meetings for founding new parties and the active role of the human rights organisations that monitored the despicable situation in jails. Numerous youth initiatives for creating new job markets grew more assertive. Voluntary associations for assisting the families of the victims, the blinded and the injured of the revolution, and associations to provide services in poor quarters flourished. All these activities channelled the spirit of the uprising during the early days of the revolution. Also, numerous debates triggered by the public visibility of the young activists in the media and television targeted issues connected to the reasons that inspired change. Reforming the police system, keeping checks and balances in the pervasive internal security apparatus, sexual harassment, repression and the authoritarian character, and a number of other acute social and economic problems were openly addressed. But unfortunately this burst of freedom of expression did not last long, giving rise to a long stream of doubts about whether the 2011 revolution had been merely a short-lived upheaval. Even if this were the case, as Paul Amar speculates, even if it was vehemently aborted as a 'social revolution' that was hampered from overthrowing class hierarchies or fostering social equality, it did succeed in instigating change in the political sphere. It did to some extent accomplish a 'revolution in consciousness' (Amar 2013a ), which was outlined by a number of specialists such as Sari Hanafi, Mohamed Bamyeh, and Benoit Challand. Each of these scholars articulated this genesis differently, while arriving at similar conclusions: that, in the end, the revolution did instigate an emerging 'new political subjectivity'.[10]

In contrast, the Zamalek Association was created just after 2011 and became a highly active organisation on the neighbourhood level, launching campaigns for collective clearing of rubbish, cleaning streets, trimming trees, closing down illegal cafés, and protesting against the large restaurant boats polluting the Nile. Is it because Zamalek is the island of the rich that this association has shown resilience, success, and continuity in its activities even after 2014?

On the other hand, just after 2011 the poor residents of the slums communally constructed stairways, ramps, and exit roads from the ring road (Nagati and Stryker 2013: 52–3), to which they had previously had no access. Numerous other initiatives were witnessed, including campaigns by architects, urban planners, and historians for public awareness of the urban problems, the systematic pillage of antiquities, and the destruction of the historic sites, parks, monuments, and *Belle Epoque* villas of Egyptian cities. But whether these initiatives and information campaigns were successful in preventing the devastating demolition of historic landmarks is another question. The area of Ramlat Bulaq and the Maspero Triangle were thoroughly cleared in 2018 and Bulaq's historic *Belle Epoque* buildings were demolished, because the area has been under close scrutiny since the Mubarak era in the interest of financial speculators, who would like to transform it into one more mini-Dubai.[11] In effect, this was the second time that evictions in the area of Maspero were undertaken by the State. The first eviction was in the seventies during Sadat's rule, when the *'Ishash al-turguman* slum was cleared by brute force. Further attempts to clear up slums (or, more accurately, 'disfavoured quarters') for speculative neo-liberal investors were repeated on the islands of Warraq and Qursaya in recent years, stirring much resistance among the residents and launching heated debates in the press and social media. It was even argued (Shakran 2016) that these ongoing confrontations with the State created new forms of 'insurgent planning', political action, and growing social awareness against evictions, as well as instigation to violent retaliations from the residents against the police forces. This was after one police officer had shot dead a resident in 2012 in the cark park of the Nile Towers on the Corniche. This incident led to further violence when the officer refused to take the wounded person to the hospital while he shot yet another resident. As a result, a large number of men from the quarter attacked the front of the Fairmont Hotel, which is located at the Nile Corniche and set fire to a number of parked cars. From the official side, this incident resulted in criminalising and collectively tagging the entire quarter for thuggery (Shakran 2016: 26).

This was not the first time that Qursaya Island witnessed violent attempts at evicting its poor residents for lucrative neo-liberal urban projects. The first occurrence was in 2007 under the reign of Mubarak. However, when evictions by the military police occurred for the second time in November 2012, the military's contention was that the island belonged to the army, even though a previous court ruling had refused the army's right to evict the residents by granting them the right to reside and work there (Chams El-Dine 2016: 196–7). Although there has been considerable debate over the success or failure of the 2011 insurrection, the failed evictions from Qursaya Island on the part of the regime proved that citizens have learned new forms of collective mobilisation, exemplified in the collaborative work between human rights organisations (like the Egyptian Initiative for Personal Rights) and the activists, journalists, and film-makers who drew intensive public attention (Rennick 2018) to the 'illegitimate' violence of the State in connection with evictions. The final result was one more court decision ordering the military to leave, and arguing in favour of the residents' rights to remain on the island (Aswat Masreya 2013).

It was in that particular spirit of post-2011 momentum that I found myself driven by two simultaneous objectives. First, because I was moving into a new place, I wanted to mobilise the tiny local community of my building to save it from its collapsing state of affairs. At that juncture, the micro-sociology of an intimate space became interwoven with the theoretical questions that I teach in my classes on urban sociology, in my course entitled 'Cairo Collages'. At the risk of sounding pretentious, the display of my emotions and reactions to the changing urban conditions was an attempt to engage in a dialogue with the literature on the megacities of the South.

I started documenting my building in Doqi, creating a bookkeeping system to keep track of my own spending for renovating the flat I was moving into. The process of documenting the spending went together with my desperate attempts to arrange repairs of the communal sewage system, the water pump, and the electrical wiring, all work that had to be done before I moved into the flat. Although I did not move to Doqi until February 2016, I had already started in 2015 to contact my neighbours face to face to organise a building residents' association that would defend the residents' rights. The continual and extensive negotiations, exchange of information, and chit-chat about the neighbourhood with the neighbours, the doorkeeper, and the downstairs shopkeepers in the building took tremendous energy and time on my part. Accordingly, my chronology of the building started during the second half of 2015, but stories and unfolding events continued until summer 2018. This explains the time lag between some of the stories, as I recounted the thread of events in certain passages that went on for three years, while I moved meanwhile into other passages. Having said that, the book should read as a collage of landscapes, striving to weave together the transmutations happening in the various Cairene geographies, moving between the *Belle Epoque* centre of town, the gated communities, and the psychological and socio-political effects of the momentum of Tahrir. It is written like a puzzle in a way, in four separate *tales*. These are made up of perhaps apparently disconnected segments, but they are overlapping stories about the city of Cairo, constituting the prelude to narrating the complexities of its microcosmic world.

## Notes

1 Some of these articles have appeared in *Theory, Culture and Society*, and on the *Jadaliyya* website.
2 I am well aware that the horrific scale of violence enacted at India's partition, leading to the displacement of some 14 million people, violence that produced a disputed number of victims estimated between several hundred thousand and 2 million, is certainly not comparable to the sporadic acts of violence perpetrated during the period of 2011–13 on demonstrators in Egypt. Still, violence during the revolution was no triviality, as it left over 848 dead and over 3,000 injured in just the first three weeks ('Egyptian revolution of 2011', Wikipedia).
3 On the question of the 'perfomative' revolution, see Abaza 2014, 2016.
4 This tour de force by Ortner consists of a survey of the major anthropological works to provide a rich panorama of what is understood by 'resistance' in a number of writings. She includes the works of James Scott (*Weapons of the Weak*, 1985), the subaltern studies school, the work of E. P. Thompson (*The Making of the English Working Class*, 1966), Jean Comaroff's *Body of Power, Spirit of Resistance* (1985), and Ashis Nandy's *The Intimate Enemy* (1983).
5 Most importantly, the steep devaluation of the Egyptian pound against the US dollar in March 2016, leading to soaring prices and the collapse of the currency, produced a collective mental state of amnesia, if not a form of denial, accompanied by a growing sentiment that precariousness has become a collective, wide-ranging concern, touching even the declining middle classes. 'The government has annihilated the middle class' is a sentence I have often heard repeated in small talk in the street.
      Not only that, middle-class Egyptians are kept constantly on the run by hearsay and gossip that prices will continue to rise the following year. Thus, in the collective imagination, it is wiser to purchase durable consumer items (like refrigerators, stoves, air conditioners, water heaters) sooner than later, before the next wave of soaring prices. These items seem to break down more often than elsewhere because of electricity cuts, improper installation, or poor-quality products.
6 During the months of August and September 2018 alone, some seven suicide cases in the Metro have been reported. On this subject, see the sardonic comments of the blogger *Egyptian Chronicles: 7000 Years and Counting* (Zeinobia 2018).
7 'Bizarre' is a bit of an exaggeration here. For example, for the descending status of the middle classes, renting out furnished flats to foreigners, and the transformation of entire residential buildings into lucrative commercial spaces, see Abaza 2016. In the past, mosques would be constructed in the ground floors of buildings to evade taxes. These flexible survival strategies teach us about how space is negotiated in Third World metropolises.
8 *Utopia* is the title of Ahmed Khaled Tawfik's novel, published in 2008. In the novel, Cairo in 2023 is imagined as a bleak dystopia, divided between militarised, protected, gated communities/compounds and the sprawling slums populated with an unwanted, disposable humanity. The poor are chased by the rich as a leisure hunting pursuit. Yet this simplistic dichotomising of the city overshadows more sophisticated and complex narratives – for example, the intertwining working-class quarters near some compounds; lively, popular/working-class markets existing within walled, gated cities like Rehab City; the migrant communities

(the ever-growing Syrian community in the Sixth of October satellite city, the Iraqi and Sudanese refugees concentrated in various quarters); and quite efficient transport systems that have already been created as parallel spaces of 'assemblages' around the compounds and gated communities. All these phenomena need further reflection in relation to the notion of 'assemblages' (Simone 2013).

9 What needs to be emphasised here is also the discomfort, if not the near impossibility, of conducting any extensive empirical, let alone quantitative, sociological research after 2013 in Egypt. A generalised sentiment of fear and suspicion has overshadowed the milieus of research ever since the brutality of the internal security apparatus was epitomised in the murder of Giulio Regini, an Italian PhD candidate from Cambridge, whose body showed horrific signs of torture when it was found along the desert highway (see Malsin 2016). Since Regini was working on sensitive topics such as social movements and the Egyptian working classes, could it be a message addressed to the circles of local and international academics that anyone who dares undertake research in Egypt had better think twice, because such research is no longer possible? This is one explanation for my retreat into the confined space of my building.

10 Sari Hanafi, Mohammed Bamyeh, and Benoit Challand all speak of the new subjectivities triggering by the Arab revolutions. See Hanafi 2012; Bamyeh 2013; Challand 2001.

11 On the aspirations for Dubaising Cairo since Mubarak's reign, see Abaza 2011b.

# Tale I: *Al-'imaara* (the building) as topos

Chapitre 1: Dans l'escalier

Oui, cela pourrait commencer ainsi, ici, comme ça, d'une manière un peu lourde et lente, dans cet endroit neutre qui est à tous et à personne, où les gens se croisent presque sans se voir, ou la vie de l'immeuble se répercute, lointaine et régulière. De ce qui se passe derrière les lourdes portes des apparte-ments, on ne perçoit le plus souvent que ces échos éclatés, ces bribes, ces débris, ces esquisses, ces amorces, ces incidents or accidents qui se déroulent dans ce que l'on appelle 'les parties communes', ces petits bruits feutrés que le tapis de laines rouge passé étouffe, ces embryons de vie communautaire qui s'arrêtent toujours aux paliers. Les habitants d'un même immeuble vivent à quelques centimètres les uns des autres, une simple cloison les séparent. (Perec 2017: 23)

(Chapter 1: In the Stairs

Yes, it could start like this, here, like that, in a way that is a little heavy and slow, in this neutral place that belongs to everyone and to no one, where people meet almost without seeing each other, where the life of the building reverberates, distant and regular. Of what happens behind the heavy doors of the apartments, we usually see only these bursting echoes, these fragments, this debris, these sketches, these breaks, these incidents or accidents that take place in what we call 'the common areas', those muffled little noises that the worn red wool carpet stifles, these embryos of community life that always stop at the landing. The inhabitants of the same building live a few centimetres from each other, a simple partition separating them.)

*Al-'imaara* (the building) as a topos, the building as a geographical site for literary imagination, the building as a microcosm narrating the major social and political transformations of the cityscape, and the building becoming the symbol of the 'literary map of the city', has been the subject of consideration by Samia Mehrez (Mehrez 2008), who analyses four contemporary novels that focus on the life of a building, each in a different quarter of Cairo. Mehrez provides a fresh reading of the megacity through the locality of the building in Sonallah Ibrahim's *Dhat* (1998), Hamdi Abu Golayyel's *Lusus mutaqa'idun* (*Thieves in Retirement*, 2004), 'Alaa Al-Aswany's *'Imaarat Ya'qubyan* (*Yacoubian Building*, 2007), and last, but not least, Mohamed Tawfik's *Tifl shaqi ismuhu Antar* (*A Naughty Boy Called Antar*, 2003). The

**Figure 5**    Stairs, my building in Harun Street, 13 October 2017.

accounts represent the fragmented spaces of the building, symbolising the chaotic globalised metropolis that takes over and dominates the narratives in contradistinction to the 'ordered' and stratified world of the *hara* (the narrow alleyway in the old Islamic Cairo). The paradox, according to Mehrez, is that it is the modern section of the metropolis of Cairo, shaped by the Western-style boulevards, which is often portrayed as ambiguous and disordered, precisely by means of an intruding, ambiguous modernity. This is just the opposite of the colonial/orientalist perspective, in which the labyrinthine old 'Islamic' Cairo seemed chaotic and incomprehensible. The so-called traditional part has been perceived in the novels as the more ordered and harmonious spaces.

For Naguib Mahfouz, who represents the earlier generation of Egyptian novelists, the main protagonist in his novels is the *hara*, the narrow alley, symbolising the architecture and soul of the traditional 'Islamic city', with its differing borderlines between private space and the specified shared public space amongst neighbours. This spatial geography is contrasted to the modern *Belle Epoque*, and 'rational' European mimicry of a city. Yet Mahfouz's characters seem to be struggling with the contradictions of moving between these two opposing Cairos, which are clearly clashing in tastes, lifestyles, languages used, and certainly classes. The protagonists agonise, not only because they move between two disparate spaces, but because of the conflicting norms which each space represents. Mehrez goes on to say that, for the generation of novelists that followed Mahfouz, the *hara* seems to vanish from literature, to be replaced by the modern and anonymous world of the apartment building. From Mahfouz's *hara*, therefore, *al-'imaara* becomes the symbol of the 'ambiguous' modernity,[1] as the antithesis of the traditional segregated space of the secluded harem, which is thoroughly associated to the forbidden (*haraam*) space. Paradoxically, in the colonial imagination, the harem is often represented as synonymous to the concept of *veiling and concealing*; its famed *mashrabiyyas* allow people only to see through, without being seen. Its protecting servants induce fantasies about the ambiguous position of the eunuchs, the highly eroticised figure of the female odalisque, the concubines and the slaves often portrayed as naked.[2] In contradistinction, it is in the modern building that 'mixity' (translated from French *mixité*) and the free movement of women were finally permissible or granted to the rising new bourgeoisies and the middle classes at the turn of the last century. But is this freedom of movement for women limitless?

Going back in time: first published in 1944, Albert Cossery's *La maison de la mort certaine* (Editions Joëlle Losfeld, 1994) is yet another intriguing novel revolving around a single building in one of the poorest areas of Cairo, just eight years before the 1952 revolution. Written in French, like all of Cossery's novels, his work earned him *Le grand prix de la francophonie* of the Académie Française. *La maison de la mort certaine* conveys an exceedingly derisive tone, for which the language of the poorest classes of Egyptians is famous. The biting sense of humour displayed in the witty cascade of Egyptian Arabic, the typical insults, the swearing, and the turn of sentences are marvellously transposed, if not always smoothly communicated in French, since Cossery never wrote in Arabic. 'Humour and derision', as Cossery's work has been often described (Temlali 2008), thoroughly depicts the *Zeitgeist* of the divided and contradictory colonial Cairo. Yet, more than half a century after its publication, this novel still evidences an amazing contemporaneity, as if timelessness is what pervades Egyptian popular life. It is only humour and derision 'that keeps Egyptians alive', as Cossery acknowledged in a long interview filmed in 1991, following his peregrinations between Cairo and Paris ('Albert Cossery: Portrait entre Paris et le Caire', 1991). Once again, humour, having always been the essence of the Egyptian soul, is what shines through the daily interactions of the poor.

The story takes place in an antiquated, decrepit building that is threatening to collapse. The building is located in the Alley of the Seven Maidens (*Venelles des Septs filles*) on a hill near the old quarter of the Citadel, which is clearly a poor, lower-class (*baladi*, popular) neighbourhood, in contrast to the *afrangi* (derived from the word 'foreign', designating the Westernised part of the city). Si-Khalil, the owner of the building, is a creepy and greedy person, who is well aware of the danger of the collapse of the building. In fact, he made his fortune mainly by purchasing failing buildings, some of which had already collapsed, taking numerous lives. Si-Khalil has on his conscience a number of deaths from previous incidents of collapsing buildings. However, he relies on the fact that no resident will ever dare protest, as they are all considered, even within this lower-class quarter, as the most wretched, poorest-of-the-poor residents. The building epitomises the life-world of the most extremely destitute, living at the bottom of society, where cruelty and the 'war of all against all' reign. Children seem to be constantly roaming around, spending all their time in the street as their natural destiny. They are constantly hungry and bully weaker kids. Hunger leads some of the young girls to offer themselves sexually to elderly men. The children do not recognise their fathers and hardly ever talk to them. The *baladi* women are constantly insulting and fighting each other in public. Many of the male residents are unemployed and feeling useless. They are portrayed as being either heavy hashish smokers, or endlessly struggling in search of errand jobs, barely able to feed their families. A third-class wedding singer; a donkey-cart driver, who had to sell his donkey out of destitution but is left with the cart; a street performer, who owns a monkey and a goat that is later stolen and eaten by a hungry neighbour, who then wanders around with the monkey; a nauseating, stinking rubbish collector, who harshly hides his ailing wife from the neighbourhood, but who is considered to be richer than the others since he can earn a regular monthly salary; a slightly better-off tram conductor; an unemployed carpenter; and a kerosene-stove repairman; they all live on the margin of society. Injustice reigns in this crumbling, terrifying ruin. The novel conveys so well the overwhelming misery during the period of the monarchy in Egypt, providing a prelude to the inevitability of the 1952 coup/ revolution as a resolution. The story ends with an incitement to rebellion. Cossery wants to convey the message that even if the building does fall apart, some will eventually survive, and they are sure to rise against tyranny. The survivors will be the ones who will trigger change by refusing injustice, as this is the only way out of the obviously deadly building, the *'mort certaine'*.

Muriel Barbery's *L'élégance du hérisson* (*The Elegance of the Hedgehog*, Gallimard, 2006) is yet another unconventional novel revolving around a building. This one is located at 7, rue de Grenelles, in Paris, on the bourgeois Left Bank. This successful novel was adapted into a movie titled *Le Hérisson*. The story is mostly narrated by a widely read, highly perceptive and intelligent, self-taught, but modest housekeeper (*la concierge*), Madame Renée Michel. It is written with irony and subtlety, as the housekeeper, who is an avid and careful reader, is well versed in the philsosophical and sociological texts of Kant, Husserl, and Bourdieu. She has even read Proust and Tolstoy, and is also an avid fan of intellectual movies, in particular the Japanese film-maker Ozu. Madame Renée interacts with another erudite, highly intelligent person, an eleven-year-old upper-class girl living in the same building, Paloma Josse. Paloma is unstable, however; through the entire course of the novel she assiduously plans to commit suicide. The two main narrators in the story are the concierge and Paloma, even though there are numerous interactions with the residents of the building, until a Japanese newcomer, Mr Ozu (who carries the same name as the famous Japanese director, but is not related to him), appears on the scene. He has just purchased the flat of the deceased, long-term resident Pierre Arthens. Mr Ozu discovers the beauty, intelligence, and erudism of Madame Renée. They share an affinity and appreciation of the aesthetics of the Japanese film director Ozu, and together they watch films in Mr Ozu's refined Japanse-style flat (with sliding doors). A bonding relationship develops during the course of the book between the concierge and Paloma, who discovers Madame Renée's impressive library and sophisticated readings. The metaphor of the hedgehog's spiky external appearance, hiding a sensitive soul, reveals much about the self-taught concierge, who believes herself to be ugly and uninteresting, but is highly perceptive. The book is fascinating to read because it refers repeatedly to academic and classical literary texts in an ironic tone, displaying a sharpened class awareness that is highly sarcastic towards the pedantic Parisian bourgeoisie. In a way, the '*pensées profondes*' that serve as chapter titles expose the pretentiousness and shallow intellectualism of French society.

First published in 1978, Georges Perec's *La Vie mode d'emploi* was written between 1969 and 1978. This is a bewildering and now classic novel about yet another Parisian building in the seventeenth arrondissement, whose intricate stories span the years between 1875 and 1975. This voluminous work consists of some 733 pages and 99 chapters. Trying to explain these 773 pages in just a few paragraphs would be unfeasible, and obviously would not do justice to this work. Perec's text is quite challenging, as it offers such a wide spectrum in its multiplicity and complexity of imaginations and readings. The novel is conceived as if the façade of the building has been stripped away, exactly what the illustration of the front cover of the *Livre de Poche* edition is conveying. As Bernard Magné's preface explains, the reader is confronted with the nearly impossible task of grasping the details when there are about 1,467 persons appearing in the novel, and when, for example, five entire pages could be dedicated to a catalogue of tools (Perec 2017: 8). Perec's genius is revealed in the unconventional style running through the entire story, as it is written like a huge puzzle, and the main protagonist, Bartlebooth, dies in the last chapter, sitting opposite his unfinished puzzle. This novel, which can hardly be read like a conventional novel, could be interpreted as a historical and documentary archive on the lifestyles, consumer habits, and culture of the French middle classes. Incredibly detailed descriptions of rooms, living rooms, bedrooms, corridors, elevators, stairs, basements, and the living and dead creatures that might possibly exist underneath the basements are likewise imagined. The way people interact in these rooms, the details of endless objects, of goods and the functions of the objects, of books and long references to literary, philosophical, and scientific works, are narrating stories behind still other stories. For instance, a detailed description is provided of the objects, the stored food, and other goods in the basement of the Altamont family in chapter 33, which is titled 'Caves, I' (pp. 221–6). Then almost two pages are dedicated solely to the names of wines and their regional differences (Perec 2017: 221–2). A large number of the life histories of the characters are narrated. These include university professors, weird and would-be artists, swindlers, disappearing ethnographers, businessmen, genius inventors, a couple with an eight-year-old child, maids, rich and poor women who have lost their fortunes. Writing like a puzzle allows the reader to follow the stories of the different characters by jumping through chapters. In other words, the chronology could be easily disregarded and the book can be read from any point one chooses, for instance from the middle by skipping chapters, except for the last chapter.

In the field of sociology, the book *Zenana: Everyday Peace in a Karachi Apartment Building*, by Laura A. King (King 2006), deserves special attention, since the social-spatial life-world of the building is made the central protagonist. King, who was married to a Pakistani, has undertaken an intriguing study on the daily exchange amongst neighbours in a building in which she lived in Karachi with her family.

Her study focuses on the intersections of emotions, gender, peacemaking, and inter-ethnic relations in a modern multi-storey apartment building. By focusing on gender politics in the confined space of her building, King attempts to narrate a grander representation, but one which ultimately draws in the long and complex history of negotiating ethnic conflict in Pakistan through the microscopic universe of the building. King argues that the various strategies of her female neighbours ought to be understood as agents of peacemaking. Since women act as astute manipulators of male anger in the building, 'women's cultural understanding of male anger is pivotal to a sensibility or praxis of peace in the building' (King 2006: 31). In contradistinction to King, while being less concerned about gender order, my work focuses on the residents' interaction in handling a situation of material decay.

## Cairo: Major urban makeovers since 2011

'Archive 858, an Archive of Resistance', created by the collective *Mosireen*, is a compilation of YouTube footage that is the testimony of the Egyptian streets in rebellion. The demonstrations, the marches, the sit-ins, the violent confrontations, and the endless incidents in the streets are today on display mostly because of the publicness of the internet. Not only that, an extensive number of interviews with street children, discussions about the imprisonment of minors,[3] encounters with the Ultras Ahli fans, interviews with citizens who were tortured and mistreated by security forces, the testimonies of the parents of the victims, and testimonies of eyewitnesses to violence are all today available to the public. These, like a number of other YouTube clips, constitute the living memory of the city in revolt, the city in pain, and the effervescent city. How does the blending of this abundant footage of virtual

**Figure 6a**    Mohamed Mahmud Street, 21 November 2013.

reality affect the reality and imaginary of the city after the event – after the so-called military securitisation and restoration of order?

Since January 2011, the nation has experienced much turmoil in the form of escalating street protests leading to successive violent confrontations, which will be remembered as demarcating geographies in the city to the escalating, unfolding events. One such image is the massacre of Maspero Street in October 2011, when army tanks ran over numerous demonstrators, killing mostly Copts, while some eyewitnesses saw victims being thrown into the Nile.[4] The photographs of piled corpses, of the crying, mourning mothers of the victims praying in the 'Abbaseyya Cathedral went viral. The portrait of the twenty-five-year-old martyr Mina Daniel, who died crushed by the tanks, spread all over the walls of the city as graffiti. More killings occurred in Moqattam when Copts demonstrated against the torching of a church in Atfiih, south of Cairo. On 8 March 2011, thirteen people were attacked by a crowd and killed while demonstrating (Human Rights Watch 2011). Then came the memorable Mohamed Mahmud Street incidents (November–December 2011), which led to the street being renamed the 'Street of the Martyrs' and the 'Street of the Eyes of Freedom' after more than 150 protesters lost their eyes and many more were killed. In the collective memory the photographs and footage of the young sniper officer Mahmud Sobhi al-Shennawi – later known as *qannas al-'uyuun* (the 'sniper' or 'eye hunter') – who specialised in targeting the eyes of leading activists, remain vividly anchored in the collective memory.[5] A number of testimonies to the extreme brutality of the police forces have been published by the human rights organisation al-Nadeem Centre.[6] The violent confrontations, the dead and wounded who resulted from them, and the widely circulated portrait of Ahmed Harara, who lost both eyes in Mohamed Mahmud Street incidents, the first in January 2011 and the second in 2012, will hardly be forgotten. The official state propaganda attempted to narrate the confrontations as if the insurrectionists were notorious thugs and outlaws, since hordes of working-class and poor young men (including a large number who had experienced police abuse on a daily basis) were in the front lines of these battles. Then in February 2012, the Port Said stadium massacre of the Ultras Ahli football fans occurred. The brutality of the confrontations led a number of Egyptian psychiatrists (who pointed to the collective neurotic behaviour of the security forces), journalists, and intellectuals to conclude that the incidents should be regarded as a sort of *tasfiyyat hissaabaat* (settling of accounts). It was a kind of vendetta exercised by inflicting pain on the bodies of the revolutionaries, in particular the poor working-class rebels who were mutilated for engaging in insurrection (Mahrous 2011). As argued earlier (Abaza 2013a), the 2011 and 2012 street battles of Mohamed Mahmud displayed a highly charged 'dramaturgical' and 'performative', Bakhtinian, carnivalesque element in defying the order of the State. When an endless series of impressive photographs, blurred with teargas, showing the canisters, exposing the violent clashes, went viral, memes and jokes also multiplied on Facebook accounts about some 'extra-terrestial creatures' (*al-kaa'enaat al-fadaa'iyya*) who must have been the main culprits, since the regime maintained a discourse of complete denial of using violence. These 'extra-terrestial creatures' were then sardonically introduced from the revolutionaries' side to mock the regime's double standards in horribly crushing the rebellious street. The imagined, fantastic, winged extra-terrestials were pasted on the photographs like cartoons, providing a highly surreal and mesmerising landscape of the localised urban war of Tahrir.

It had also been argued previously (Abaza 2013a) that when the second Mohamed Mahmud clashes occurred in 2012, repertoire could be a key concept for deciphering the regular use of violence by the authorities and the recycling of similar methods of violence in the discourses of both the two previous regimes and the rule of the Muslim Brotherhood. Repertoire might also have explained the persistence of graffiti artists, who kept on painting and repainting the same murals over and over, most notably a portrait that was half Mubarak and half Mohamed Hussein Tantawi (Abaza 2013a). Using the same language of the repertoire, one could have viewed the graffiti and murals of the corner where Mohamed Mahmoud Street meets Tahrir Square as the site of an unfolding continuous dramaturgical performance from January 2011 until 2013 that visually narrated the history of the revolution.[7]

**Figure 6b**  Street of the Eye of Freedom, 9 April 2015.

The following passages provide a close-up of some vital testimonies of the incidents of the 'Street of the Eyes of Freedom' – the most valuable sources for the disputed versions and multiple archives of the revolution.

### Time and again, Mohamed Mahmud Street

This battle was far from being on equal terms ... There was one side that had all amunition and weapons. It controlled the space of the combat ... This means that the internal security forces could have instantly created a checkpoint to gather the soldiers and arrest people as they wanted, they had the power to do so ... We did not have any authority over space, or over time, or even the massive amount of weapons they had. We were just bodies ... with rocks, and fireworks (*shamaariiskh*), in particular when the Ultras football team introduced these in the battles ... When a soldier would fall down, which was rare, no one from the protesters' side collected his gun, for instance ... There was no point in retaliating with weapons ... The internal security's prime aim was not to kill the protesters. They wanted mainly to carve a life-long mark (on bodies) ... what happened ... happened and people died, but it was meant that we should not have been left without being stained, so that we remember the pain forever. So that it becomes a lesson for those who want to go to the street not do it again ...

It was like a fight ... a vendetta that evolved mainly on a daily basis ... but there was no clear long-term plan about what was to be done ... I don't think that

the Ministry of Interior had any plans or tactics either ... they mainly wanted
to evacuate the square.

(H. H. participated in the 2011 and 2012 Mohamed Mahmud incidents. He was
born in 1994, and was eighteen years old when he actively participated in the
2011 events. H. H. was violently beaten by the security forces. Interview, 10
December 2017.)

Activist Nawara Negm, daugher of the late renowned leftist poet Ahmed
Fuad Negm, was at the forefront of the first and second Mohamed Mahmud
confrontations. Negm, who was an established columnist writing for newspapers from the very start of the revolution, published her testimony in a
series of articles in the *al-Tahrir* newspaper, which were reproduced in the
years that followed on different websites. In an article published on 18
November 2013, while throwing the blame on those who wanted to commemorate the Mohamed Mahmud incidents in public at that time, Negm
recounts the central elements that triggered the first confrontations in 2011
(Negm 2013). Negm once again accused the Salafists, whom she held responsible for the first Mohamed Mahmud killings. She seemed to imply that
there was a kind of bribery over the martyrs. The Government wanted to
commemorate their own martyrs, meaning the police officers, while Negm
insisted that no officer was killed during the incidents. According to Negm
the incidents were sparked by the Salafist leader Hazem Abu Ismail, whose
demand was the retreat of SCAF, after he had given a highly charged speech
in Tahrir. This was followed by encouragement to organise a sit-in (*itissam*)
in the square. Apparently Abu Ismail postponed it to 18 November. The
wounded and disabled of the revolution were already squatting in the square,
hoping that the people would return en masse to rejoin the revolution. The
followers of the Muslim Brotherhood had also been in the square, but had
left earlier that night. Only a small group of Islamists who started shouting
'*Islamiyya, islamiyya*' (in support of an Islamic rule) remained. Abu Ismail
arrived later and ordered his followers to retreat from the square, after
negotiating with the Government (it was, however, unclear with whom in
the Government these negotiations had been conducted). The revolutionaries,
Negm amongst them, started to protest by pointing out that this level of
disorganisation would lead to a massacre, while Abu Ismail was tagged a
traitor. Suddenly, the square was attacked by thugs of the regime (*baltaguiyya*)
who resorted to violence. While Negm left the square briefly to get some
sleep at home, attacks on the square had continued. Upon her return to the
square, she found a small group of protesters, all gathered at the entrance
of Mohamed Mahmud Street. Negm recalls that the scene had quickly turned
against the army when the body of a dead protester was dumped in a rubbish
pit. The shocking scene, ironically, did not deter the Muslim Brotherhood's
plans, as they quickly denounced the protesters, accusing them of derailing
the parliamentary elections that they hoped would grant them new powers.

Negm recalls how on the first day of the incidents, 19 November 2011, when she went for the second time to Tahrir, the police forces were clearly the ones who started the offensive by fiercely attacking the relatively small number of demonstrators. Negm describes how her friend, the activist Malek Mustafa, was transported to the hospital with a number of other wounded protesters. Mustafa, like a number of young people, lost an eye that day after being targeted by snipers (Negm 2012a). The next day, the confrontations escalated further (Negm 2012b). Negm continued her testimony regarding the second day, which she published in *al-Tahrir* on 15 November 2012. In the following days, the war between the protesters and the army and police forces took a new turn, and a number of demonstrators were shot. But the fights were restricted to Mohamed Mahmud Street, while the day before, the battles had been seen to spread all over Kasr al-Aini and Mohamed Mahmud Streets. Negm states that the bullets fired from the police forces from the front were synchronised with the attacks from the army from the side streets. Symbolic, theatrical, and often performative elements in displaying resistance and bold acts of insurrection were dominant in these confrontations. For example, Negm recalls that the protester who was carrying a large flag with the portrait of martyr Mina Daniel was shot several times, but he courageously resisted and held the flag higher. The endless footage revealing the way the protesters swiftly returned the tear-gas canisters directed towards them, the fireworks of the Ultras Ahli fans directed against the police forces, the motorcycles transporting the wounded, the attacks of the security forces and the retreats are evidence of this performativity.

The shocking footage of the dead demonstrator thrown in the rubbish by the police forces, which went viral, resulted in even more protesters joining the numbers on the square. The demonstrators were all united in their belief that SCAF rule had to end. Negm recalls phoning the journalist Ibrahim Issa asking him about an alternative to demonstrating, in the form of contacting the Muslim Brothers to form a national consensus to cease the killings.

There are a number of meaningful observations to be noted in Negm's testimony. While depressing, it is a thoughtful narrative that deciphers well the landscape of the urban warfare at that moment. From what she recalls, the protesters were entrapped in a self-defensive position, while all the battlefronts and attacks seemed to have been dominated by the army and the police forces, who apparently never lost their control of the situation. The police forces were consciously wounding and killing the protesters. Negm observes that on the fourth day, dozens of protesters died from the lethal gas (Negm 2012c). She also described the truce between the police forces and the demonstrators initiated by Sheikh Mazhar Shahin, later celebrated as the 'preacher of the revolution'. During the dawn prayers a group of activists stood as shields to protect the front-line activists while they were praying. Negm later received information that the truce was disrupted when the police shot the backs of the protecting human shields, killing most of them. The blame was put on Sheikh Mazhar Shahin, who felt responsible for the carnage.

On the fourth day, the bearded youths (meaning the Salafis, according to Negm) tried to mediate between the revolutionaries and the police. A truce was negotiated, the revolutionaries followed it, but as happened earlier, they were once again shot in the back by the police forces and many were killed. Negm argues that these repetitive truces, followed by an obvious betrayal, turned out to be a repertoire that exposed the naivety of the revolutionaries. It was the same story over and over: the mediators between the police forces and the revolutionaries were the Salafis and Muslim Brotherhood members. The request for a truce repeatedly happened when the protesters advanced, nearing the Ministry of Interior, when the police's ammunition and weapons were almost exhausted. Then the truce was repeatedly broken exactly at the time when activists were performing their prayers. This betrayal happened three times, and with each truce more killings.

The most moving episodes of Negm's narrative are the visits she paid to the morgue in search of missing friends. She once met there the famous activist Asma Mahfouz[8] in tears, mourning the numerous martyrs of the clashes. Negm told her that the demonstrators did not enter Mohamed Mahmud by their own will, but that whenever they retreated to the square, they were then attacked and followed by the police. Those who died were mostly poor and working-class youngsters. In the morgue, she saw the restless mourning parents, who could hardly understand why their children went to Mohamed Mahmud to be killed with such brutality. Activist Malek 'Adly was endlessly checking on the autopsy reports, written by the doctors and state employees, in which the cause of death was 'registered as dangerous and a criminal'. 'Adly persisted in redrafting the reports, adding: 'death, shot by bullets'. He had to insert his fingers into every single wound of the dead bodies and take out the countless bullets as evidence of the killings, as a testimony against the falsified reports of the state employees (Negm 2012d).

### Landmarks and snapshots

> The aim at that time (Mohamed Mahmud 2011) was to stop these people (the police forces) from entering the street and beating us. On the other hand, the Ministry of Interior had then lost its standing as a ministry, they were just a bunch of thugs (*baltaguiyya*) who were hitting us ... so we had to respond. (H. H.)

Landmarks and signs transform the collective memory of the geographies of the city. A bird's-eye shot of Tahrir Square, the single most widely circulated image from the revolution, overshadowed the equally significant protests in cities like Alexandria, Suez, and Ismailiyya. But then Cairo witnessed the Itihadiyya (the Presidential Palace in the district of Heliopolis) filled with millions of protesters before the ouster of Morsi in summer 2013, and earlier, in the same location, in December 2012, when the militias of the Muslim Brotherhood violently attacked and killed protesters. Copts in the Moqattam district were killed, and the headquarters of the Muslim Brotherhood was attacked. When the Muslim Brotherhood were in power from 2012 until June 2013, confrontations also took place between demonstrators and the security forces in the cities of Port Said and Suez, leading to further deaths. Then the lynching of four Shi'a citizens in June 2013, after the hate speech of former President Morsi (the major incident that fostered Morsi's collapse nationwide), followed by attacks on Copts by Salafis and Islamists, severely shook the nation.[9] Then after Morsi's ouster, the violence in Rabe'a Square killed an estimated 800–1,000 people during the evacuation of the square. Nahda Square in Giza and the Orman Garden were occupied by Muslim Brotherhood sympathisers after Morsi was removed. This was followed by the burning, looting, and vandalising of a large number of churches, as well as houses and shops of Copts, and open killings of Copts by Morsi's followers all over the country.

One more memorable snapshot is the public performances of ballet and dancing to Greek music in front of the Ministry of Culture in Zamalek as a protest against Morsi's cultural policies in summer 2013, just before he was removed.

Even today, for many people, certain streets and lower-class neighbourhoods evoke endless memories and symbols of rebellion: images of cars running over and killing protesters in the early days of January, canisters of tear gas, live amunition, bullets, text messages, tents, masks against tear gas, motorcycles transporting the wounded, graffiti, bandaged eyes, one of the iconic lions of the Kasr al-Nil bridge with a covered eye, outrageous insults and poems against the regime on walls all over the city. Meeting points during the long marches when more protesters merged into the main march. Sexual assault, rape, and undressing of women, for the purpose of intimidating, if not terrorising and humiliating, them. Organised Ultras Ahli fans performing marches and outrageous, impressive chants. Extraordinarily abusive insults directed towards the Ministry of Interior. The anti-police catchword ACAB ('All Cops Are Bastards') that filled endless walls all over the city. Public displays of coffins – actually, of moving cenotaphs – the display of photographs and portraits of martyrs in the squares and during marches, a large number of whom were children. Chanting slogans, drumming in marches. Para-phernalia and gadgets sold by the poor street peddlers in the square and in marches, who seemed fearless during confrontations. Street children and poor itinerant sweet-potato sellers, peddlers selling drinks, and cheap food carts spread all around the square. The flood of Egyptian flags and their commercialisation as a consumer item. Walls and more walls being erected by the military in the centre of town. Pedestrians trying to jump or climb over these walls. More and more people trying to pierce these walls. The removal of some of the walls. Then, after 2013, even more and higher concrete walls being built around ministries, embassies, and government buildings. The impossibility of moving around these impenetrable boundaries.

The city of Cairo experienced two parallel but contradictory phenomena. First, the occupation of public spaces as an emerging global configuration of political activism witnessed a novel turn after 2011. It proved ephemeral, however, as it was terminated by the predictable, overwhelming military intervention. It was an immense disappointment that the brief, euphoric momentum of the Tahrir effect brought about the further militarisation of urban life and increased public visibility or tactility of the military in all aspects of civil life. And yet, some would argue that the army's obvious involvement represents a form of 'natural' continuity rather than a change. For example, already in the early 2000s, the Cairo region was managed by three military governors appointed by presidential decrees, as Eric Denis has reported (Denis 2006: 60).

The centre of Cairo was 'targeted' (Bishop, Clancey, and Phillips 2012; Conley 2012: 135–47) for the early stages of the revolt, and in the process, the city centre became the epicentre of violent confrontations, killings, exposure to lethal tear gas, an escalating military presence, and the erection of check-points. This may well be the reason that the gated satellite compounds/communities have gained increasing popularity in the collective conscience, as isolated havens of safety, cleanliness, and complete absence of the unwanted poor. This development paralleled the massive exodus of the middle and upper classes towards the consumerist lifestyles in the satellite cities. As Paul Amar observed, the takeover by SCAF after Mubarak's fall was translated into a discourse built around what he calls 'armed humanitarian interventions', a scheme that operates in paradoxical and contradictory approaches to urban rule that are both repressive and liberating (Amar 2013b: 7). These 'humanitarian' measures gave legitimacy, if not exactly popularity, to the military in its early days of rule through the pervasive campaign on the 'war on terror' against Islamic terrorism, which went hand in hand with restoring the so-called order after the chaos that accompanied the retreat of the police forces from 2011 until 2013. Following Amar's argument on armed humanitarianism, the Sisi regime, for example, also championed public morality as a way of protecting women against sexual harassment in public spaces after 2013.[10] For a significant number of women, at least in the official media channels, Sisi was welcomed as the rescuer from the rule of the Muslim Brotherhood, who had issued on several previous occasions a number of gender-biased statements, hinting at his approval of misogynistic practices. On the other hand, exaggeratedly macho representations of Sisi as *al-dakar* (literally, the virile 'male') are quite revealing of the prevailing attitudes of his regime. A number of times he has been portrayed as a lion (not without a grain of salt), an image that became popular on consumer gadgets, paraphernalia, and other items – even chocolate cupcakes. The regime also hedges its gender bets by resorting to politically correct feminist language to balance the hypermasculine symbols. After 2014, the army became one of the most important distributors of food supplies, announcing that it would sell boxes of food at half of their market price to assist the poor and needy, thus assuming yet another function of civil life by taking over the duties of the Ministry of *Tamwin* (Food Supplies) ('Egypt's army distributes "largest food supplies"', 2016).

On another level, we were then reminded by Oikonomakis and Roos (2013) that by the second half of 2011, the planet had witnessed protests in more than a thousand cities across eighty countries. Inspired by the moving images of the Arab Spring, similar tactics of occupying public spaces were replicated worldwide. The insurrection in Kiev's Maidan testifies to the infectious impact of travelling images.[11] 'Encampment', together with the 'tent', the emblem of nomadism, of the rootless refugee's shelter, became the most circulated and celebrated images in global media (Mitchell 2012; Oikonomakis and Roos 2013). Novel artistic, public expressions, and highly inventive urban ways of protest and action evidently travelled swiftly, though with a number of local variants.

The power of the street in Egypt produced a surreal energy causing 'a hundred flowers to bloom' in public. It also fostered collective acts of performance, social interaction, unexpected encounters, and an unprecedented proximity between classes, who found themselves gazing at lifestyles that were alien to their way of life. It is possible to argue that the early years of the revolution constituted a fantastic laboratory for experiencing a '*dérive*' in the city. Every march, every confrontation between various opposing political forces, the lethal urban wars, the erecting of concrete buffer walls by the army and their destruction by the protesters, detouring around and jumping the walls, the attacks and retreats, all these activities created the most unexpected and fascinating euphoric moments that reshaped what Guy Debord calls the 'psychogeographical' morphology of the city.[12] People have learned to read their own cities in a new light, through protests, marches, urban wars, and the refinement of the tactics of attack and confrontations with police forces; as a result, a novel relationship to the street was witnessed. The continuous, improvised human interaction in the streets might remind us of one of Bruegel's surreal paintings. After Tahrir was occupied in January 2011, Salafis and Islamists, street children, the poor lower classes, the middle and upper classes, veiled women, peasants and protesters from the provinces of Egypt, sheikhs and Coptic priests and unveiled young women, representing the broad spectrum of society, were all visible in the square. The occupation succeeded in imposing an entirely unprecedented new choreography for the city, in which the 'stage' of Tahrir[13] was the exemplary moment that triggered extended, dramatic, violent public confrontations, public performances, and occupations that were replicated in all the squares of Cairo and in other cities of Egypt. This coincided with a key juncture in the emerging public visibility of an unprecedented and powerful visual culture (Abaza 2013b), which is associated with the reconfiguration of what Mitchell calls 'the rhetoric of space' (Mitchell 2012: 11). These transformations teach us that one of the main material transformations of the city of Cairo since January 2011 has been, precisely, over the fascinating art and tactics of squatting in public spaces.

Having said that, the paradoxical effect of the representation of Tahrir as 'an image, a symbol, and an icon' from its early days led to a much-contested visual saturation of images that quickly turned into a cliché, which accordingly drained the signifiers of their meaning, as Angela Harutyunyan has argued (Harutyunyan 2012: 11). Numerous observers commented on the fact that the Egyptian revolution, with the central focus on Tahrir Square, was more thoroughly covered by international media than almost any other revolution in history, raising questions about the effect of the continuous overflow of images into memory and written accounts. That said, of all these images, the best-remembered remains the panorama of the square filled with masses of people, an image which reduced the complexity of the revolutionary narrative.

One more reversal in the role of photography can be identified. The effect of the overabundant flow of the millions of photographs and videos, producing what Mitchell called a 'tsunami of material' (Mitchell 2012: 14), has evidently enhanced the further commodification and iconising of 'revolution photographs'. This phenomenon is quite similar to the invasion of paraphernalia, in concert with the disproportionate proliferation of the icon of the Egyptian flag and its pervasive commercialisation, resulting in a banalisation of its symbolism. The circulation of the bird's-eye shot of the square,[14] the most emblematic photograph of the revolution, produced this reversal, which served the counter-revolution more than anyone else. In 2013, vertical filming was appropriated by the military to good effect, using highly sophisticated aerial shots from helicopters of the mass demonstrations on 30 June 2013, just before the ouster of former president Morsi.[15] Certainly, the diffusion of these professional videos and photographs worldwide, displaying a much larger number of protesters in the street than in January 2011, were crucial both in speeding Morsi's departure and in enhancing at that moment the popularity of the military. This brings us to *Colonizing Egypt*, by Timothy Mitchell (Mitchell 1991), who once again critiqued orientalist and colonial representations in the production of knowledge, and as a consequence the interpretation of the 'reality' of Egypt, which was constructed via the effect of the 'spectacle' and staging (at the Exposition Universelle), and the 'conquest of the world as picture' (Martin Heidegger, cited in Mitchell 1991), further blurring the line between reality and representation.[16] Being in accord with Mitchell, I am tempted to raise the question of whether the 'staging' and the spectacle effect of Tahrir, heightened by the iconic bird's-eye panoramic[17] perspective, was not in the end merely an effect, an entrapment of the image freezing the revolutionary momentum.

But to control this euphoric moment meant that Cairo typically witnessed what Stephen Graham, in his brilliant, futuristic work *Cities under Siege: The*

*New Military Urbanism* (Graham 2010), argues is a growing process of urban militarisation, which merges military and surveillance strategies with civilian and consumer urban life. Nothing could be more apt than Graham's theorisation to explain what Cairo has witnessed during the past three years by becoming the site of an ongoing battlefield. The following quotation by Eyal Weizman (Weizman 2005), extracted from Graham's book, says it all: 'The City is not just the site, but the very medium of warfare, a flexible, almost liquid medium that is forever contingent and in flux' (Graham 2010: 21). This form of 'militarisation', so to speak, of urban life ran parallel to the paradox of a thriving public cultural scene that merits much attention. Helicopters became visible after the first few days of the revolution in January 2011. I recall how they hovered over Tahrir Square the entire night of the memorable Battle of the Camel on 2 February 2011 and continued to be visible in the capital thereafter.[18]

Graham's predictions make Cairo a stimulating laboratory for experimenting with the erection of walls as an urban-warfare strategy and as a way of counteracting demonstrators by military planning to reinvent and subvert space (Adey 2010). So many of the army's actions remain in the collective memory as vivid images of the mounting militarisation of daily urban life: the presence of the army tanks in the streets of the centre of town (constantly appearing, disappearing, and reappearing from 2011 until 2014); the erection of concrete walls as barriers between the protesters and police forces; the piercing and demolition of these isolating and paralysing walls by the citizens; the blockading of entire areas for security reasons; checkpoints, barbed wire, the various forms of urban combat; the vertical control of the city through the presence of helicopters at peak moments in Tahrir in January 2011 and on 30 June 2013; the numerous attacks and retreats and killings by the police forces in various busy central streets of the city between 2011 and 2013; the tear gas, resulting in numerous deaths and epileptic attacks; the emergence of newly created paramilitary troops parading in the city; and finally, the Rabe'a al-'Adaweyya massacre and its aftermath, the escalating number of militarised terrorist attacks by opposing Islamists. These attacks not only targeted state representatives and police forces but also torched a large number of churches in summer 2013, killing many innocent citizens.

### Divided Cairo

Control is discipline without walls.

(Diken and Laustsen 2002: 298)

If the late Janet Abu-Lughod took a stroll around Downtown Cairo today, she would be delighted that the thesis of her 'Tale of Two Cities', which is the title of an article published in *Comparative Studies in Society and History* in 1965, and which she developed later into an invaluable work (posthumously

**Figure 7**   Block wall with prayers for the martyrs of Mohamed Mahmud Street, 15 December 2015.

published), still vividly describes Cairo's contradictions and unrelenting dualities.

Having said that, Cairo's paradoxes and dualities, which resulted from the post-January 2011 urban reshaping, turned out to be completely divergent from Abu-Lughod's lively account of post-colonial, 1960s Cairo (Abu-Lughod 1971), which was trying to come to terms with the duality between the colonial boulevard-shaped, *Belle Epoque, khawagaat* ('foreigners') city with its *grands magasins*, French-style cafés, and modern apartment buildings, in contradistinction to the so-called Islamic city of the local Egyptians, demarcated by the border of 'Ataba Square. Of course the two-cities thesis was meant to depict two entirely different life-worlds and lifestyles that resulted in clear contrasts in dress and language – for example, French, Italian, English, and Greek in Downtown versus Arabic in the Moski and Khan el Khalili area.

Today's Downtown spatial dualities look contrastingly different. The spatial segregation seems to be the outcome of four years of urban-war confrontation, resulting in wiring, fencing, and zoning of entire areas. This could be simply and graphically translated through the creation of two clearly divided Downtowns. And we if we add the desert satellite cityscapes, one could then speak of a mosaic of clashing Cairene cities, or of numerous multiple Cairos, with clashing autonomous lifestyles and sprawling slums. Even in the rich residential satellite city of Sixth of October, public spaces have been occupied by the poor, and a working-class population that caters to the rich coexists in parallel nearby cities. There, too, emerging large communities of Syrian and Iraqi refugees are in the making, reproducing 'little Syrias', spaces filled with cafés, restaurants, and shops, reinventing a life-world of émigrés. This phenomenon is replicated in various places in Cairo.

On the one hand, there is one part of the *Belle Epoque* Downtown that, since 2013, has been experiencing an ongoing gentrification and beautification by painting façades and refurbishing the entrances of buildings, and which is the main theme of the Creative Cities Conference. This gentrification, which was underway well before January 2011, has been taking place in certain buildings on 'Adly Street, the entire Orabi Square, and El-Alfi pedestrian area, up to Talaat Harb Square, where intensive real-estate speculation by mega-companies has invested in both nostalgic sentiments and neo-liberal dreams. The gentrification plans were interrupted by the revolution, but they have picked up pace recently. These plans seem to be undergoing a kind of repertoire or déjà vu scene of downtown refurbishment undertaken with a long-lasting bureaucratic mindset, revealing a steady continuity with Mubarak's rule.

At the same moment, there is another part of the city in which the borderline between the gentrified area and the previous war zone is epitomised in the iconic 'Street of the Eyes of Freedom' or 'Street of Martyrs', i.e. Mohamed Mahmud Street. It is also important to note that Mohamed Mahmud Street is one of the main entrance streets to Tahrir, which explains why it became a strategic battle space.

This demarcated spatial zone of the city includes Kasr al-Aini/Sheikh Rehan Street and Yussef El Guindi Street, up to Nubar Street and 'Abdin Square. Since 2011, this area has witnessed violent confrontations and urban wars. The centre of that state of exception is the colossal Ministry of Interior building, which has been turned into a fierce citadel surrounded by numerous walls, checkpoints, and barbed wire. Life continues to be difficult for its residents in terms of mobility and parking. That specific zone of Downtown, during the past few years, was protected by tanks, police vehicles, barbed wire, armoured cars, and countless permanently camping soldiers, and today by newly erected iron gates. Recently, even more walls were erected and checkpoints installed at the four corners. But Mohamed Mahmud Street remains the demarcating line of the previous war zone area, with its growing fences and walls that kept on appearing and reappearing, long after the violent incidents of November and December 2011 and 2012 occurred. Some walls have been removed, like the Falaki wall and the Kasr al-Aini walls, to be replaced by iron gates that can be closed, but remain open almost all the time. However, even more walls were added much later after the violent incidents. These are fierce walls that are meant to prevent car bombs and terrorist attacks.

Immediately obvious are the concrete-block walls, which were erected by the army during the Mohamed Mahmud violence. The entrance to Sheikh

Rihan Street from Kasr al-Aini Street remained barricaded until recently by yet another concrete wall. The concrete wall that blocked off Kasr al-Aini Street from Tahrir Square, erected at the end of 2011, was replaced in 2014–15 by iron gates that can be closed at any time. Across from the l'Institut d'Egypte, situated near several ministries at the intersection of Kasr al-Aini Street and Sheikh Rihan Street, is the Garden City quarter, the site of the British and American embassies. The area around these embassies remains a closed-off, heavily protected security zone. This quarter has been transformed into a policed-cum-militarised space. During summer 2015, one more concrete barricade was added around l'Institut d'Egypte, just opposite the Sheikh Rehan Gate of the American University in Cairo.

I argue that these concave bunkered walls and the surrounding fences – which have multiplied, for example, around the Itihadiyya Palace in Heliopolis, the Ministry of Justice in Doqi, the Internal Security building in Nasr City, the main Internal Security Ministry compound around Lazugly Street, and the huge, Egyptian-style Great Wall of China around the People's Parliament passing through Kasr al-Aini Street up to Lazugly Square and Falaki Street – all these walls, replicated all over Cairo, are becoming spaces that incite 'terror' and fear. Perhaps, too, the walls remain witness to the painful political memory of the Mohamed Mahmud Street massacre in 2011, the dragging of the iconic 'blue bra woman', and the dumping of the corpse of a demonstrator in rubbish, images that went globally viral in 2011.

The Ministry of Interior in Lazugly Street was transformed into a citadel, with black iron gates and terrifying fences surrounding it. And the public visibility of the might of the powers, exemplified by these walls, is what is at stake.

Most of these fences and walls have been constructed well after the violent clashes and confrontations took place. It is possible to argue that they have no real utilitarian function, since the million-marches and demonstrations ceased to occur after August 2013. Nonetheless, the State remains seriously concerned about potential terror attacks by the Islamists. However, the magnitude, length, and concave form of the walls, built to resist car bombs, are basically functioning as a means to 'terrorise' citizens, as reminders of possible punishment for insurrection. These walls certainly intimidate passers-by from daring to imagine what is behind the walled areas, since they are mostly surveilled by round-the-clock internal security plainclothes guards. These spaces have become constant panopticons for the residents. With the increasing terrorist attacks within the country after 2011, the 'war on terror' provided legitimation for erecting these multiple walls.

In spite of the multiplying concrete walls around the ministries, the dramaturgy of Mohammed Mahmud Street continues. Ironically, after 2014 the street witnessed a rapid process of gentrification, as the former Greek Campus (renamed the GrEEK Campus) of the American University in Cairo was rented out to tycoon Ahmed El Alfi. The campus was transformed it into a 'technology and innovation park', entrance to which is restricted to 'entrepreneurs'. Thus this space now serves a new public, who could be viewed as the emerging, Egyptian-style Yuppies and professionals.

This renewed pattern of gentrification of the street went together with the growing phenomenon of Western-style cappuccino cafés and bakeries alongside the already existing local, popular cafés (*qahwa baladi*) catering for the poorer public, which offer cheap water pipes and are crowded with night owls, mostly youth. The side streets off of Mohamed Mahmud Street at the Tahrir end have witnessed one further transmutation: the flowering of a large number of electrical appliance shops catering to middle-class consumerist lifestyles.

Today Mohamed Mahmud Street looks like a hip, neo-liberal, fashionable space. The annual Downtown Contemporary Arts Festival ('D-CAF') has transformed the quarter once again into an attractive area for middle- and upper-class youngsters to attend concerts, street performances, films, and exhibitions. With extensive sponsorship from the Al-Ismailiyya Company, which has purchased a large number of buildings in Downtown as part of a massive process of renovation (Abaza 2016), D-CAF is marking its eighth year as a successful festival attracting young artists from overseas (D-CAF)).

The street art on the entire wall of the main gate of the American University along Mohamed Mahmud Street was wiped out, with the exception of a few metres that were intentionally left by the administration as a reminder of the street as a 'memorial space' (Abaza 2012). After the abundant insults and offenses against the regime, and the many portraits of the martyrs, have been whitewashed, what remains today is a sort of decorative, aimless street art that has actually been sponsored by the neo-liberal tycoon Al-Alfi. On the walls of the former Greek Campus remains some apolitical graffiti drawn by young female artists who were part of the project of 'Women on Walls' (WOW) launched by Mia Gröndahl, a Swedish photographer residing in Cairo. This specially commissioned art is considered tolerable, inoffensive, and orderly by the Government, but it clearly has little to do with the offensive political graffiti produced between 2011 and 2013. This case reveals the tensions among artists, art gatekeepers, and foreign funders, as it raised much controversy among the scene of graffiti artists (see Abaza 2017).

## Nostalgias and the city

In spite of all this recent gentrification, the present is tough enough, which explains why there is such a pervasive, collective nostalgic mood about an imagined, beautified past. For if I spoke previously of the violence of the revolution, what followed after 2014 was another form of violence in the urban reshaping of the city, resulting in the erasure of an entire historic quarter.

This is a logical consequence of the dreams of utopias instigated by the revolutionary momentum. Svetlana Boym (2007: 7–8) reminds us that the twentieth century began with utopia and terminated with nostalgia. She furthermore asserts that nostalgia in the seventeenth century was perceived as a disease that could be cured with opium and wandering in the Alps. Her fascinating reading of nostalgia conveys the idea that the desire for the lost place can be translated into a longing for a slower past time, i.e. the time of childhood. As she says:

> The nostalgic desires to turn history into private or collective mythology, to revisit time like space, refusing to surrender to the irreversibility of time that plagues the human condition. Hence the past of nostalgia, to paraphrase William Faulkner, is not even past. It could be merely better time, or slower time – time out of time, not encumbered by appointment books. (Boym 2007: 8)

This brings Boym to her next point: that the imaginaries of the past time, fostered by nostalgia, can be decisive with respect to the desires of the present. I find Boym's explication of nostalgia quite timely in deciphering the current overwhelming, post-traumatic, counter-revolutionary momentum in Egypt that seeks to cope with an unbearable present. It equally explains why various competing, if not clashing, camps are resurfacing with diverse nostalgic visions. The first of these visions is the fresh and extreme nostalgia of those supporting the 2011 revolution, who experienced the unique moment of the eighteen magical days and the two years of turbulent, effervescent, performative street politics that followed, triggering dreams of the possibility for improving life – dreams which were then harshly crushed. The second vision is maintained by the pervasive counter-revolutionary forces. Paradoxically, I would include here the supporters of the Sisi regime together with the opposing camp, the Muslim Brotherhood, who were victims of military killings in Rabe'a al-'Adaweyya Square in summer 2013. Over the past three years, Sisi's military regime has adopted a nationalist tone,[19] while borrowing symbols of socialist realism that contradict the obvious state of the globalised region. Meanwhile, the Islamist camp seems to be fixated on a golden period of the early years of Islam. The complex ideology of the counter-revolutionary camp encompasses both of these doppelgängers, as the two share the elective affinity towards authoritarianism. Both camps have worked hard against the forces of civil society, which advocates the reinstating of human rights, workers' rights, social justice, and a renewed sense of citizenship. Ironically, the two forces are entrapped as mirror images of each other in perpetrating authoritarian and anti-democratic practices, as well as in their obsession with public morality.

The third vision is that of the Nasserite camp, which glorifies the past post-colonial military regime of Nasser at the expense of a complete denial of its non-democratic rule. Nostalgia is spilled on the golden times of Nasser with the celebration of independence movements, nationalism, the times of the Bandung Conference and the non-aligned movement, the era of socialism with its grandiose projects like the High Dam, and the democratisation of education that opened opportunities to millions.

The fourth vision, in direct opposition to the third, is held by the supporters of an imagined, over-glorified, pre-1952 colonial-royal elite, which denied the flagrant social inequalities existing at the time and the economic deprivation for the majority that led to yet another revolution. A nostalgic trend persists amongst those who continue to lament the disappearance of colonial times in Egypt, together with the glorious times of the former, deposed royal family. All four visions, however, express multiple understandings of nostalgia, through a prevailing, overwhelming sentiment of defeat.

'The Beautiful Times', '*al-zaman al-gamiil*', is a Facebook page that posts symbols of the lost and glorious past: images from Egyptian films of the 1940s, 1950s, and 1960s; concerts of diva singers like Om Kalthum, Fairuz, and Warda; performances by 'Abdel Halim Hafez and other famous Middle Eastern oldies stars; and other vintage artefacts and photographs. These are displayed in opposition to our supposedly miserable and tasteless present. 'The Beautiful Times' has also become a popular expression in Egypt that refers to a specific image of past relics and landmarks that have now disappeared. For the minds in this camp, these 'beautiful times' represent an idealised, simplistic, imaginary Cairo, when stunning, European-dressed Egyptian women could wear bikinis without being harassed by the 'vulgar' masses; when the streets of Cairo and Alexandria were clean (free of beggars and street children) and uncrowded; and when the centre of Downtown Cairo looked like a replica of a European city. More precisely, it is a way to mourn the lost 'Paris along the Nile'[20] city. No bearded Islamists or women wearing hijabs existed (at least in the photographs). No poor street vendors were seen in the European part of the city – although that certainly does not mean that they did not exist.

In today's discourses of denial about the 'beautiful old times', a fact is often overlooked, that the *Belle Epoque* city, including its prominent Jewish-owned *grands magasins*, its apartment buildings, and its residents, who consisted mostly of the foreign communities, was strongly associated with the so-called ordered, colonial, European-dominated space, in contradistinction to the 'disordered', 'oriental' part of the city with its forest of minarets, chaotic bazaars, and labyrinths. Timothy Mitchell provides a Foucauldian reading of the colonial mechanisms of power that were in effect at that time (Mitchell 1991).

Further blurring the meaning of the term, Egyptian architects have equated '*Belle Epoque*', as a label for the modern European architecture of nineteenth-century Downtown Cairo, with '*al-zaman al-gamiil*'. This leads to further overlap between a nostalgic vision of the glorious past that produced such flourishing arts – albeit under colonial rule – with an obvious denial of the rigid and unequal spatial and class structure that led to the 1952 revolution/military coup (depending on one's political affiliations).

The imagined old (and 'beautiful' yet colonial) Cairo cannot conceal the fact that in our present times, vulgarity and greed are rampant. In fact, this nostalgic feeling coexists with a form of conscious destruction on the part of the powers that be. Although they cannot annihilate the histories of the major cities like Alexandria, Mansura, and Cairo, they do nothing to stop the organised mafias who have got hold of large amounts of real estate and monopolise the construction sector. In Alexandria, for instance, and all along the Mediterranean coast, no one is concerned about the aesthetics of the ugly, crowded, nightmarish towers. Instead, the worry is that these towers have started to collapse like houses of cards, and thousands may die under the rubble in the decades to come. Indeed, it needs little intelligence to conclude that these buildings defy any logical architectural laws.

In the current case, the unbridled nostalgia for Tahrir has been submerged in a traumatic sentiment of depression after the ephemeral, euphoric moment of the military takeover. Has the revolution failed when the country has never witnessed such violations of human rights, and such clampdowns on activists, journalists, and intellectuals, as under the Sisi regime?

But above all, it is the feeling of absolute exhaustion, accompanied by a perpetual *'mal de vivre'*, that overwhelms our daily lives. Simply walking out of one's apartment door sets off a 'war of all against all'. This coincides with the constant erasure of the memory as an involuntary self-defence against the targeted and conscious erasures of landscapes, of public expressions, of the art, the music, the graffiti, the signs and symbols experienced since 2011, of the nature we moved in for decades, of the trees and the architecture that surrounded us. Violence takes different shades, as it is not restricted to confrontations with the regime. Entire neighbourhoods, like the Ramlat Bulaq area, have been erased in 2018 and their population expelled to make way for wealth-seeking investors, as it has been targeted by speculation for almost a decade now. It only needed the army to accomplish a project of cleansing the place of its population, which Mubarak had been reluctant to undertake.

Simply stated, greed, corruption, and money, working superbly in concert, have consciously managed to destroy the urban texture of Cairo, and even more so of Alexandria. One might think that the counter-revolutionary forces blame the 2011 revolution for causing a massive eradication of the city's landmarks, of its rich Coptic, Islamic, and European patrimony, of its wonderful old villas and colonial buildings that continue to disappear at a dizzying speed. This has been accompanied by the explosion of informal construction on agrarian land all over the countryside. Soon the entire country will look like a huge conglomerate of ugly, frightening, red cement-brick towers sticking to each other. The population explosion, together with the degradation of the agricultural sector, leaves no option for the rural poor but to convert agrarian land into dwellings that keep on growing vertically. The sole exception will be the isolated gated communities and compounds that have so little to do with the reality of the old centre of Cairo.

It is true that the erasure of the city's landmarks has been going on for decades, since well before 2011. However, it is as if the powers that be now excel in destroying the little beauty that remained, as if anything that might look ancient has to be erased and replaced. The cities of Cairo and Alexandria have broken aesthetic records in ugliness and incoherence. It is no coincidence that the rich heritage in Mamluk Cairo threatens to disappear due to organised, collective theft since 2011, as architects have been warning. The pillage of antiquities has reached an unprecedented scale, prompting alarmed Egyptian architects and historians to lead relentless campaigns to track down the countless valuable pieces that too often turn up in Sotheby's and Christie's auctions.

The unstated main issue is the bargaining over reality. Official sources seek to erase what has really happened during the past six years: the fact that numerous protesters were killed, others tortured, many disappearing, blinded, or disfigured, while no official has been held accountable for these crimes. The refusal to commemorate the martyrs of the revolution, the regime's denial that the violation of human rights is what triggered the events of 2011, and the fact that injustices continue in an even harsher mode, is what makes obsessive urban dystopias so pervasive. The erasure becomes the point of departure.

### The Dubai/Singapore models of transnational cities

In what follows I will attempt to raise questions about the future of the urban reshaping of the cities of the Middle East that is currently taking place, in order to provide a mosaic of contradictions between the further militarisation of urban life and the burning theme of the disappearing cities, increasingly surrounded with walled islands of consumer culture and 'smart' and 'informational' cities while sprawling slums continue to expand. I will then move to some questions social scientists have raised concerning the future and the shape of the kind of cities we will end up living in, if the dominant and hegemonic neo-liberal mindset we are all subjected to will continue to dominate. It seems that we are confronted with restrained models – or rather, very limited 'ideal types' in the Weberian sense – with respect to the future of urban life in the Middle East.

The Dubai model – the Singapore of the Middle East, the 'Arab Riviera', the dream world of conspicuous consumption – has been both vehemently demonised and applauded for being imagined as either a uniquely artificially constructed utopia, or an immanent dystopia pushing surreal and lavish consumerist lifestyles only for the happy few, pairing with 'smart' high technologies of surveillance and control running the city port. This runs parallel with pervasive feudal bonds to the rule of the al-Maktum family, who run the country like a big neo-liberal city-corporation (Kanna 2010: 110). This dream world exists alongside harsh labour conditions for the large imported population of immigrants, mostly Asian. It is no secret that the securitised archipelago has flourished at the expense of the over-exploitation of Asian workers. Mike Davis has also criticised Dubai for being a paradise for money laundering and for its much-contested gargantuan mega-projects like the World Islands, which are apparently doomed to fail, not only due to ecological impediments, but also through the impact of the fluctuating global financial markets that directly affected Dubai's growth in particular after the last global recession of 2007 (Davis 2006b). Davis's metaphors, describing in negative terms the highly acclaimed architectural wonders of Dubai, are deeply cynical, as if the entire landscape of the country were an inflated mimicry turning into a monstrosity. I would like to quote him: 'Although compared variously to Las Vegas, Manhattan, Orlando, Monaco, Singapore, The Shiekhdom is more like their collective summation of mythologization: a hallucinatory pastiche of the big, the bad and the ugly' (Davis 2006b: 51) Yet Davis seems to argue that 'copying' the finished product to the point of perfection in backward societies attaining capitalism at a later stage has the appearance of trying to meet an 'ideal type' – an ideal type, ironically enough, that can be even more perfected than its original conception in advanced societies because it is viewed as a finished product (Davis 2006b: 54).

Stephen Graham's fascinating work on elevators, which I will be engaging with in the forthcoming chapters, describes one particular apocalyptic moment at the Burj Khalifa towers, which encompass some 1,000 apartments, as a nightmarish dystopia. This happened when a large number of the residential tenants ended up being locked up electronically in various spaces of the tower, such as the spas and gyms. This occurred when the flat owners refused to pay the astronomical maintenance charges. These charges were reportedly as high as £155,000 for an apartment worth £1 million (Graham 2014: 256).

On the other hand, the works of both Yasser Elsheshtawi and Ahmed Kanna (Elsheshtawy 2010; Kanna 2011) are fresh attempts at providing an alternative, realistic, and perhaps more sensitive representation of the city from below, as well as from an insider's view. Both works demystify a number of simplistic assumptions about Dubai by providing profounder ethnographic analyses of the interaction between the immigrants and the local residents. Elsheshtawi focused on the life-world of 'informal urbanism', and of the numerous nationalities of immigrants (in particular the areas where Indians, Pakistanis, Egyptians, and Kazakhs live) and how they interacted in the various urban spaces in the city. Elsheshtawi looked at Dubai as the ultimate migrant city to focus on the spacial sites of resistance, which led him to meditate on the locations of bus stops from which the immigrants commute to the labour camps.

Elsheshtawi narrates how he started his Dubai journey by searching for the area previously named Gamal 'Abd al-Nasser Square (a name that many people do not know) and now renamed Baniyas Square in Dubai. He then links Dubai's emergence and development to the specific history of that square, now a neighbourhood of Indian immigrants, as epitomising a pattern of 'globalisation from below'. His work also looks at the relationship between the *longue durée* trade connections uniting Africa and the Indian subcontinent and the life-worlds of the immigrants (Elsheshtawy 2014). Kanna, in contrast, analysed the emergence of the corporate culture amongst the younger generation of local professional men and women and the ways in which globalisation is affecting urban life and reshaping novel understandings of citizenship. Dubai stands as an interesting example of hybridising corporate capitalist worldviews with feudal forms of rule, as Kanna has argued (Kanna 2010). However, Ahmed Kanna also speaks of a differing 'subjectivity', here in relationship to an emergent neo-liberal, individualistic, 'valuable citizenship'. He borrows from Aihwa Ong's concepts of 'flexible' and 'valuable' citizenships in order to apply them to Dubai's struggle with the modernity/tradition paradox. He convincingly weaves the discourse of global corporatist ideology – self-made solutions achieved within the intricate local ethnic hierarchical specificities. However, these two positions – Kanna on the one hand, in contrast to Bamyeh (2013) and Hanafi (2012) on the other – seem to converge on similar conclusions: that these novel figurations of subjectivities, both revolutionary and neo-liberal, point once again to fresh understandings of individuality and forms of self-reflexive individuality, which nonetheless can be different from neo-liberal individualism.

Egypt, standing at the crossroads of a counter-revolutionary moment, seems to suggest that the future appropriation of the post-revolutionary city of Cairo will arise from the struggle between these two opposing 'subjectivities': a struggle between preserving the memory, knowledge, and experience of urban wars and performative revolutionary advocacies, on the one hand, and neo-liberal agendas obsessed with erasure on the other; a struggle today confronted by a neo-liberal gentrification supported by a military 'order'.

## Dreams about escape while in Cairo: The shopping mall

Ski Egypt Price List

> Snow Go: Adult = 300 L.E.; Child = 300 L.E.
>
> North Pole: Adult = 450 L.E.; Child = 450 L.E.
>
> Snow View: Adult = 100 L.E.; Child = 100 L.E.
>
> Ski pass: Adult = 300 L.E.; Child = 250 L.E.
>
> Gloves voucher: Special = 50 L.E.
>
> Locker = 50 L.E.
>
> Key card deposit = 50 L.E.

Ski School

> Discovery lesson: Adult = 200 L.E.; Child = 200 L.E.
>
> Group lesson: Adult = 300 L.E.; Child = 200 L.E.

Private lesson 60 minutes: Adult = 750 L.E.; Child = 750 L.E.

Private additional guest 60 minutes: Adult = 250 L.E.; Child = 250 L.E.

90 min. session: Adult = 855 L.E.; Child = 60 min. session 570 L.E.

3 days' camp 3 sessions package: Adult = 855 L.E.; Child = 570 L.E.

5 days' camp 5 sessions package: Adult = 1,455 L.E.; Child = 970 L.E.

Alpine group lesson package (6 group lessons for price of 5): Adult = 1,500 L.E.; Child = 1,000 L.E.

Alpine private lesson package (6 group lessons for price of 5): Adult = 3,750 L.E.; Child = 2,750 L.E.

Terms and conditions apply. Please note that it is compulsory for all skiers to wear gloves.

This is the price list on the large board behind the ticket stand of Ski Egypt, situated in the grandiose, newly opened (2017) Mall of Egypt. Clearly, these are not cheap entrance fees. Ski Egypt, like the Magic Planet and Vox Cinemas companies, are all exact replicas of attractions in Dubai's famed mega-malls. The fascination of skiing, of white and bright snow and cold surrounded by endless sand and unfinished construction landscapes, is certainly catching. The mirage-like malls are surreal constructions, lost in the vast spaces of the desert surrounding the satellite city of the Sixth of October.

The question keeps arising: why are so many wealthy Arabs mesmerised by the simulacra of mini-Switzerlands, of artificial snow landscapes in the confined spaces of closed-up, glassed-in malls all over the Middle East? Does the sensation of skiing on artificial snow in compulsory gloves provide a sensual, self-elevating feeling of 'conspicuous leisure' and 'conspicuous consumption', so strikingly prophesied by the late sociologist Thorstein Veblen (Veblen 1953) as the grand malaise of modernity? Anything that is rare is highly desired, and in Egypt nothing is more available than sand. Snow is just the opposite.

When you enter a Cairene mall, forget all about the *Weight of the World*.[21] Just keep on strolling through the endless kilometres of shops, cafés, restaurants, and whatnot, and keep on staring, for life there looks different from the one you know. And if you visit the Mall of Egypt, don't get hung up watching people wearing rented winter jackets and gloves for playing in the snow, or be mesmerised by the mass of digital photographs of the people skiing and playing in the snowy hall, displayed on computers nearby. Take the escalator one floor up; observe the poorer visitors with their children who can't afford the entrance tickets. Do they get their satisfaction by just staring for long moments at the other people through the barrier of the huge window? Isn't it enough of a relief to simply walk around in cool, air-conditioned space? Window shopping still costs nothing, and so far no entrance ticket to the mall itself is required, which has actually happened in some of the earlier-generation big malls that fear the invasion of the riff-raff.

These are excerpts from an article I wrote after paying a visit to the Mall of Egypt in April 2018.

Having said that, the clichéd orientalist and yet orientalised Dubai deserves attention, as it is what fascinates and catches the attention of most of the current Arab ruling classes. Dubai – so admired for building the largest shopping malls and tallest towers in the world, segregated compounds, palm islands, and futuristic postmodern architecture, the magnet for world-class architects – is idealised as the only possible utopia for the entire Middle East. It is precisely the 'gigantism', if not megalomania pushed to the extreme, that stands as the last counterweight between the war zones of the collapsing states (Yemen, Libya, Iraq, Syria) and the occupation of Palestine. Why has the insatiable desire to mimic Dubai, the dream world of abundance and luxury, become so imperative since 2011 in Egypt? The neo-liberal powers seem to regard this kind of development as an urgently needed face-lift after the troubled years of the Arab revolutions, the devastating civil wars, the unprecedented massive migration of refugees to Europe, the acute humanitarian disaster of the greatest population displacements in modern history, and the emergence of the threat of ISIS on a global scale.

The replication of copied and pasted shopping malls in the entire region epitomises this utter fascination with Dubai, since mimicking is coming to be imperative. Since the early 2000s, the Emirati Majid al-Futtaim group has extended their financial empire by building numerous gigantic malls not only in Egypt but across the Middle East. In response, nearly a decade ago, I wrote that the Middle East was suffering from the construction of a racial segregation wall around Israel, and that the horrific war in Iraq was happening simultaneously with the opening of more mega-malls in Dubai and in a number of cities in the Gulf (Abaza 2006). Also, in the early 2000s, a snow city and an ice rink in a shopping mall in Cairo's Nasr City were simultaneously erected and celebrated. And yet the shopping mall was quickly shut down because snow cities, like ice rinks, were not sustainable financially.

The number of malls has more than quadrupled since about 2008 in Cairo's suburbs of New Cairo, Sixth of October, and Sheikh Zayed. These malls are replicated in standardised, monotonous shapes. It is this sameness that creates a semblance of democracy, so that we can all feel elevated to dream of being elsewhere, as long as we are in the confines of the mall, while in reality we remain in Cairo, but oblivious towards the *'ashwaa'iyyaat*.[22] This mesmerising replicability has been led by the Majid al-Futtaim group in the Middle Eastern cities of Beirut, Sharjah, Bahrain, Alexandria, and Muscat.

Middle Eastern countries have now entered a race to see which Arab country has the biggest mall in the world. This also means that the next generation of malls will be even larger. Today, the Al-Futtaim group runs twenty-one huge shopping malls. They advertise their success story on their website by claiming that these spaces welcome 178 million visitors annually. They also boast that they employ over 40,000 people, and enjoy 'the highest credit rating (BBB) among privately-held corporates in the region'.[23] This pride in extreme dimensions verges on megalomania.

But it is Dubai, rather than the replicable malls, that is most frequently the proposed model, which begs for systematic comparison with Singapore. I am referring here to the working paper of Ahmed Kanna, published in 2009 (Kanna 2009). Kanna draws an appealing comparison between these two 'Asian', global city-states. Dubai and Singapore have both been labelled as neo-liberal. Both city-states were part of the British Empire and the Indian Ocean trade routes. Both have very important ports with voluminous shipping traffic, and both are considered free-trade zones. Oil and the refinery industries also unite the two city-states. And both sell a specific global image of luxurious tourism and leisure (Kanna 2009: 12). Above all, the two cities are advertised as the perfect utopias or empires of consumption (the positive side) while clearly their workers' rights are suppressed (the negative side). In spite of numerous similarities between these two countries, the 'feudal capitalism' style of rule, whereby power is monopolised by the al-Maktum family in Dubai, clearly diverges from the meritocratic system on which Singapore was founded, or at least it is regarded as such, even if it doesn't function in that way, since inequalities are far from being erased (Teo 2017: 21).

My aim is to transpose the discussion raised by Chua Beng Huat on 'Singapore as model' and its practical implications in our part of the world. More precisely, it examines how 'mimicking' and 'cloning' (Chua 2011: 36) this frequently cited model can lead to distasteful unintended consequences elsewhere, since no other place is quite the same as Singapore. In the Middle East, the similar idea of promoting Dubai as a model continues to create multiplying dystopias – even more so since the 'Arab Spring'.

It is actually the virtual dream of an imagined Singapore/Dubai model that is being encouraged by the military and decaying authoritarian/neo-liberal regimes. The giant real-estate companies, one of the most lucrative economic sectors in the Middle East today – companies like Emaar, SODIC, and Solidere, or the Ismailiyya Company and the Gulf Investors in Egypt – continue, with pervasive aggression, to sell 'the success story of Singapore/Dubai', of the 'possibility of success', of imagined tropical greenery in the new 'walled cities', the mushrooming gated communities in the Arab deserts. No matter how loudly the official discourse advertises, for example, the new capital city of Cairo as a virtual Dubai, neither the twenty-million-population megacity of Cairo nor any other Middle Eastern city will ever be Dubai or Singapore. To the contrary, it is estimated that, by 2020, some 66 per cent of Greater Cairo's population will be living in what are called 'informal areas' (Sims and Séjourné 2000).

Equally fascinating, as Ahmed Kanna argues, is the way in which the Dubai model has come to predominate over the Singapore one. It is astonishing how Singapore emulated Dubai, or was inspired by Dubai, in investing in huge real-estate projects and in the promotion of gated communities and new cities. These are advertised today in Egypt, by the way, as the only so-called decent and livable spaces, feeding on middle-class neuroses and enhancing further physical segregation between the sprawling slums and the new walled cities. Kanna argues that the Sentosa Cove mega-project in Singapore is a replica of Dubai's Palm Jumeirah (Kanna 2009: 24). Furthermore, it is no coincidence that the late Zaha Hadid, whose remarkable architecture remains strongly associated with Dubai, was invited to develop the billion-dollar residential project d'Leedon (Sklair 2017: 162), which is now being advertised as 'Singapore's Zaha-Topia' (Choe 2015).

The repertoire of aspiring to replicate the utopia of Dubai since January 2011 remains not only an obsession for the neo-liberal military establishment, but a dream of countless youngsters (who participated in Tahrir) who wish to escape Cairo's pollution.

But where is the novelty in these virtual magnifications? This is, regretfully, a déjà vu that was well manipulated by the former neo-liberal Mubarakist tycoons. One need only recall the pre-January 2011 television advertisements for the satellite city *Madinaty* (My City), constructed in the northeastern desert by the real-estate mogul Hisham Talaat Mustafa, to be assured that we are experiencing continuity rather than change with respect to desert cityscapes.

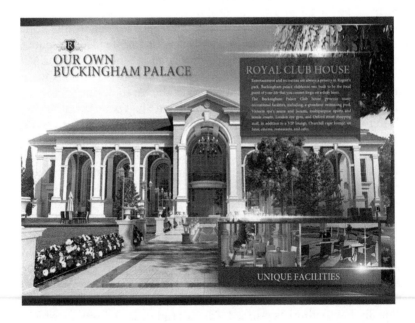

**Figure 8** 'Our Own Buckingham Palace'. Advertisement for Regent Park New Cairo Apartments.

## Notes

1 This point will be discussed later in Naguib Mahfouz's *Al-Qahira al-jadida (Modern Cairo)* – specifically, how the European quarter becomes a space that allows greater sexual promiscuity, in contrast to the tight social control of the older quarters.

2 For one of the most visually intriguing works dissecting colonial phantasms of the harem in Algeria through postcards, see Alloula 1986.

3 Concerning the imprisonment of minors, see www.youtube.com/watch?v=tQLUWNUVylw (accessed 14 May 2018) and www.youtube.com/watch?v=S35ygVttECw&list=UUXEM0XN_OzK_rScQKP8hYFg&index=44 (accessed 14 May 2018).

4 The number of victims is disputed, ranging from 30 to 300 deaths ('Maspero Demonstrations', Wikipedia).

5 See 'Sniper targeting eyes'.

6 'Testimonies of Mohamed Mahmud'. See also 'Mohamed Mahmud Street's incidents'.

7 For an interesting reading of the revolution as a 'performance' and as dramaturgy, see Alexander 2011; Taha and Combs 2012.

8 Asma Mahfouz's YouTube clip inciting people to take to the streets went viral before 25 January 2011. It was vital in triggering the spark of the revolution.

9 See YouTube: www.youtube.com/watch?v=satudpo5xWQ&list=UUXEM0XN_OzK_rScQKP8hYFg&index=37&has_verified=1 (accessed 15 May 2018).

10 Government efforts to protect women against sexual assaults were part of Sisi's propaganda to enhance his popularity, even though he is blamed for having issued the order to conduct 'virginity tests' on female protesters in March 2011. Furthermore, it was clear that the thugs who assaulted female protesters in Tahrir in 2011 and 2012 were paid by the regime to discourage them from protesting. Also, even if, under the rule of the Muslim Brotherhood, it was not the Brothers but the internal security who instigated these public assaults, the Brotherhood members who were in the regime were mostly complacent about such acts. They blamed women for taking to the streets.

11 It is mesmerising to observe the striking similarities in actions and resistance, such as the creation of mobile clinics, communal action, the display of text messages, and the art of resistance to violent police forces between Tahrir, Gesi, and the Maidan in Kiev. The very fact alone that the word '*Maidan*' means literally 'square' in Arabic raised strong emotions for Middle Easterners who were observing the unfolding events in Kiev.

12 Debord 1956; first appeared in *Les Lèvres nues* 9.

13 Regarding Cairo's transformations during the past years and the political turmoil that is fundamentally redesigning the cityscape, I could not think of a better analogy for Cairo than Lewis Mumford's earlier observations on the city as 'a theatre of social action' (Mumford 2002: 92) and as a space that 'fosters art and is art. The city creates the theater and is the theater' (Mumford 2002: 94).

14 On the point of the iconic image of the bird's-eye shot of the millions filling the square becoming, so to speak, the most representative photograph of the revolution, globally going viral and producing the effect of a 'faceless' revolution, see Westmoreland 2016.

15 The Islamist Mohamed Morsi was elected as president on 30 June 2012 and served until 3 July 2013. He was removed from office as a result of spectacular demonstrations against his regime, which gave the army the golden opportunity to interfere and oust him.

16 Tahrir as a spectacle was a point that was further elaborated in the edited volume of Samia Mehrez (2012).

17 Timothy Mitchell dwells at length on the significance of panoramas and panoramic perspectives amongst European photographers, as a drive to dominate the city from above, and to try to comprehend the logic behind the labyrinthine, visually chaotic, and opaque oriental cities.

18 Regarding the role of vertical control via helicopters, see Adey 2010.

19 While still remaining the second-largest recipient of US aid, after Israel.

20 This is the title of Cynthia Myntti's book on Cairo's *Belle Epoque* architecture (Myntti 1999).

21 Title of the celebrated work of the late French sociologist Pierre Bourdieu, *La misère du monde* (Bourdieu 1999).

22 The word *'ashwaa'i* (pl. *'ashwaa'iyyaat*) refers to the spontaneous, unplanned, informal constructions of squatters or simply slums; the *'ashwaa'i* spontaneity is thus associated with chaos. These informal areas are not exactly like Latin American slums. Some of them were previously agrarian land, around the fringes of the city, turned illegally into red-brick buildings, up to seven to ten storeys high, tightly glued to each other.

23 See Majid al-Futtuaim.

**2**

# Tale II: Commute

**Meanderings and wanderings through regular commutes
to the desert**

English/Arabic advertisements of real estate on billboards on the Sixth of
October Bridge, up to 90th Road, New Cairo, 15 February 2018:

'*Madinaty* ... your life investment. Call: 19691.' (in Arabic)

'Customise your space and pick your view, Lake Park Studios, Taj City. Call:
16750.'

'Capital Heights, New Capital, New Home. Luxurious apartments and duplex.
0% down payment, up to 7 years instalment. Developed by Safwa Urban
Development.'

'In Cairo's future, there's Sun Capital and then there's everywhere else. Sun
Capital. 6th October.'

'Beta Egypt: *enwan gadid lil sa'ada* [a new address for happiness]. Beta Greens
New Cairo. Call: 19231.'

'Investing in a lifetime. California Homes in New Cairo, Golden Square Villas.
Call: 16050.'

'*La Mirada el-Mostakbal*: Near everywhere. La Mirada. The future starts now.
New Cairo. Call: 16632.'

'Hassan Allam Properties: Looking after heritage. From our family to yours.'

'Hassan Allam Properties: For generations to come. From our family to yours.'

'Steer your mind. I love New Giza. Call: 16656.'

'Delivering Phase 1, Galleria, The Golden Square Fifth Settlement. Arabia
Holding. Call: 19217.'

'The leading developer in Mostakbal City. A tradition of trust. Sabbour. Call:
16033.'

'*Stella Di Mare*, Ain Sokhna. Call: 19565.'

'*Jebal al-Sokhna* launching marvel. Sky Bridge Development. Call: 16752.'

**Figure 9**   'Have a "Lushly" Life'. Advertisement for the Lush Plateaus
development over Sixth October Bridge, 7 June 2018.

'Granda Life, launching in al-Shorouk. Egygab Development. Call: 19961.'

'A new star launching. Tucana. Your own dreamy private beach. Town homes,
twin houses, villas. Call: 16643.'

'Liberty Village, New Capital. Redefining essentials. Fully finished luxury
apartments. Novus Stanza. Call: 19625.'

'Heliopolis Hills. 10 minutes from Heliopolis. Security and guards. 30% green
space. A social club 300 metres. Oriental Weavers Group. Call: 16234.' (in Arabic)

More and more advertisement billboards on the Sixth of October Bridge up
to New Cairo.

26 February 2018. Personal observation: I am mesmerised at the velocity
of the change in advertisements on the huge billboards. Every week, when
I drive to the new campus via the Sixth of October Bridge, I discover more
real-estate advertisements that have popped up recently, and through them,
an endless display of mysterious companies and developers:

'Stella Park New Capital. Redefining luxury. Remco. Call. 19565.'

'It's happening. Hassan Alam Properties.'

'Sun Capital, own tomorrow. Arabia Holding, 6th of October. Call. 19217.'

'We are culture. 9,800 units delivered – We are Oud. An Oriental Weavers
sister company, Oud Orientals. Call: 16234.'

Billboard on top of a building in Ramses: 'Take part in the next industrial hub. ElSewedy Development, Industria Sokhna. Call: 19107.'

'Architectural sophistication, cozy cabanas to one-storey villas. Tatweer Misr. Call: 16094.'

'*Il Monte Galala Sokhna*, delivering in 2019. PUKKA, New Capital, launching now, luxury apartments, up to seven years payment plan. Call: 16603.'

'*Aria*, now fully finished. Landmark Sabbour. Call: 16295.'

'*Azzar*, New Cairo, California Homes, in New Cairo, Golden Square. Call: 16050.'

28 February 2018:

'The lush plateaus. Have a "lushy" life. Zizinia El-Mostakbal, New Cairo. Ground floor with garden. Ardic Developments Co. Let's talk: 16348.'

'Life like never before. Lake Side.'

Small billboards in New Cairo on Road 90:

'Al Rowad Group, 20 years, since 1997. Call: 19211.'

'Diar. Call: 19053.'

'Alfth Group. Call: 19571.'

'Bonyan. Call: 19084.'

'Royal. Baytak mamalaktak [Your house is your kingdom]. Call: 19657.'

'Tatawur. Hayaat afdal, istithmaar afdal [Better life, better investment]. Tel. 010 22113111.'

'Karma Construction. Call: 19569.'

'Jadeer Group Real Estate. Call: 19820.'

## Modernisation and spatial alienation

'In Palm Hills we dream of the return of love and beauty ... and clear enjoyment ... and the return of mercy to our heart ... and the dream of the return of culture and the arts ... and enlightened thought ... Palm Hills for construction ... the return of the Egyptian spirit.' (Advertisement on ONTV channel, during Ramadan, June 2016)

'*La Vie en Rose*. Located in the 5th Compound Service Centre, New Cairo.'

'*La Vie en Vert*. Villette New Cairo, SODIC. For more information visit us at the SODIC Sales Centre Headquarters KM 38 Cairo–Alexandria Desert Road.'

'Projects realised by Beverly Hills Development, founded in 1998, one of the most visible real estate developers in Egypt: Skymall, Swiss Medical Centre (Egypt), City Plaza Mall (Egypt), Hilton Sabangali Resort (Chad), Dream Resort (Juba).' ('Beverley Hills Development')

'Your dream, our mission.' ('Arkan Real Estate')

**Figure 10**    Developer advertisement on the way to Road 90, New Cairo,
8 February 2018.

'Do you wish to escape the noise and traffic of the city and live in a park and
be surrounded by stunning lakes and breath-taking greenery? Regent's Park
offers Maadi Sports & Yacht Club members the opportunity to explore a new
experience in fine living.'

'Regent's Park, a new experience in fine living at New Cairo.' ('Regent's Park')
[Followed by an avalanche of photographs, with massive, lavish, and imposing
villas, condos with waterfalls, ponds, and swimming pools, in the desert sea.
Simulated photographs of futuristic would-be landscapes.]

'*La Vie en Vert*' is an advertisement I encountered in 2016, on a daily basis,
on the depressing desert road that takes me to my simulated-shopping
mall-cum-American University campus located in the Eastern Desert of
New Cairo. The commute is roughly fifty kilometres one way, thus about a
one-hundred-kilometre round trip. For an American such a commute might
not be an issue at all, were it not for the deadly, interminable traffic jams
paralysing the city on a daily basis. One could easily argue that the chief
predicament of modern life for Egyptians is that they squander almost half
of their lives in commuting from one end of the city to the other. Not only
that, one way of defining who belongs to the working class today in Egypt is
by their means of transport, and whether the commuter uses three different
means of transportation to reach one destination on a daily basis (public
buses, microbuses, collective taxis, the metro, and *tok-toks*).[1] *Toks-toks*, as

a reminder, the typical means of mobility for the poor working class, are restricted mostly to popular quarters. In a clear way, *toks-toks* are inevitably paired with *'ashwaa'iyyaat* (informal areas), precisely because they remain one of the most practical and efficient means of mobility in the extremely narrow and unpaved streets in slums. Recently, these engines have been forbidden circulation in the main arteries of the centre of Downtown, and in residential quarters. The fact that these three-wheeled cars are relatively cheap (about 22,000 L.E. in 2015) explains why driving them has become one of the main means of livelihood for working-class young men (Alaa El-Din 2015). For state officials, and for their faithful devotees who believe their propaganda, as well as for large sections of the middle classes, *tok-tok* drivers, most of whom are barely eighteen, are often perceived as quasi-delinquent polluters, to be constantly harassed and chased by police officers and traffic controllers.

The construction costs of the 260-acre AUC campus, inaugurated in 2008, rocketed to some US$400 million.[2] The idea was to hybridise elements of Islamic architectural traditions into modern lines, which succeeds as a first impression. It seems, however, that the designers of this colossal construction neglected functionality. Almost a decade of exposure has not been sufficient to conciliate my alienation from the new campus. At the start of every term, I have trouble finding my classes. I constantly doubt myself. Am I ageing prematurely? Perhaps I am suffering from an everlasting disorientation that has to do with a creeping erasure of memory, inflicted on me by the powers that be, and I keep on wondering whether obliviousness is not becoming a national collective malaise? Or is it perhaps a blessing to constantly remain in a state of vagueness?

My nostalgia and sense of loss towards the old Tahrir campus, where I grew up and taught for many years, has been growing by the year. But the Tahrir campus has been altered too, and the Cairo I grew up with no longer really exists. To my comfort, I am certainly not the only one who finds the identically replicated units around the campus, inspired, so to say, by the labyrinth in Islamic architecture, so disorienting, and in truth intimidating.

The spatial alienation I encounter every time I am on campus goes together with harsh budget cuts, so that faculty have had barely any rise in salary for many years. What's new about that, you ask? Isn't the global neo-liberal virus infecting academia 'equitably' like the rest of the world? Are we not the tenured academics located in the South, still fortunate to continue to earn a fixed salary? When the neo-liberal policies that were established under Mubarak's 'cabinet of businessmen' and their entourage of crony capitalists, following the dominant 'laissez-faire' free-market economic policies, accompanied by the massive deregulation of working conditions and firing of workers, is still in operation under the current military regime? For example, workers have been detained, as in the attacks on bus and shipyard workers in October 2016 (Abaza 2013b; Egypt Solidarity 2016). So why complain about long commuting hours when I am still quite fortunate?

The inevitable integration of our small university into the world system of nasty neo-liberalising policies corresponded to an unrelenting heavy teaching load and competitive measures affecting research, with adjuncts always the worst remunerated in the hierarchical scale. But these quite common observations are not new to any academic. It is just the evidence that our university has been emulating the metropolises and thus has finally globalised. The hearsay is that tenure positions will be soon extinct, while a number of tenure cases have been poorly handled, as has occurred in some other American overseas universities, leading to younger scholars leaving and adding to a growing collective resentment amongst their colleagues who remain. After the military takeover in 2013, and because of the curtailment of academic space and even more of political freedom, numerous young, untenured, foreign-hired academics have left AUC. The running joke is that this university has been converted into a collective graveyard.

With the sharp devaluation of the Egyptian pound in 2016 through the pressure and interference of the World Bank, resulting in the loss of nearly 80 per cent of its value, and the constant increase of student fees, which are expected to be paid in hard currency, an explosion of massive student demonstrations occurred, forcing the administration to change its hard-currency payment policies. Student demonstrations, it should be noted, had already been going on since 2011, just after the revolution, when the fees had already rocketed to US$17,000 a year for undergraduates (Shenker 2011). 'My father is not a thief, you are the thief' (abuuya mish harrami, enta elli harrami), the slogan chanted by many students during the 2016 demonstrations, hit the point. It touched upon the burning issue of the unsustainability of private education for the increasingly impoverished upper middle classes in a country facing a serious economic crisis.

But that is not all. Campus life has changed, and all those who have experienced the old Tahrir campus will assert that when old-fashioned AUC underwent its modernisation by expanding into a grandiose simulation of American campuses in the Eastern Desert, it lost its unique identity. In fact, it has lost the intellectual life that gravitated around Oriental Hall, which has hosted so many memorable lectures during the past decades: Edward Said and Mahmud Darwish for many consecutive years, the late Annemarie Schimmel, Judith Butler, Jürgen Habermas, Tarik Ali, Amitav Gosh, Marguerite Duras, and Bruno Latour. Its famed and pleasant sociability fostered intellectual exchange around the gardens of the fountain area in the main campus and the Greek campus, as well as in the numerous cafés, bars like al-Horreyya, and restaurants such as Estoril, Grillon, and Felfela, all within walking distance – the Downtown life that was such a joy after long hours of teaching.

The commute to the new campus transformed the commuters into neurotic beings, extremely frugal with time. Once one has reached the new campus, the race to reach the classroom starts, then one has to rush out to run in panic for fear of missing the scheduled buses. There is hardly any time to

**Figure 11**    Mock graves and display of photographs of the martyrs of the
revolution, Tahrir Square, 8 June 2012.

even purchase food, as food stalls are always filled with endless queues for
poor-quality products at insane prices. On some days, one hardly has time
to visit the toilet, and even less time for socialising.

The arrival of Uber and Careem taxis did solve significant inconveniences.
The cars are far more comfortable and faster than the University buses.

### Everyday indoctrination

'Grab your last opportunity for clean air ... grab the last place in heaven ...
invest in the clean and beautiful life of the compounds of upscale New Cairo.
We provide you with your dream villa and a swimming pool ... all you need
is to sign a down payment ... pay in seven years of instalments to be in paradise
... choose a worthy life in a gated compound ... You deserve a more beautiful
life.' These sentences are witch-hunting me everywhere, on billboards, in
newspapers, on television, and last but not least they are sent repeatedly as
messages on my mobile phone. Villas, villettes, condos, and compounds ...

'You deserve a decent life.' This is an advertisement I read somewhere.
But what's a decent life today in Cairo? My Facebook account is constantly
invaded by advertisements for lavish villas and walled-off condominiums
worth millions, which I cannot afford anyway. And who cares? The last thing
I would want is to live in such walled-off spaces amongst neighbours I would

certainly dread. Billboard after billboard selling virtual dreams ... because life at the heart of Cairo has turned into hell. Truly unsustainable. How long can disposable humanity remain disposable?

We all know that human life here is cheap and worthless; this is certainly no novelty. I know ... I know that I am still deeply privileged. Above all, I am not a political activist ... I do not really fear forced disappearance or incarceration, since I am not in the age group clearly targeted by the authorities. I am in fact too old to be suspected by the regime. I do not really fear torture or death or being asphyxiated in a police truck by tear gas, as was the dramatic case in August 2013 (Kingsley 2014). Nor do I fear being banned from travel, as has been the case for a number of human rights activists, journalists, and critics of the military regime. But who knows? Big Brother is expanding by the day.

I am perplexed at how apolitical I have been in the last two years. More disturbing is that being apolitical does not make life easier; neither does it solve the problem of an infernal chaotic daily life under authoritarian rule and the mounting corruption scandals, which confirm unbridled disasters of food, air, and water pollution day after day.[3] Thus we were told by certain official circles in April 2015, when some five hundred tons of phosphates were spilled by accident in the Nile in the governorate of Qena, that such a disaster would not affect drinking water, while the Ministry of Environment declared it an emergency situation.[4] What is worrying is not merely the frequency of pollution and industrial accidents and the traffic disasters that give Egypt one of the highest rates of traffic fatalities. It is the ever-constant denial on the part of the Government that the problems even exist.

I often speculate about potential, and all too possible, car accidents on my daily ride. The depressing ring road leading to the new campus is lined with endless red-brick slums, and then ugly and cheap high-rise buildings.

But, but ... 'We are fortunate, we are not Syria or Libya, we have managed to avoid a civil war and remain the only secure oasis in an abysmal region', as countless taxi drivers, several low-income individuals, and above all, the *feloul* class (the pro-Mubarakists) keep saying, over and over again, perhaps as a self-deluding strategy that life has to go on. Even if one lives by endurance, even if life is unbearable, is not stability irreplaceable? Have we not seen how hard it is to experience the turmoil and violence of revolutions? But what is harder: revolutions or slow torture in daily life?

## Internal migration, or the flight to the gated communities

> ... for counter-revolution – the word having been coined by Condorcet in the course of the French Revolution – has always remained bound to revolution as reaction is bound to action. (Arendt 1963[1965]: 18)

Internal migration? Or when to decide in favour of exodus, to leave this nightmare for good? So many people I know have already left Egypt, not to mention some of the young activists, who keep on leaving one after the other. It looks as if I will never have the nerve to leave Egypt once more for good. I seem to be in denial of my past in this connection: I have already migrated once to the North, determined never to come back, and did come back nonetheless. How archetypal is this return to one's roots or origins after the classical, colonial/post-colonial, Ulyssean experience of travelling overseas for the sake of learning? There is nothing really original in such meanderings. It just compels me to be reminded of the work the late French anthropologist Fanny Colonna did in her gaze towards the numerous Egyptians who, after long sojourns overseas, felt compelled to return back to their villages, with 'missionary' endeavours for changing and improving the world, while eternally rethinking or reinventing their identity (Colonna 2004).

### Alienating aesthetics or landscapes

Some of my acquaintances who, just like me, are caught in the dilemma of escaping Cairo's inferno, repeatedly tell me: 'We all seem to be bound to follow the urban exodus to the desert. It is the only portal for clean air; go with the better-off to the newly built satellite cities.' Head for New Cairo in the Eastern Desert, Sheikh Zayed, City View, the ever-expanding projects of SODIC in both the Eastern and Western Deserts, or the Sixth of October City in the Western Desert. I have had several students who have watched their quiet residences on the Cairo–Alexandria desert road turn into a densely urbanised area. I cannot help regarding such an exodus as anything except speeding up the already nightmarish dystopia I am confronted with regularly. I cannot help thinking that in one of my writings I once called New Cairo the *'ashwaa'iyyaat* (the slums) of the rich, and I still perceive it as such.

Could my utter distaste for the so-called upscale New Cairo simply stem from my elitist hallucinations? Snobbishness perhaps? But if this is Cairo's future, then I certainly don't want to get old here. The schizophrenic aesthetics and the alienating architecture of New Cairo lead me to believe that this must be a conscious erasure of reminiscence. For me, at least, my past life-world has withered away, and my sense of loss is growing by the day with each commute to the new campus. These desert landscapes of unfinished, mushrooming, hideous constructions I encounter on my daily commute, after crossing the city slums via the Sixth of October flyover, clearly have little to do with the old Cairo I grew up in. I am far from saying that there were no slums in earlier times, for I recall quite well what the poor decrepit neighbourhoods looked like some four decades ago, and I know, too, that poverty hurts. However, the architectural ugliness induced by quick money and wealth have become a rule exacerbating the atrocious space/class divide of the city. Time and again, the sense of alienation is renewed.

Coming from the centre of town, my drive over the Sixth of October Bridge glosses over Downtown. Shubra, Ramses station, and the wild, new, ugly high-rise buildings are in close vicinity, with slums that can be seen from afar, then the 'Abbaseyya quarter, then heading towards Nasr City. Billboards and more billboards, shockingly indecent with luxury dreams, bombarding passers-by with the promised paradise of compound life.

After leaving the Sixth of October Bridge, the frightening Ministry of Interior, with its huge bunkered concrete walls and sandbags blocking all the windows, inspires unsettling images. Then one enters the gigantic and extended zone of the army barracks. One can observe some of their industries, the bottled mineral water and soft drinks factories, and privatised spaces, then military clubs, hotels, the gigantic Tantawi complex that includes numerous halls and buildings, then one more large shopping mall, the air force stadium, and endless desert land that we are told is managed by the army. On Mahmud al-Shahid Street, it is written on the walls of the army barracks that it is strictly forbidden to take photographs: 'No photo'. These walls are lined with photographs and propaganda slogans like *Masr lam wa lan tasqut* (Egypt did not and will not fall down/collapse), *Masr al-hadaara* (Egypt the civilisation), *Masr awalan* (Egypt first), *Masr um al-dunya* (Egypt, the mother of the world), *Tahya Masr* (Long live Egypt), *Al-nasr li-Masr* (Victory for Egypt), *Al-gaish wa-l-sha'ab iid wahda* (The army and the people are one), *Masr fawq al gamii'* (Egypt over all), *Masr betefrah* (Egypt is happy). The most eye-catching thing on these walls is the photograph of a soldier carrying a baby, which was strategically hung all over the city during the times when demonstrators shouted the slogan '*Yasqut, yasqut hukm al-asqar*' (Down, down with the military) in 2011 and 2012. The military area starts at Nasr City, just beyond the Sixth of October Bridge. Then a recently constructed flyover by the army is lined with smaller billboards with '*Masr al-watan*' (Egypt, home-land), '*Masr al-mustaqbal*' (Egypt, the future), '*Al-gaish wa-l-sha'ab iid wahdah*' (the army and the people are one hand). These are side by side in the desert landscape with its endless billboards and unfinished 'luxurious' cities, gated communities, and condos, destined to be walled off.

After the new flyover, one drives along the famed *al-Sharei al-Tess'iin*, Road 90. This iconic but otherwise nameless road is the symbolic aperture to the future Cairo: the 'new upscale Cairo', with its large shopping complexes including the gigantic Cairo Festival Centre, its endless office spaces, and the villas, villettes, and gated communities of the rich. This cityscape gives me a sense of déjà vu, but of a worse quality, because it reminds me of the relatively new satellite quarter of Kuala Lumpur called Bandar Utama where I once lived for half a year in the mid-1990s. Perhaps, too, the five-star hotel *Dusit Thani*, Lake View, located on Road 90 with its Thai management, advertising on its website graceful Thai hostesses, Thai design, cuisine, and luxurious *Devarana* spas, along with its elaborate landscaping, is a good representation of the brave new world of New Cairo. A bit further away, off Road 90, at Cairo Festival City and Cairo Festival City Mall, the dream world of shopping has come true for Egyptians: Asian furniture, Kian, Marks &

Spencer, IKEA, the German insurance company Allianz, a huge parking garage, promenades,[5] all these agglomerations of companies seem like a déjà vu landscape. This transplanted consumer dream world in the desert clashes with the public visibility of the floating mass of poor seasonal workers carrying shabby bags with meagre belongings, standing in long queues in the main bus stations on Road 90. One often sees miserable workers packed into trucks that are either transporting them to work in an endless multiplication of compounds or bringing them back to the meeting points of the bus stations. These informal pick-up stations have actually expanded into spontaneous spaces for popular cafés.

In reality, in a couple of years, Road 90 will look like a replica of Nasr City in its former days. Originally, Nasr City was a military zone overflowing with army barracks. It eventually evolved into the then new and modern post-colonial satellite city constructed under Nasser, and today it is an agony of unbearable traffic jams, mushrooming shops, and wild, falling-apart construction.

But in 2018, Road 90 already looked like a second Nasr City. It has turned into a loud and busy highway with interminable traffic jams, as if Cairene city planners excel in replicating the same unresolved problems in each newly built satellite city. As the French would say, these newly constructed replicas are the best example of '*la fuite en avant*' (the headlong rush forwards). If the traffic jams are just as hellish on Road 90, why leave the centre and move so far away to the desert? On the right side of the road, sticking to each other and competing in ugliness, one large villa after another and two- or three-storey buildings; on the left side, offices, shopping malls, banks, and endless spaces for business. Every morning I ask myself who these lunatics are who have given away millions for these monstrosities that are just a few metres away from the daily movement of thousands of vehicles. But being located along a horrible highway for the newly rich equates to being modern and moving rapidly towards one's destination.

But these interminable traffic jams have become an indicator of a new consumerist and professional lifestyle in the urban reshaping of the Eastern Desert. Numerous international banks, office complexes, and large shopping centres packed with visitors at their peak hours have sprung up along Road 90, which leads to New Cairo City. In other words, New Cairo today looks like a bustling, lively city, except that it caters to a specific and limited public. Instead of expressing the essential traits of Cairo, it evokes the imported *Khaliijii* (Gulf) tastes and lifestyles, analysed in an earlier work of mine on consumer culture in Egypt (Abaza 2006).

The commute I confront is a nightmare not only for being stuck in a bus or car for hours, but even more because the alienating aesthetics depress me. These horrific, grotesque, larger-than-life villas of the nouveaux riches, glued to each other, filled with fake quasi-Roman columns, jammed with flowered wrought-iron gates, replicated everywhere, invariably make me melancholic. It is a sin that these villas fill up with construction all the space that could have surrounded them with gardens or greenery. Then, just a few kilometres before I reach the campus, there is the surreal Future University with its kitsch pseudo-Roman construction. And kitsch followed by more kitsch seems to be the destiny of modern New Cairo.

This dystopia might not be seen as such by the younger generation, and strangely enough the 2011 Tahrir effect did not manage to undo it. My friends M. and A., who are in their early thirties, and whose apartment was turned into a roundabout to shelter the protesters during the January revolution in Downtown – because of its ideal location exactly opposite the Ministry of Interior – have finally made the decision to exit to the satellite city of Sheikh Zayed. They purchased a spacious flat in 2014, right after they experienced the heavy tear gas and killings of Mohamed Mahmud. The main reason that M. sank into a nervous breakdown in the early years of the revolution was the heavy tear gas they had been exposed to. I would have never thought that this young couple, whose dream was to live as semi-bohemian artists in the centre of the city, would finally opt for the gated and ordered community life. But they expected a baby and it was out of question to undergo the daily harassment from the disguised plain-clothes internal security policemen squatting opposite their building, in front of the ministry, when they were parking their car. The ritual and daily harassment, the investigation everyone underwent when visiting them, was an ordeal. My other friend A. moved to another semi-detached villa near Sheikh Zayed. Several cousins and acquaintances are all slowly but surely leaving the city. A distant aunt had serious clashes for many years with the people who ran a nearby mosque because its amplifiers were aimed right into her bedroom. After long battles for years at the police stations, she finally moved with her daughter into a large villa in the Sixth of October. My sister, several of my cousins, and numerous friends are now out in the desert. Whenever I visit any of them, I have to go through these desert moonscapes and the endless, empty, unfinished houses. But purchasing real estate in New Cairo is a good investment, everyone tells me, 'you can simply double the price in a couple of years'. Real estate never loses value in Egypt, we are told. How many people in my circle have done that? I remain, with only a few of my friends, in the weird minority that abides solid in the centre.

The commute, time and again. Interminable, unbearable commutes. I choose another road, but it is worse. The routine of being stuck on the Sixth of October Bridge. Time and again dreaming to flee the country?

The urban downtown centre became militarised after the bloody incidents of Mohamed Mahmud Street. Militarisation goes perfectly with the gentrification of another part of the city. New concave walls are continually added around the ministries, embassies, and security offices, making movement in the centre of the city impossible.

If the main benefit of being rich is that people can easily plan their life thanks to their assets and reserves, which become a 'natural' device for predicting and thus efficiently shaping the future, this is exactly why the mindset of the poor is mainly caught in the spiral of fatalism. The hardship of everyday survival implies that one can never really be able to predict or plan much, particularly about where to live. Yet what makes Cairo's urban texture unique is that even if one is considered well-to-do, one can never really predict how the residential quarter so 'rationally' chosen will evolve, or how fast the deterioration of the surrounding public space, noise, and air pollution will be. This could be understood as a kind of unplanned form of equality or divine justice, in the sense that even the rich cannot really be spared from the 'invasion of the riff-raff' (a term used with a grain of salt). It is only that the rich have more liquidity, which allows them to keep on constantly moving outwards to the fringes of the city, leaving behind them spaces occupied by the newly ascending middle and lower classes. This brings me to the next question: how long can the gated communities and walled-off spaces of the satellite cities be maintained as clean and exclusive, and what could guarantee their continuity?

### Flashback, time and again, early 2016

January 2011 is so remote, almost like a mirage. Has Tahrir been completely deleted from our memory? An endless, growing sense of loss and desolation reigns in my surroundings; Tahrir has been reduced to a nostalgic and utopian memory amongst those who have experienced it.[6] This nostalgic moment translates naturally into a constant struggle to retain, if not freeze, memory, even if it is painful and sad, since it is coupled with an eagerness to record and archive the unfolding events of the past five years, as many have been hopelessly attempting to do. That might also explain why there is an urge to recall, invent, and reinvent the '*lieux de mémoire*' (Nora 1989) of the past five years' turmoil. This effort is coming to be seen almost as a calling in order to stop the withering away of a vivid memory. Such is the fate of counter-revolutionary moments. Once again, we have been overwhelmingly overpowered. The dream of change, and the possibility of dreaming, was just a dream turned into a nightmare. This translates into bipolar and pessimistic, if not bleak, sentiments. But the present consists of a hard, counter-revolutionary, ruthless moment. The old regime has never really departed from the stage. The wounded counter-revolutionary powers that be have learned the lesson; Tahrir is not repeatable and our present is not quite exactly identical to Mubarak's time. It is certainly much worse.

### Berlin, June 2016

The start of my sabbatical year. I spend endless hours watching on YouTube this year's *musalsalaat*, the highly popular thirty episodes of television, aired every Ramadan season. They are posted on YouTube one day after being aired in Cairo. For the past few years these episodes have been often widely commented and discussed amongst countless Facebook members. These are constantly interrupted by advertisements for the endless merits of compound life.

The nightmarish compounds chase me even to the lakes and remote farmhouse where I live, one and a half hours east of Berlin. It seems much easier to watch these episodes with the true remoteness and distance offered by the country life in a village in the former East Germany, isolated by forests. Actually, I don't know why I never have the patience to watch these long and highly repetitive episodes in Cairo. However, over the past few years the standards of the television serials have risen significantly, because they address acute social questions in a much more sophisticated way.

In what follows, I would like to point to one *musalsal* that caught my attention, compelling me to watch the entire thirty episodes, as it depicted such a surreal representation of a Cairo unfamiliar to me: the walled-compound Cairo of the rich. Yet although it is unfamiliar it appears real, a sign of what is yet to come in terms of the forms of segregation experienced by cities of the global South.[7]

*Fawq mustawa al-shubuhaat* (*Above Reproach*)[8] is one of the most successful series of *musalsalaat*. It has much to reveal about the new lifestyles of rich Cairenes. The year 2016 was marked by an unprecedented tour de force in advertising the Ramadan *musalsalaat*, with portrait displays of numerous actors and actresses, who all look alike, on countless billboards all along the Sixth of October Bridge. These seemed to compete with the never-ending billboards of real-estate companies all along Cairo's highways and roads.

The script of *Above Reproach* was written by 'Abdallah Hassan and Amin Gamaal. The episodes were directed by Hani Khalifa, starring the prominent actress Yussra as the main protagonist of the story. Of interest here is the fact that most of the episodes were filmed in the very real and lavish Palm Hills compound located in the Eastern Desert.

The first episode opens with a scene that says it all. The plot starts with the birthday of a one-year-old infant taking place in the public communal garden of a compound, with a large number of neighbours wishing the child happy birthday and socialising with various parents. In the open space of the compound we see clowns dressed à la Walt Disney moving around, loud Western music, decorations, fashionable children's outdoor inflatable bouncers, games, and balloons. English words are constantly mixed with Arabic dialect in conversations, such as 'Oh my God', 'negative energy', 'she is over', 'light', 'the right track', and 'deal'. The most important point, however, is how the birthday of a baby becomes the major event for socialising amongst the neighbours on the wider scale of the compound. The event serves as a platform for gossiping and getting to know the newcomers. The protagonist, Rahmah Halim (Yussra), obviously a newcomer, is introduced over the loudspeaker by her neighbour, the rich housewife Inji (Shereen Reda), as a special guest, since she has recently been elected to Parliament. But we also get a glimpse of the resentful waiters, who express their frustration while they are catering to the rich. One waiter complains to his colleague that he cannot finish paying for the necessary items for his wedding, while all this wasteful spending is devoted to nothing more than an infant's birthday. Then, in a subsequent scene, Rahmah asks one of the two waiters whether he could provide her with a Philippine maid, since hers has just left her.

The Sixth of October police station appears and reappears in the various episodes as a well-maintained building, and the young, 'efficient', American-style police officers who are investigating a murder case are portrayed as positive. The police station is lavish, with clean, modern offices. In other words, it is an attempt at polishing, if not selling, a new look of young policemen – not by coincidence, after so many police stations were burnt in January 2011 and the image of the police officers tarnished.

A murder occurs in a compound, leading to a series of misfortunes that will affect the entire community, as one neighbour after the other ends up being implicated as a suspect through the sophisticated manipulations of Rahmah Halim. She is portrayed as a politically ambitious social climber, but also as a mentally disturbed person, as we learn in the final episodes. It is no coincidence that the three main female characters – Rahmah, her sister Maha, and the neighbour Inji – are all blonde, fair, Westernised types. The Westernised stereotype of upper-class women is here targeted as entirely negative.

Rahmah murders a psychiatrist who lives in the same compound on grounds that he has incriminating evidence to prove she had consigned her younger sister to a mental asylum and had accidentally killed a British student in a boarding school in the UK because of severe bullying. He is also officially assigned to conduct psychological tests on her before she can be authorised to become a Member of Parliament.

As events unfold, Rahmah is unveiled as a bleak psychopath. The Arabic name Rahmah translates as 'mercy', but Rahmah, who turns out to be nothing but a devilish murderer, triggers a series of attempted murders within the neighbourhood. The psychiatrist maintains an archive of numerous records of his patients, who all end up cohabiting with each other as neighbours in the same compound. After killing the psychiatrist, Rahmah gets hold of the taped sessions of the patients in the compound. She uses confidential records to blackmail en masse the network of neighbours and acquaintances. Here the plot weaves the spatial vicinity with a web of networks, gossip, and distribution of information amongst the neighbours, highly revealing of the nature of the tight and controlled social relations in these compounds. We are given to believe that the rich live in separate villas, while the younger, upper middle-class yuppies and professionals move spatially in modern flats in four- or five-storey buildings.

As events continue to unfold, we are told that each neighbour has some sort of shameful deed to conceal. These are either illicit love affairs and betrayals between couples, financial frauds, corruption cases, or husbands leading double lives by having a secret second wife. These are all secrets that Rahmah will use to her own advantage.

Rahmah, we are told, is well connected to influential political circles, which, throughout the show, are clearly corrupt. She is portrayed as a social climber who lives in a lavish villa on her own, with a trained shepherd dog. She managed to take away (or embezzle) the villa from her ex-husband, whom she succeeded in sending to prison through her machinations. However, Rahmah originates from a well-to-do family, which runs counter to the often portrayed, stereotypical image of the social climber from a poor and popular origin. Rahmah claims to hold a PhD in 'human resources', which is clearly another hoax. As the *musalsal* progresses, she mesmerises the audience with her destructive but highly intelligent capacities for harm. Particularly remarkable is the fact that Rahmah is portrayed as a powerful and articulate *doktoorah* (PhD, although of course hers is fake). This is the recurrent negative image in the popular imagination of the powerful, active, and modern-looking woman, visibly single (with a dog), turning into a swindler; so emblematic of the current misogyny and associated with the so-called social critique of the new rich today. Rahmah is a public figure, with frequent appearances on television and in the press. She has countless followers on Facebook, and furthermore, she is soon to be appointed to Parliament. But once she commits the murder, she multiplies disasters and cannot refrain from further murder attempts.

Yet the main hero/protagonist of the story is in fact the modern compound in the desert and its artificially constructed landscapes that appeal to the new rich. The life of the compound, as imagined in the episodes, turns out to be an excellent barometer of the consumerist lifestyles of the new rich. We see various fashionable types of villas, side by side with modern, well-constructed, three- or four-storey buildings, targeting the younger generation of the rising middle classes. We see how the neighbours jog and walk their dogs together in the open areas of the compound. We notice that some owners have multiple television screens connected to cameras to monitor all the entrances of the compound. We also gaze at fancy and modern interior decorations, and large modern paintings on walls. Fashionable, IKEA-furnished kitchens abound, along with large gardens with greenery like Southeast Asian flora and private swimming pools. We also see Rahmah training on a regular basis in a well-equipped fitness club. These ordered, clean, and modern spaces keep on appearing and reappearing. We also observe how well-off women are socialising, gossiping, and interacting in modern clubs and restaurants within the compound.

We are impressed by the fashionable, modern decor of the psychiatrist's office, which is a section of his villa. We learn that he records every single conversation with his patients and archives them in the form of CDs. It is with these CDs that Rahmah blackmails several of her neighbours, by transferring the records to a Macintosh computer storage system, then sending the information as messages through mobile phones. In other words, we learn of the many other uses this sophisticated technology has for the rich.

The function of the psychiatrist deserves special attention, as he fulfils the role of the repository of 'confessions' for his patients. The many patients residing in the compound, who have resorted to him, show that he carries out quite an ancient task, albeit dressed in new attire. Namely, his function has allowed him to put together a type of archive on the collective secret life of this secluded compound of the rich. In other words, as Foucault tells us, the 'obligation of confession' (Foucault 1978: 33) – in this case, to the 'modern' psychiatrist through the process of talking, listening, recording, and developing sophisticated techniques of confession – creates a discourse about the acts that enhances a form of power through this codified and 'scientificated' knowledge. But one could read the resort to the psychiatrist as an ambition to appear modern, and thus Westernised. An alternative reading to the function of the psychiatrist would position him as the fashionable replacement for the traditional religious sheikh and the popular healer (who both appeared quite often in the television *musalsalaat* of the 1960s and 1970s), practitioners of popular medicine who were resorted to for reversing evil, magical spells and for providing protective amulets.

We also see endless commutes to the centre of Cairo, with cars as the main means of transport, and many mobile-phone conversations taking place. African and Asian maids are constantly moving around and receiving guests at the door, and the heavy presence of security guards around the compound is evident. An increasingly resentful lower class of waiters serve in the restaurants of the compound. They end up working as informants for the various wealthy residents, who are constantly either corrupting them with money or threatening them if they provide misinformation.

We also see young professional couples. One young female neighbour, who runs a radio programme, is critical of the political situation and becomes quite antagonistic to Rahmah's hypocrisy. While she supports the January 2011 revolution, her husband becomes a corrupt real-estate employee, who takes percentages under the table for each sale and is eventually fired.

The *'liaisons dangereuses'* seem inevitable in the confined space of the compound. An affair between a married woman and her young, good-looking neighbour obviously has to occur. The morality of the story evolves so that the wife has to be punished in the end by being divorced on the spot and deprived of her child, whom 'she will never see for the rest of her life' (says her angry husband), even though she repented earlier and discovered that she truly loved her husband. We also see how the well-to-do Jihan (Rahmah's neighbour), a housewife married to a medical doctor, lands in jail once again thanks to Rahmah's conspiracies. Meanwhile, the second, secretly married wife of Jihan's husband insists on occupying the villa while Jihan is in prison, once again due to Rahmah's advice.

The main point of analysis of the choice of this soap is: does *Above Suspicion* serve as an appraisal of the luxurious life of compounds? Or does it, on the contrary, constitute a social critique of the superficial inner circles, gossip mechanisms, and lavish lifestyles of the new Egyptian rich in the walled-off gated communities? Perhaps it is both. One thing is clear: that the enormous gap in lifestyles in Egypt between the rich and the poor, now in the making, is leading to an unprecedented physical and mental chasm in society.

*Ahram Online* reported that almost all the Ramadan series of 2016 were perceived by the National Council of Women as conveying a pretty grim image of contemporary Egyptian women. 'The mid-month report states that "The dancer, the call girl, the psychologically ill, the divorcee who steals another woman's husband, and the working woman who is unsuccessful in her family life are the most notable portrayals of women in the 2016 Ramadan series"' ('Ramadan series feature violence', 2016).

Once again, it seems that it is women who end up being targeted as scapegoats when a collective disorientation dominated by a counter-revolutionary moment clearly prevails in society. This is occurring precisely after the dominant public presence in the streets that women have occupied for the past five years – and precisely after so many women's organisations, empowered by their public visibility, began speaking out against sexual harassment and discrimination. Are we facing here, once again, an act of erasing one's memory?

### Burgeoning dystopian novels on Cairo

In addition to immersing myself in the *musalsalaat*, I have compiled a number of recently published Egyptian novels written by the younger generation,[9] which I read simultaneously. Revolutions are about fostering hope and dreams of the possibility of changing the world. As Agnes Heller argues, the strength of revolutions is that they trigger the anticipation, or the possibility, of dreaming to achieve a utopia, a better world. Since utopias are by definition imaginaries of an ideal future society (Heller 2016), when these dreams are not fulfilled, hope can swiftly be transformed into fear and despair. Heller refers to the feeling of being cheated or betrayal that is often associated with unfulfilled revolutions, which can quickly twist a utopia to dystopia (Heller 2016: 39). Dystopias, according to Heller, are located at the opposite pole from utopias. They are counter-mirror images that feed on utopias and engender exactly opposite feelings. Heller argues that utopias and dystopias are in close proximity to each other because they constitute the product of the power of imagination.

Interesting here is how the counter-revolutionary momentum in Egypt has degenerated during the past five years into a collective dystopian feeling of depression, which numerous observers have written about recently, in

**Figure 12** 'Entrance forbidden to the Muslim Brotherhood', Mohamed Mahmud Street, 23 November 2012.

which the daily life of the divided and clashing city of Cairo is depicted as a collective conflagration (Abaza 2016). If the dream of a utopian world has been closely connected to a collective belief in 'progress' and change, through the possibility of improving life by dissenting or rebelling (Heller 2016: 35), this was attested to by the Arab Spring revolutions, which, however, turned into an 'Arab winter' and became nearly unreachable, at least in the short run. The successive regime changes (through the ouster of Mubarak, then the military takeover by SCAF, then the regime of the Muslim Brotherhood, then the armed forces again under Sisi) all proved to be repertoires, variations on the same melody (Abaza 2016). In fact, no possible change could have taken place in the bureaucracy, the internal security and the police forces, the judicial sector, and the media and information sectors when the players of the 'deep State' remained the same, and the identical previous elite of crony capitalists was rescued from trial and their untouched wealth was transferred overseas. To the contrary, we are today witnessing excessive corruption and even more brutal violations of human rights than under Mubarak. The targeted witch-hunting of activists, feminists, and academics, the freezing of their assets, travel bans, massive jailing, and finally forced disappearances are perpetrated like never before.

Consequently, it is no coincidence that all these recently published novels[10] portray a dystopian and bleak environment, in which Cairo becomes the epicentre of either urban wars, natural disasters such as earthquakes and sand/desert tsunamis (e.g. in Naaji's *Istikhdaam al-Hayaat*, 2014), or as landscapes of ruins and utmost destitution, in which surreal masked snipers,[11] posted on the highest points, such as the Cairo Tower located on the residential island of Zamalek, are routinely killing citizens (as in *'Utaarid*, by Muhamad Rabii').[12] Pollution, destitution, and chaos reign in the city. *'Utaarid* opens with a horrific scene of cannibalism: a man who hacks his children and his wife to death, and cooks them in a large pot. He then ties up the grandfather and forces him to eat large quantities of the meal he prepared, after which the grandfather dies.

Terrorist attacks are countless, just as Egypt has experienced recently. The army and the police forces degenerate into fragmented, lawless militias. The country is invaded by a possible mercenary army from Malta, speaking numerous foreign languages, including central Asian languages. Cairo's social divisions are pushed to the extreme into infernal, outsized, inhuman underworlds of prostitution, violence, and underground checkpoints. The city descends into localised urban wars and dangerous zones, with numerous snipers who enjoy killing passers-by en masse without any clear purpose or even political motives. Dead, disfigured, and tortured bodies linger in the streets of Cairo. These are left to rot, to be stripped of their clothes and all their belongings by a series of passing gangs, each specialising in particular items, until they are left naked. Depressing descriptions of people searching for their loved ones amongst endless unrecognised corpses in morgues, evoking déjà vu scenes of what occurred to the martyrs of the revolution and their disappearing bodies, abound in the novel. As the story unfolds, the question becomes what to do about the missing bodies and those killed by coincidence just because they were in the street. Are they martyrs? Are these vanished bodies with no proper burial, nor proper prayers and ritual ablutions according to Islamic traditions, still considered as martyrs, wonders Rabii'? In that sense, *'Utaarid* could be classified as a dystopian science-fiction thriller.[13] It is a projection of the future Cairo in 2025, twelve years after the 2013 Rabe'a al-'Adaweyya massacre, in which the city witnessed the widespread use of thugs to beat up and terrorise the protesters of Tahrir, and when numerous insurrections that took place on university campuses were violently crushed with live ammunition.

Alternatively, the city becomes an oppressive, open-air prison, where Big Brother is omnipresent, as in Basma 'Abd al-'Aziz's *al-Taabuur* (*The Queue*). In the words of Hannah Arendt on the essence of violence, the city in this case is dominated by the 'rule of Nobody', constituting the very essence of tyranny (Arendt 1969[1970]: 38).

'Abd al-'Aziz immerses the reader in yet another dreary and apocalyptic Orwellian landscape. The events are clearly taking place in Cairo, even though the city is not named. The streets and districts are numbered, and accordingly nameless, evoking the newly built districts of New Cairo in the Eastern

**Figure 13**  'Martyrs produced according to demand (or supply and demand)' (*shuhadaa' taht al-talab*), Tahrir Square, 4 June 2012.

Desert as well as some quarters of Nasr City, which was built in the late 1960s and has expanded as district numbers. However, the description of the sites, the popular cafés, the minute details, depicts the daily lives and practices of the underprivileged floating mass roaming around, as well as street vending and vagabonding. All of this evokes the memorable scenes of Tahrir and its environs during the early years of the revolution. More precisely, it evokes the bizarre life-world of the colossal Mugamma' building where all Egyptian bureaucracy is concentrated. 'Abd al-'Aziz stretches the imagination by pushing to the extreme the Kafkaesque bureaucratic practices that no Egyptian can avoid. She invites the reader to move in an oppressive atmosphere, filled with stubborn and nasty employees, so familiar to any Egyptian. Even nastier doctors and horrid hospitals are described, together with endless unsigned official papers and disappearing reports that are never stamped. It is the world in which the invisible Big Brother is felt around every corner through on-the-spot monitoring, secret reports, and all-encompassing collective forms of intelligence. The state propaganda and media manipulations against the insurrections, which are labelled as '*al-ahdaaath al-mushiina*' (the despicable or shameful incidents), immediately evoke the unfolding confrontations between the revolutionaries and the police forces after January 2011, which were labelled the same way by the regime. The modes of monitoring and spying on the conversations and actions of those standing in the queue for endless days, if not for months, by the omnipresent 'Purple Mobile Company', which holds the monopoly on communication, would certainly evoke parallels. The déjà vu quality of the endless ordeals with hospitals and official media asserting that those who disappeared from the street were never shot because no bullets were used by the police, the torture, and all the other details pertaining to the violation of human rights that truly occurred would certainly ring a bell to anyone who experienced the urban wars during the three years that followed 2011. The parallels here with the November–December 2011 killings on Mohamed Mahmud Street are quite remarkable. This novel was evidently written after the revolution, since it conveys the mood and the collective pessimism that followed it.

The main protagonist, Yahya, a clearly apolitical young employee, is by coincidence wounded by a bullet while on his way to work. He is caught in warfare between the rebellious crowds – which remain unnamed and unidentified right up to the end of the story – and the police forces. As a consequence, Yahya is stigmatised, because the official state version insists that no ammunition has ever been used in the streets. Yahya has to get an authorisation to undergo the operation to remove the bullet. This is not possible without the authorisation of the opaque and frightening 'Gate' (*tassriih min al-bawaabah*, 'the authorisation from the Gate'), which is overcrowded by the endless queuing masses. But the Gate never actually opens and the citizens remain queuing forever. They end up squatting and sleeping in the street. They socialise, fight, and share their worries, while every detail of their conversations is being spied on.

*The Queue* is a surreal story about an endless queue of desperate citizens, waiting eternally in front of a terrifying state organism. Each person queuing has a story to narrate about the injustice and humiliation he or she underwent, while the queue takes on a life of its own. The citizens end up coming on a daily basis in the hope that they can get the authorisation of 'valid citizenship' in order to proceed with their papers. Until the end of the story, Yahya is unable to have his operation because his papers have disappeared, or rather were confiscated by the powers that be.

As the story unfolds, the characters start doubting themselves, since reality becomes as uncertain as illusion. The regime and the media insist that no bullets were ever shot in the street, and thus that no one was killed, while those who disappeared are never seen again. By the end of the story, the regime issues a statement that the shooting and confrontations were part of an international crew filming in the streets. Therefore, the confrontations were just a simulation for a feature film – in other words, an illusion.

'Abd al-'Aziz's surreal cityscape sounds so real in its description of past events. It once again draws out the denials of the successive regimes (the Mubarak regime, the SCAF, and the Muslim Brothers), who all rejected the accusation of using live ammunition against the protesters. For those who have experienced Cairo since the 2011 revolution, this novel is a rich and playful narrative on the propaganda discourse that was used by the successive counter-revolutionary regimes.

In these three novels, one can trace a common denominator – namely, the fact that they are inspired by the collapse and decay of the city. The descriptions all draw upon the violent confrontations and urban wars, the killings, and above all the sufferings, disfigurement, and high toll of martyrs that unfolded after January 2011. The concern with the mutilated, suffering, and ailing bodies moving around the city is omnipresent in both Rabii' and 'Abd al-'Aziz, evoking once again the disfigured face of the young, middle-class Alexandrian Khaled Said, who was tortured and killed at a police station in 2010, after a bag of hashish was forced into his mouth in an attempt to incriminate him in his own death.[14]

The militarisation of urban life, the erection of buffer walls by the army, and the checkpoints that devastated the Downtown landscape are all present in these novels. Last but not least, the life-world of the sprawling *'ashwaa'iyyaat* is clearly imagined as a decadent, violent, and uncontrolled underworld. This may be a simplistic kind of symbolism, as there is in fact a long tradition in official circles of demonising the slums as polluted sites, generating violence and Islamic fundamentalism. The *'ashwaa'iyyaat* have been designated by the spokesmen of the regime, time and again, as a malignant cancer that needs to be eradicated from the so-called healthy urban life.

What unites these three novels is the graphic descriptions of poor and chaotic neighbourhoods and the unique human encounters and situations which Cairene life has been famed for, such as fist fights with taxi drivers or spontaneous conversations while queuing. But above all, it is the blurred line between the utmost surrealism and the utterly real moments in urban life that make these literary works both timely and sociologically rich. Ahmad Naaji (in colloquial Arabic Naagui) portrays, ironically, a sexually frustrated and perverted collective male population, as well as a largely subservient, circumcised, and also sexually frustrated female population. The situation sounds so real, but the author stretches it into a state of collapse, with decaying human beings unable to express feelings. They are apathetic and unable to take control of their lives in the grip of a faceless, unspoken fascism. Naaji's graphic sexual descriptions, which resulted in the banning of his novel and a two-year prison sentence, depict sex lives suffocated by interruptions and surveillance that produce a feeling of constant angst.

Here the dystopia takes the form of a brutal, polluted state under constant surveillance, by neighbours, house guardians, or officials, in this large, depressing, and suffocating metropolis. The suffocation is literal (through pollution, lack of proper building maintenance, and accumulating dirt), as well as metaphorical and psychological. A pervasive collective decadence and perverse crimes tainted with cannibalism (*'Utaarid*) and repression dominate in all of the novels.

As in almost all writing about Cairo, the Nile itself plays a role. In two of the novels under discussion, the residential island of Zamalek either disappears (*Istikhdaam al-Hayaat*) or is completely unpopulated (*'Utaarid*). In *Istikhdaam al-Hayaat*, the Nile is diverted and the proposed solution to rescue decaying Cairo is to destroy the river so that the population is forced to move away to the fringes. In fact, *Istikhdaam al-Hayaat* is mocking the multiplying satellite cities in the desert, which are indeed causing the diversion of the Nile, or at least the appropriation of the diminishing supply of water at the expense of depriving the old and poor quarters.

The main characteristic of the dystopia in the literary works mentioned here is the complete control of the citizens by uncontrollable and violent governmental powers. In this way, dystopia is revealed as the antithesis to Georg Simmel's evaluation of urban life in his famous brief work, *The Metropolis and Mental Life*, in which he asserts that the evolution and tensions of individuality are the factors that render urban life the location of intellectual and cultural creativity.[15] In other words, individuality ceases to exist in dystopias.

These apocalyptic scenarios and imaginations go well together with the equally dystopian counter-images of the TV series analysed earlier, since in reality a number of these unfinished and scattered desert satellite ghost compounds and cities are still sometimes perceived as genuine dystopias.

David Sims asserts that the desert cities conceived since Sadat's regime have not succeeded in attracting the population figures that the Government was hoping for. Quite a few of the newly built industrial satellite cities in the early 1980s managed to attract more people than the residential areas, but not the desired numbers of the working-class population (Sims 2014: 126). Sims states that, after forty years of existence, the satellite cities have attracted less than a million people, for various reasons. Sims presents a list of unresolved problems, explaining why these cities are such spectacular failures. One main problem has been the remoteness of these cities from the established commercial areas. This means the majority of the numerous working and poor classes, who cannot afford to own a car, cannot live in the satellite cities. But above all, these desert cities are evidence of poor planning, which went together with a high level of state corruption, as well as extensive land speculation by private investors. The simple fact is that the Government has been obsessed with a modernist dream of conquering the desert, following models from elsewhere without taking into account the ecological specificities of desert life, especially the acute problem of water shortage (Sims 2014: 174). Even though most of these cities originally included plans for large blocks of public housing, the successive regimes have been too willing to abandon these plans in favour of the more lucrative market speculation. Thus, the satellite cities have brought no benefit to the poor classes, while enriching the speculators.[16]

For the past three years, I have taught both a graduate and an undergraduate course on urban sociology with a focus on Cairo. As a rough estimate, almost

70 per cent of the well-off AUC students who took my urban sociology courses reside in the satellite cities.[17] Although the commute is dreadful for those residing in the 'old' centre of Cairo, life looks quite different for the new generation raised within the compound boundaries.

For a large number of my students who were assigned to describe their neighbourhoods, how they spent their leisure time, and where they consume, it was a discovery that they lived in an entirely different 'cityscape' from those living in the 'old' centre of Cairo. The cineplexes of Sheikh Zayed City where they hang around on weekends, or the gigantic shopping plaza of Rehab City with its high-quality Iranian, Lebanese, Syrian, and Italian restaurants and multiple cappuccino-style cafés, or the privilege of frequenting the spa and pool facilities of the Thailand-based *Dusit Thani* Hotel, located on Road 90, or the possibility of shopping at the Cairo Festival City shopping complex with international franchises and imported brands, or purchasing furniture from IKEA, or shopping regularly at Carrefour or Spinneys in City Scape Mall in Sixth of October City, all express the fact that we are witnessing multiple, unconnected Cairos with increasingly separate lifestyles.

Some of my youngest students who grew up in New Cairo City have visited Downtown for the first time in their lives only through the field trips and walks assigned in my course. To my astonishment, some students have never been to Tahrir. This leads me to disagree with Sims on one point. One can hardly deny his dystopian diagnosis of the causes for the failure of the desert dreams. However, the push factors from the centre of Cairo, such as air and noise pollution, stress, traffic jams, and decaying housing, seem so pervasive that I would assert that the massive exodus to the desert seems to have intensified, rather than slowed, after 2011. In other words, in spite of the multiplying nightmarish landscapes, these cities seem to have gained a considerable number of middle- and upper-class residents. Many predict that in less than a decade New Cairo's Road 90 will be a replica of the jammed Nasr City district built in the late 1950s, in particular its famous central Tayaraan Street. Many also predict that the commercial activities and offices will succeed in New Cairo.

The ugly villas filled with kitschy pseudo-Roman columns and overworked wrought iron of the new rich, and the jammed buildings on Road 90 leading to New Cairo, all crowd next to each other, as a symbol of the neo-liberal greed in landscaping as well as in land speculation. No space in between the fences for greenery, nor adequate distance for privacy from neighbours, is to be expected. But even if some people – particularly the lovers of the Downtown *Belle Epoque* architecture – perceive the compound life as a dystopia, it remains the only possible, close-at-hand 'imagined' utopia for the middle and upper classes, who today are experiencing suffocation at the heart of the city. However, it would be incorrect to lump together all satellite cities as mainly containing the compounds of the rich. This vision would ignore the large working-class area of Sixth of October City not far from the area of Hussary Mosque, the large Syrian population that has created a kind of 'little Syria' market life there, and the more affordable flats and cheaper housing blocks that have been constructed in the Sixth of October City, Sheikh Zayed, al-Shuruuk, and al-Rehab Cities, attracting younger generations, the middle classes, and also African and Iraqi exile populations.[18]

It all depends on one's class affiliations. How many times have I heard, not only from taxi drivers, but in numerous conversations with acquaintances, that Tahrir Square and the area of Downtown constitute a nightmare, as if these were polluted sites to be avoided. It is in the centre, they point out, that all the violent events occurred. Would it not be healthier to consciously erase from one's memory these painful recent years? Since the daily present is so enduring, would it not be better to start anew in the clean desert landscape? This is what so many acquaintances, including some former participants in the revolution whom I personally know, have done, taking the path of internal migration to the desert.

These apocalyptic sceneries and imaginations go well together with the dystopian counter-images of the episodes analysed earlier. Dystopia is expressed in utmost control of the citizens by uncontrollable and violent governing powers that be. Dystopia is revealed as the antithesis to Simmel's concern regarding the evolution and tensions of individuality in urban life. In other words, individuality is extinct.

CAIRO – 17 July 2017: Clashes erupted Sunday between security forces and residents of the Warraq district in Giza during a campaign to remove squatters, resulting in injuries on both sides.

A citizen was killed, and 37 security personnel, including two major generals, were wounded in clashes between citizens and security forces, the Interior Ministry said on Sunday. Four of those are in critical condition.

Also, 19 rioters were injured in the face-off and 10 others were arrested, the ministry said.

The clashes erupted after security forces started removing encroachments and retaking state-owned lands from their illegal residents in the district. ('Details of Warraq riots against campaign to remove squatters', 2017)

### Notes

1  A *tok-tok* is a motorised tricycle, open on both sides. Its concept is an import from India, and it is also to be found in Indonesia under the name of *bajaj*. Its main advantage is that is can be cheaply and locally manufactured.
2  See 'New Cairo Campus'.
3  Questions about the quality of tap water emerge repeatedly every summer with the rise in temperatures and the increasingly widespread problem of water shortage in the governorates (in particular Upper Egypt) and in popular quarters. In recent years there were numerous cases of water poisoning in different governorates, including Mansura. Most recent is the *Mada Masr* article of Isabel Esterman (Esterman 2016).

4 'Government officials', 2015.

5 See 'Cairo Festival City Mall'. See also 'Oriana Villas'.

6 On the question of growing nostalgia and the sense of loss with respect to the revolution, see Abou El-Naga 2015.

7 The theme of the outrageous and growing class disparities between the residents of compound life and the rest of Cairo's popular quarters, the contrast between the servants' life-world and the rich, is intelligently addressed in the recent film *Nawara* (2015), directed by Hala Khalil, starring Menna Shalabi and Mahmud Hemmeida.

8 'Fawq mustawa al-shubuhaat', 2016.

9 I will focus here on Ahmad Naaji's *Istikhdaam al-Hayaat* (*The Use of Life*, 2014), Basma 'Abd al-'Aziz's *al-Taabuur* (*The Queue*, 2013), and Muhamad Rabii''s '*Utaarid* (*Mercury*, 2014), which is the name of the policeman and protagonist of the novel.

10 I am aware that these three novels are not the first in the Arabic dystopian genre.

11 Masked snipers evoke, in the collective memory, the early days of January 2011, when they killed a large number of protesters. Later on, special police squads with their faces covered became an everyday scene in the streets of Cairo, in particular whenever demonstrations were to be expected.

12 For a review of '*Utaarid*, see al-Jibali 2016.

13 In the same genre of a science-fiction thriller, in which the revolution becomes the epicentre of events, is Ezzeddin Choukri Fishere's *Baab al-Khuruug* (*The Exit Door*) (Fishere 2012). The novel speculates on the *longue durée*, the forthcoming massacres, and urban wars resulting from the power struggles between the old guard, the army, the Muslim Brotherhood, and the Salafis. The cityscape of Cairo becomes, once again, the main protagonist of the unfolding violent events.

14 The famous Khaled Said murder was one of the main triggers of the revolution. It inspired graffiti artists in the years that followed to paint on walls his smashed and tortured face, images that went viral in social media as a reminder of the brutality of the old regime. The depiction of Said's disfigured portrait in graffiti triggered much controversy (see Abaza 2013b).

15 For a stimulating analysis of the question of anonymity in the city and how the Middle East differs from Europe in this respect, as well as a way to rethink Georg Simmel's concept of the 'blasé' and the city, together with Norbert Elias's concept of 'civility' and whether 'individuality' in relation to modernity would entail an entirely different dimension in the Middle East, see Mermier 2015.

16 For the reasons why Sims considers the satellite cities as failures, see Sims (2014: 140–74).

17 See the description of the neighbourhoods of some of my students in 'AUC students describing their neighborhood', 2015.

18 The Tenth of Ramadan City hosts large manufacturing complexes and cheap working-class housing. Sadat City and Fifteenth of May City have also developed cheap housing. See Sims (2014: 122–5).

# 3

# Tale III: My exhausted and exhausting building

In effect, neo-liberal discourse is not just one discourse amongst many. Rather, it is a 'strong discourse' – the way psychiatric discourse is in an asylum, in Erving Goffman's analysis. It is so strong and so hard to combat only because it has on its side all of the forces of a world of relations of forces, a world that it contributes to making what it is. In this way, a Darwinian world emerges – it is the struggle of all against all at all levels of the hierarchy, which finds support through everyone clinging to their job and organisation under conditions of insecurity, suffering, and stress. (Bourdieu 1998)

## An imagined conversation with Stephen Graham

Indeed, super-fast elevators are now being lauded by the world's business press as proxy indicators of what's really going on in the fast changing economic geographies of globalisation, urban growth and the real estate speculation. 'If you want to know where the world's hottest economies are', Forbes Magazine gushes, 'skip the GDP reports, employment statistics and consumer spending trends.' All you need to do is answer one question: Where are the fastest elevators? (Graham 2014: 249)

Before meditating on the state of affairs in my building,[1] I wish to start my narrative with the antiquated, characteristic elevator, which, in our archetypal building, stands as a living attestation to the urban reshaping of the city. I wish to engage in a speculative one-way dialogue with Stephen Graham's fascinating work, whose timely speculations on the 'new military urbanism' have been highly applicable to Cairo's urban reinvention since 2011. I will concentrate on Graham's recent reflections on the geographies of 'horizontal mobilities' and 'vertically structured city-scapes', with the mushrooming skyscrapers as symbols of power and modernity. More precisely, I will consider Graham's focus on what he defines as the practices of 'elevator urbanism' as emblematic of modernity. Graham expresses the drive in Taiwan, Japan, the Gulf, and the United States for taller skyscrapers than ever before, in terms of faster elevators with highly sophisticated, digitised technologies, as a leading architectural characteristic of the ideal, futuristic global city. He equates the vertical expansion of the modern metropolis

**Figure 14**    The elevator, 6 April 2016.

with high-velocity upward travel. Graham's ahead-of-its-time analysis of the elevator in modern times informs us that 'Hitachi's research elevators are now running at speeds that are 300 times as fast as those in New York 100 years ago' (Graham 2014: 245). To meditate on Graham's work is to indulge in a science-fiction novel or a film from a lagging time machine. Graham is quite conscious of the class disparities and alienations which dysfunctional elevators can cause, in the wake of the retreat of the welfare state from cheap housing schemes and their collapse in Europe, due to aggressive neo-liberal policies in the reshaping and planning of its cities. The daily struggle in the constrained space of my once-charming, now decaying environment not only engenders a straining physical nervosity, it has above all shaped a particular psychological mindset, cultivated by an abysmal sentiment of backwardness amongst many of its users. The daily deployment of our slow and ageing elevator evokes a specific response: a feeling of detachment from the global forces that Graham so brilliantly dissects. It is as if our building has been edited out of the map of the 'civilised' and, abused by the forces of time, undergone a process of 'demodernisation', a term I borrow from Stephen Graham's military urbanism.

> The experience of elevator travel is also overcoded with a rich history of fictional, filmic poetic and science fictional imagination. From the mysterious and secret seventh-and-a-half floor in the 1999 film *Being John Malkovitch*, to a whole chapter of urban folklore, or a myriad of unfortunate filmic deaths and catastrophes, the elevator stalks the interface between the banal and the fearful or unknown within the vertical and the technological cultures of the contemporary metropolis.

> 'Public yet private, enclosing yet permeable, separate from but integral to the architectural spaces that surround them', elevators, Susan Garfinkel (2003: 176) writes, 'invite us to expect the unexpected in certain predictable ways'. She shows how, in film, elevators have variously been used to symbolise the 'corporate ladder', aspirations of social or economic advancement or sexual liaison (or sexual predation); the democratisation of public space; anxieties of technological collapse: the monotony of corporate life and anxieties of urban anomie. (Graham 2014: 245)

*Between the Sky and Earth* (1959 or 1960),[2] with screenplay by the late Nobel laureate Naguib Mahfouz and directed by Salah Abu Seif, is a testimony that Egyptians, too, were inspired by the foreign, Anglo-Saxon, 'civilised' world, and made a pretty successful adaptation of the elevator as the hero or the epicentre of a movie. In *Between the Sky and Earth*, the elevator typically gets stuck between high floors for a few hours with a group of passengers (not by coincidence, the mystic number of thirteen takes on a certain relevance to the number of passengers it held) from various contrasting, if not clashing, classes, representing differing tastes and lifestyles. Their enclosure in this tightly confined space creates a collective state of moral panic. When *Between the Sky and Earth* came out, it must have been perceived as a biting social criticism of the rigid and unrelenting class system that still persisted some seven years after a disruptive anti-colonial revolution (or coup d'état) led by the Free Officers. Seen from a contemporary perspective, even though all the characters are portrayed in a farcical, stereotypical, and one-dimensional fashion, the film remains a significant testimony to the *Zeitgeist* and an indication of what the aspirations for modernity might have been in the Cairo of the early 1960s.

The story takes place during the summer, in an extreme heat wave that puts animals and human beings alike in a total state of inertia. In the miniature universe of the elevator, clashing classes end up being confined for a few hours, leading to a series of comical situations. We see Upper Egyptian servants and Nubians fighting with the elevator operator. The servants are all scolded and shouted at for their physical appearance by the better-off passengers. The elevator operator wants to forbid a servant from taking the elevator and the servant answers him back that the times of servitude have come to an end. He continues to argue that a servant is surely better off than an elevator operator, because a servant works for one family only, while the operator is subservient to the entire building.

An archetypal sexy film star, played by iconic blonde Hind Rustum, parodies upper-class Egyptians by mixing French words with Arabic (*c'est trop, oh non ...jamais, merci*). The scene in which Rustum enters the building nonchalantly after promenading her dog is particularly satirical. The men are completely distracted by her eroticised way of walking, à la Marilyn Monroe. Sexy, high-heeled Hind Rustum is headed to the rooftop with her dog, where a movie crew is waiting for her to shoot a film. But a passer-by, clearly a sexual harasser, follows her to the elevator. He sticks to her in an obscene manner; the viewer understands Rustum's reaction through her angry facial expression. At the same moment, an upper-class Egyptian, snobbish but visibly fallen, arrives in the lobby. Played by the late, gifted comedian 'Abdel Salam al-Naboulsi, he arrogantly but comically slaps the servants around. He uses hilarious expressions in his obviously classist jokes. He complains constantly about the horrible underprivileged people, the 'onion-stinking servants' and 'riff-raff'. When the elevator operator calls al-Naboulsi 'effendi' (a title less senior than the more elevated rank of 'pasha'), al-Naboulsi screams back at him, '*Afandi fi 'aynak! Gilf, ya 'adiim al-symitriya wa-l-nathar*' (Effendi, my arse! You undiscerning, unperceptive oaf). Al-Naboulsi continues to insult the operator: 'You are a zero [implying a "nothing"], you only press buttons.' Obviously, class tensions and hierarchy are being satirised to show how deeply ingrained class sensitivities were in this period.

The scenario progresses to include a pregnant woman who ends up delivering in the elevator, assisted by Hind Rustum, who in the latter part of the film transmutes from the role of the sexy arrogant star into a public-spirited character who holds the newborn baby while retaining her down-to-earth mettle. As the repertoire of characters expands, we encounter a married woman secretly following her lover up to a flat, and the madman who has escaped from the mental hospital but speaks wise words and several times becomes, as Michel Foucault put it, 'the harbinger of truth' (Foucault 2006: 13). There is a decrepit old married man on his way to marry a much younger woman, who dreads him but is forced into this arrangement by her greedy mother because he is obviously a catch; the distressed old man's first wife and children attend the wedding in the hope of disrupting the deal. More characters continue to join this cast, such as the young woman on the verge of rescuing her lover, who is about to commit suicide because her father's refusal to give them his consent has driven him to contemplate ending his life, which leads the young woman to desperately rush to stop him from leaping from the rooftop. We also see a religious old man who is continuously reciting verses of the Quran and religious sayings, a pickpocket, and a supposedly much-feared gangster who is on his way to commit a rather serious burglary. In a nutshell, the group becomes a miniature of the society of the late 1950s. The building's Nubian doorkeepers are portrayed in a stereotypic manner of that era, adopting a dialect that is heavy, distorted, even comical, its peculiar accent just part of the way they are portrayed in this framework as lazy and a bit idiotic. Their perceived mismanagement of the elevator engines seems to be one main reason why the elevator ends up stuck in between floors.

The movie is filmed in the ornamented and famed *Lebon* building on the residential island of Zamalek. It was one of the few modernist skyscrapers of the time, symbolising Westernised Cairo, the Cairo of the rich and powerful, with women going in and out in décolleté fashions. Famous actors and actresses, politicians and wealthy families, who resided in *Lebon*, certainly contributed to the notoriety of this iconic building, whose spacious apartments even today are traded at the highest amounts ever in Zamalek. The *Lebon* building, constructed in the early 1950s, was conceived by the Levantine architect Antoine Selim Nahas, who is considered the pioneer of modernist architecture in Egypt (Elamrani 2001). The *Lebon* building, together with the Union and the Ali Labib Gabr buildings, all three adjacent to each other, are located at a few minutes' walk from the once 'prestigious' Gezira Club. As the historian and journalist Samir Raafat, a prominent and astute recorder of the *Belle Epoque* period, reports with a note of nostalgia, these buildings were called 'the three grand ladies of Zamalek' by the Egyptian bourgeoisie of the period (Raafat 1999).

When the elevator gets stuck between floors, people collapse one after the other and tensions grow. Particularly significant is the way in which the passengers are eventually rescued by firemen. The Nubians, portrayed as a bit incompetent, push and pull on the elevator machinery, with the result that they manage only to terrify the passengers even more. The firemen decide to pierce the wall and remove the passengers from the upper floors using a ladder, instead of actually fixing the motors. This Egyptian cinematic depiction of elevators is a colourful representation of modernity and class disparities in 1960s Egypt.

### Recurring nightmares: Deadly elevator incidents

In February 2018, at the hospital of Banha University, an elevator collapsed. It dropped from the sixth floor, resulting in the death of six passengers (al-Guindi 2018a). This was a significant incident that triggered a series of articles in the media on the large number of unreported previous fatal elevator incidents, highlighting the neglect on the part of elevator companies of any regulations related to health and safety. This curious avalanche of critical articles pointed to the time bomb of other perilous collapsing elevators in Egypt's buildings.[3] Ironically, this incident turned into an exemplar for evaluating the state of the art of the poorly built, swelling, informal high-rise buildings. Press and website articles pointed to a number of previous deadly elevator accidents that went together with the increasing trade in unlicensed elevators, as an essential element of a larger corruption pattern in the construction business. The collapsing 'collective coffins', the 'moving tombs', the 'Ezra messenger', were all sardonic and yet depressing epithets for the innumerable deadly elevators. The press went as far as advertising, so to speak, six steps or protective measures, illustrated with photographs of proper possible postures (such as how to hold onto bars before falling down, or how to kneel in order to alleviate the shock of the fall, and above all, to caution against jumping out of the elevator), all basic measures to deal with the calamitous conditions related to collapsing elevators (al-Gallad 2018).

The trend of failing elevators led to other, more in-depth, investigations by the media, exposing the long series of previous deadly incidents. In one, a woman met her death in the elevator shaft in the Abnud town hospital. Four people were injured when an elevator in a private hospital in the town of Zaqaziik collapsed. A doctor died in the cancer hospital in Mansura in another similar incident. In the town of Beni Sweif, three people were seriously injured when the elevator collapsed from the second floor. Children, too, were victims of elevators. In the town of Tanta, a child fell down an elevator shaft, and another child in the town of Marsa Matruuh met a similar fate ('Abdel Qader 2015).

Most important is the spreading phenomenon of some one thousand or more unlicensed elevator companies. A recurrent cause of disaster in the high-rise buildings in the densely populated quarter of Dar al-Salam is the poor quality of spare parts, whether locally made or imported from China. Obviously, the imported spare parts and elevators do not conform to any regulation. The necessary specialists do not seem to exist in the neighbourhood, and the local licence is given without any inspection. Numberless elevators have no safety parachute or amortiser, nor are there any safety measures against fire. According to the Ministry of Electricity, the number of open and licensed flats all over Egypt has expanded to some 19.5 million, while sealed and unoccupied flats have reached some 3.5 million. The number of flats that have been constructed without proper licensing has rocketed to some 6 million. The number of unlicensed constructions between 2009 and 2013 alone has reached some 318,000, which means that none of these buildings would have licensed elevators ('Abdel Qader 2015). Egyptians elevators are evidently a ticking time bomb, but who really cares? There are already too many ticking bombs within the Cairene urban texture.

## The majestic, ailing elevator

But then again, who is afraid of Cairene elevators? Cairene elevators are unique, fascinating, exceptional spaces, as no two look alike. Their slowness, their antiquated appearance, the picturesque Art Nouveau or Art Deco doors in the Downtown buildings, are a charming reminder that these objects have been left behind as colonial memorabilia. Many have commented on the fact that so many Cairene elevators contain a system that automatically begins to chant the Quran the moment they start to travel up and down. Others, counterbalancing the Quran ones, play the theme of the movie *Love Story* when you open their doors.[4] The use of 'elevator music' is not at all an Egyptian innovation. It actually emanates from the United States, an American invention that dates back as early as 1928. According to Stephen Graham, the music was meant to appease fears of delays and breakdowns (Graham 2014: 244). Elevator phobia seems to be widespread amongst Cairenes, but it is not necessarily culturally specific, since American history displays identical fears related to this installation. Scores of Cairene elevators are ideal spaces for staging claustrophobic horror films, which is of course a well-established genre in the American film industry. Still, almost all my guests would politely mention how they began to be afraid the moment the doors of my antiquated elevator closed.

I can recall two frightening elevator incidents as a child with my mother – who with age became a claustrophobic hater of elevators, which did not come as a surprise to anyone. In one of them, which is typical, we were trapped for almost an hour in an elevator that hung between floors.[5]

Many elevators don't have real doors. One can enjoy jumping out of them as one pleases. These genuinely inflame the feeling of living dangerously, as one can toy with adventurous suicidal leaps into the void. Other elevators – like ours – are absolutely terrifying, and unpredictable on any given day.

With this long list of misgivings, the archaic and ill-managed elevator of our building has turned into the spiritual epicentre of the place. In a way, it constitutes the symbolic cosmos holding the collapsing edifice together. Around our dying elevator, so many tragicomic stories are recalled, such as endless fights and quarrels. Ever since I purchased my flat, eleven years ago, the residents of the building have been engaged in an endless war of arguing, negotiating, and fighting with one another in order to ascertain whether to repair the elevator or replace it with a new one. The only conclusion after long years of bargaining is to fix bits and pieces by scouring the market for spare parts. But nothing fundamental had been done about the matter.[6] Instead, the 1950s-style, round glass windows in the door of each of the five floors disappeared one after the other, to become holes through which people push the door open. The door latches followed, becoming mostly inoperable. Many of the users, including my friends and I, were terrified of getting stuck in between floors if the elevator came to a sudden unexplained halt. After frightening moments of suspense, followed by the usual shouting and screams, the users have to be lifted up, with the help of Y., the *bawaab* (doorkeeper), who pulls them out into safety, with the understanding that such rescue efforts have to be rewarded by a handsome *bakshish* (tip). And if one carelessly opens any of the doors without looking to see whether the elevator has reached the designated floor, one can risk simply dropping into the void, although fortunately this has not happened yet. I have, however, heard of a few tragic incidents that occurred as recently as 2017, in a building located in the residential quarter of Garden City, when someone fell into an open elevator shaft and died a few hours later.

However, such rescue efforts tilt the power relations in our building, and constitute a double-edged sword. There are instances when Y., the *bawaab*, wanted to retaliate against Madam Mx., because she had not paid him the monthly amount of money he requested. He had within his arsenal the power to stop the elevator completely by pushing the key (the *sikkina*, literally 'the knife'). This resulted in Madam Mx. taking a dramatic victimhood approach, also known as the 'Amina Rizq'[7] role, by reciting lines from a famous Egyptian soap opera that we came to know by heart as a result of their frequent rendition. Madam Mx. associates her continued poor health (although it isn't that poor) with the failing elevator, and blames the *bawaab*, whom she absolutely hates. She exults in declaring how she landed in the hospital the week before because of the loathsome *bawaab*. This is then followed by the claim that she is on the verge of a heart attack because the only alternative to using the lift is taking the stairs.

The *bawaab*'s youngest son, who is not yet nine years old, is willing and intelligent enough to be able to stop the elevator if one of the tenants orders him to do so. Four of the tenants, myself included, proposed in 2016 to shut down the elevator for a few hours each day to let it 'rest', so to speak, in the afternoons, just when the masses frequenting the fifth-floor internet-café-cum-co-working-space would be flooding and overloading the elevator. Our proposal did not last long, since many of the neighbours felt that this was an insult to their status and respectability. But how many of the users were careful to close the fifth-floor door properly so that the elevator wouldn't just sit there? How many of them felt that they had to scream at the *bawaab*'s son, in a harsh, authoritarian voice, to climb the five floors to close the door because it is his duty to do so?[8] These variations of 'inborn' class affectations are quickly absorbed by the newly arrived foreigners who frequent our building – for example, the female Palestinian students living at the nearby Palestinian women's hostel. It is as if the users of our building are automatically rehearsing a déjà vu repertoire, excelling in mimicking the scenes of the *Yacoubian Building* movie but, alas, totally losing its sardonic twist.

How many times have I screamed at the foot of the stairs that the elevator cannot take more than four persons at a time? It seems that the feeling of being squeezed into this stinking, dirty wooden box must be an alluring sport for some. Another habit is that of throwing rubbish underneath the moving wooden box as a challenge to the *bawaab*, who first has to immobilise the elevator on an upper floor, until he can reach into the pit beneath the elevator and retrieve the rubbish. The hole underneath the elevator then attracted an enormous number of fleas, leading me to set aside a special budget for the *bawaab* to purchase insect spray, which he apparently kept for personal use and his living space instead.

Then there are the endless boxes expected to be delivered to the perfume company on the third floor every second day, to say nothing of the delivery orders of food, the electricity and gas collectors, and others who use the elevator.

Since October 2017, a wild group of quite angry-looking deaf beggars have called at each door on a weekly basis. Last but not least, there came the nightmarish internet/co-working-space-cum-café on the fifth floor, which forms the heart of this story later on. Then there is 'Amm Sayyed, the elevator repair man, whom I have never met, prophesying every month that our elevator is on the verge of an imminent, final, and dramatic apocalypse that will take our lives and the lives of others, as reported by Y., the *bawaab*. Needless to say, 'Amm Sayyed has never been paid properly by the residents, so that he disappears for months at a time, and with some justification.

### Moving to Doqi

UPDATE November 18, 2012: Military and security forces stormed the island (of Qursaya) during the early hours of November 18, burned fields, and when the farmers defended themselves, at least two have been reported dead and 10 injured. It is known since the 2007 attacks that investors, Egyptian and Saudi, have been wanting to confiscate the island and turn it from a productive farming community to an exclusive tourist complex. (Cairobserver 2011)

I am exhausted from the visible material degradation in my daily life since I moved to the neighbourhood of Doqi in February 2016, after having lived on the residential island of Zamalek. Some friends have teasingly told me that the psychological process I have been undergoing is an obvious form of '*déclassement social*'. Such a statement would not be an extreme exaggeration, since countless Cairenes would immediately identify with the descriptions of deteriorating standards in urban life that I have traced in my meanderings. The city in which we grew up, its nature, streets, and landscapes, has been distorted by the increasing urban problems haunting neighbourhoods. As early as the mid-1980s, I began to notice a growing sense of the decay and decomposition of the city, which is a collective experience shared by many people I know, including my family, and had been the prime push factor for them to move into other neighbourhoods, such as the massive exodus to the areas of Maadi, Heliopolis, or the desert cities. Yet it also seems that the older Doqi residents have either left for quieter places, or reached some sort of modus vivendi with their neighbours, since hostilities and extremely violent acts of aggression are rare, although not unknown. These hostilities replace fights with words, and are a daily sport for many residents in our quarter.

It is true that this feeling is certainly not specific to my neighbourhood but is more widespread. It is as if a large part of Cairo is experiencing the 'all against all' Darwinian war that Bourdieu depicted so eloquently in his analysis of neo-liberalism. On one point, however, Zamalek is different. Its insular character has certainly been much less affected by the recent spectacular urban decomposition that has marked the other older quarters of the city. Zamalek residents organised themselves well after January 2011, through the association they created and its Facebook account.[9] The latter circulates valuable information on sales, gatherings, and collective organising for cleaning streets and cutting trees, the constant problem of how to collect rubbish in a well-managed way, and attempts at restraining the chaotic mushrooming of cafés that remain open until dawn, disturbing the residents. Above all, the Zamalek Association has proved to be quite efficient at organising public events at the Fish Garden over the past few years, bringing together musicians and artists and providing spaces for sales of books, arts and crafts, and homemade food. The communal work of Zamalekites through this association, which emerged after the January revolution, became the target of attacks by official circles and the media. Its residents were stigmatised as the rich 'bourgeois', often publicly attacked as 'egoists' for refusing to allow the future subway line to pass through the middle of the island, right through the very narrow Ismail Mohamed Street (and incidentally revealing how impractical the metro line will be, as some Zamalekites have incessantly argued). The skirmishes between the residents of Zamalek and the regime revealed the complexities that underlie civil initiatives, since the metro line will seriously affect the old and (by today's standards) historical buildings of Zamalek, like the Sedqui buildings overlooking the Nile. Yet regardless of whether or not such a project is feasible on these justifications, there are certainly issues that go beyond the question of bourgeois class interests: the questionable ecological sustainability of the metro project, in addition to the uncontrollable occupation, if not the colonisation, of public spaces and street vending.[10] One thing is clear: the Zamalek Association has clearly revealed the impact of the revolution in opening new paths for collective work (ironically, working well for the better off) on the local-neighbourhood level for issues like rubbish collection and the serious challenge of reordering public space.[11]

Having said that, the building into which I moved in Doqi is a good case in point of class mobility in a quarter that once witnessed a particular magnificence, but has been left to degenerate into decay (a view that is certainly tainted with a biased, middle-class outlook). There are various reasons for this, but the most important is the fact that many of the older residents, mostly representing the higher middle classes of the 1960s, have left for better neighbourhoods like Zamalek, Maadi, or the satellite cities like the Sixth of October and New Cairo. This older generation has largely been replaced during the past decade by newcomers, not without wealth, but who sprang from the lower strata of the middle classes,[12] with clearly different lifestyles and expectations. The newcomers harbour different sets of ideas regarding the usage of public space, sanitary and hygiene concerns, aesthetics, and exteriors of buildings. They seem to have little grasp of the intellectual aspirations of the more established middle classes of the 1950s and 1960s. This neglect is reflected in the spaces not only outside the main entrance but even the entrances of the individual flats. No square centimetre deemed a public space is seen as falling within the responsibility of any individual. The prevailing sentiment is the famous injunction of '_Après moi, le déluge_'.

The majority of the residents of my building are over sixty years old, which may go some way to explaining why they are mostly politically and socially conservative in their attitudes. It has been practically impossible to get them to agree on anything, least of all to organise any collective framework to improve the infrastructure of the building such as the entrance hall, the stairwells, or the garage. Clearly, there is something constrained and impractical about rescuing the declining conditions of life amongst Cairene middle classes, who are in constant denial of the material culture surrounding them. Perhaps this denial of the expanding rubbish, dirt, and miasmas in one's vicinity is actually an effective survival mechanism. Unconsciously or consciously training oneself not to see displeasing things, or ceasing to react to the long hours of the dreadful amplifiers of the nearby schools, damaging to our senses, might plunge us into either a deep depression or a state of utter lightness, as the only sane survival strategy. The aphorism 'After me the deluge' also encompasses the notion that any physical exertion, such as taking the stairs, has to be perceived as demeaning for both the 'new' (ascending) and the 'old' (declining) middle classes. Meanwhile, day after day, all the buildings on my street are invaded by multiplying offices and commercial spaces, noisy working-class cafés, chaotic signboards, countless satellite discs on the balconies and roofs, and a multitude of informal street activities, all of which conspire to openly defy the very notion of privacy.

### Mahfouz's _al-Qahira al-jadida_

CAIRO, 14 August 2018: The Maspero Triangle Development project is progressing so well, and about 75% of the area has been already demolished, Khalil Shaath, head of the development of slums department in Cairo governorate, said on Monday.

Prime Minister and Minister of Housing, Utilities and Urban Communities, Mostafa Madbouly, witnessed on July 9 the signing ceremony of two cooperation protocols between Cairo governorate and the new Urban Communities Authority.

**Figure 15** 'Looking over modern residential part of Cairo, El Duqqi, from above English Bridge to the Pyramids [picture]: [Cairo, Egypt, World War II]'. Created and published between 1938 and 1945.

The agreements aim to transfer the ownership of a 5.5-feddan area in Maspero Triangle to the authority to build new housing units and provide the necessary services for the residents. (Egypt Today 2018)

In several unique and prominent literary works, the Doqi/Giza complex of the early 1930s typifies the space of promise – of progress, so to say – epitomised in the newly founded, 'modern', and spacious Cairo University, which had then just opened its doors to women. But by the 1950s and 1960s, the Egyptian film industry had begun to portray the Orman and Zoo gardens as the clichéd meeting spaces for lovers to date and wander around, while the neighbourhood of Doqi enjoyed a reputation for its pleasant streets. *Al-Qahira al-jadida/gadida* (*Modern Cairo*, 2006), Naguib Mahfouz's much-acclaimed novel, first published in 1945 and adapted into film as *al-Qahira 30* by director Salah Abu Seif in 1966, deserves attention as an illustration of the changing topography of space. In this novel, the Doqi/Giza complex is the main stage of the narrative. While the story is a portrayal of Cairo in the 1930s, the film adaptation was made in the 1960s, and the script was written by Lutfi al-Khuli (Youssef 2014), a militant intellectual who was known for his communist leanings. In al-Khuli's treatment, the film's emphasis on the burning question of class inequalities and the politics of space gained a visual prominence and contemporaneity under the Nasser regime, as if class inequalities had remained unresolved. However, it is possible to speculate that the Doqi neighbourhood of the 1930s epitomised aspirations for healthier, more spacious residences, imagined as the futuristic 'Cairo modern'. This portrayal of Doqi can be seen as the equivalent of today's dream of the middle class to move into the spacious satellite cities of 'New Cairo'. Once more, this pertains to the contemporaneous redefinition of 'becoming modern' through the necessity of commuting primarily by cars, and frequenting shopping malls and Western cafés in Cairo Festival City, for example. These new satellite cities are sold for their radiant future, clean air, greenery, enclosure security, and above all slum-free neighbourhoods.

Mahfouz's *al-Qahira al-jadida* astutely portrays the turmoil of the 1930s, brilliantly exposing the disarray and confusion that reigned in colonial Egypt. It does not hesitate to display the flagrant class disparities between the palaces of the rich and the huts of the destitute, or the corruption and carelessness of the dominant classes vis-à-vis the poor, since the rich could easily corrupt anyone by means of money and power. The cultural alienation of the rich is shown through their lifestyle and their preference of foreign languages to Arabic. The utmost poverty and deprivation are depicted in the character of the nihilistic student Mahgoub 'Abdel Daa'em, who turns into a creepy, opportunistic social climber. The beautiful but terribly poor Ihsaan Shahata al-Turki, played by the late star Suad Hosny, discontentedly marries the slimy Mahgoub as a result of her parents' blackmail. Even though Ihsaan is in love with the idealistic socialist Taha Ali, she willingly accepts the marriage arrangement with Mahgoub as a cover so that she can become the lover of the well-off Bek, who in exchange provides the newlywed couple with a flat in a *hay affrangi* (a European quarter), where social control is lax. As part of the deal, Mahgoub Affandi also obtains a well-paid job as an employee in a government ministry.

Mahfouz sets the first part of the novel in a geographic landscape inspired by reality in which all the protagonists live, commute, and move between the Doqi and Giza quarters. The lovers and students often meet and walk at the Orman Garden and the university campus, ending their walk by passing through the *mudirriya* (the police station that still exists today) located opposite the main entrance of the gardens. The students' hostel was located at the corner of Rashad Pasha Street (which now has a different name), in the vicinity of the Orman Garden and Cairo University. The shabby and dilapidated dwelling of the poor family of Ihsaan Shahata al-Turki seemed to be located in the vicinity of the magnificent palaces of Rashad Pasha Street. In the film, almost all the male students are constantly glimpsing the lovely Ihsaan from the hostel, and following her as she goes in and out of the shabby building. They stare at her from the window in the hope that she will notice them. This implies that a sort of a visual public interaction across classes is happening within the same neighbourhood. Mahfouz describes in the novel the marvellous villas located on Rashad Pasha Street, including the Green Villa – which arouses much envy and resentment in Mahgoub. It was originally owned by an Italian businessman, but was later purchased by the rich and corrupt Egyptian Bek, who takes Ihsaan as a 'concubine'. There is also a reference in Mahfouz's novel to an 'Ezbat Street not far away from the students' hostel, and another reference to the 'Ezbat al-Doqi. Rashad Pasha Street, we are informed, was located behind Giza Street. When Mahgoub became even poorer, forced to survive on merely one pound a month after his father became bedridden, he often went to Giza Square to eat cheap *fuul* (fava) sandwiches as the only way to overcome biting hunger.

The opening scene of *al-Qahira 30* is a long shot fixed on the venerated cupola of Cairo University. Then three students who are close friends, including the idealistic socialist Taha Ali, who dreams of changing the world, walk out of the entrance of the university, talking about politics and Egypt's future, the pervasive and intolerable colonial presence, and the unresolved class inequalities. They discuss their dreams and aspirations, talking about how they could apply Auguste Comte's sociology and Saint-Simonian ideals to the harsh Egyptian colonial reality, having just heard a lecture about these two positivist thinkers, such great believers in progress. In the background, just opposite the entrance of the university, hang posters stating 'Boycott English goods'.

Mahfouz conveys marvellously the poignant class disparities, and how the poorer classes remain trapped in the vicious circle of mere survival. But since the rich and the poor live in such close vicinity in Doqi, the display of luxurious cars, the fine dresses of upper-class women, and the blatant consumer lifestyle sharpen the awareness of class disparities. This is what both the novel and the film successfully managed to convey by focusing on the topography of the Doqi neighbourhood. In the Doqi/Giza complex the breath-taking villas and palaces (quite well portrayed in Abu Seif's film adaptation), surrounded by magical gardens, are visually near the dwellings of the poor. The beautiful but extremely poor Ihsaan Shahata al-Turki has evidently been seduced by the Bek's lavish car entering his palace as she passes by it on her daily walks. It is not a coincidence that to his last days, Naguib Mahfouz resided in a building located in Gamal 'Abd al-Nasser/al-Nil Street, in the neighbourhood of 'Aguza, which is an extension of the Doqi quarter and which was evidently his major source of inspiration.

### False nostalgia: Doqi

When today I see the Park (the Azbakeyya park) in a film, or passing by what is left of it, or even just hearing its name, I feel a pride mixed with sadness and nostalgia. I knew Azbakeyya in its days of splendour. I witnessed its decline, and since I have lived in its immediate vicinity, I began studying its history. I wanted to search through the historic layers that have accumulated in this place over time, making it a magnet for the collective memory of all Egyptians. Individual memories or the momentous events are passed down from generation to generation, and few Egyptians can claim not to know Azbakeyya: once to have wandered around its park, sat in the shade of its tall acacias, smelled the scent of its flowers, sat down at one of the nearby cafés, lingered about outside it in search of some out-of-print or forbidden work, visited its bars and its brothels, or attended a concert where the Egyptian diva Om Kalsoum was singing. This temple to lust, pleasure, leisure, and entertainment was also that of great assemblies, celebrations, protests, but above all a place of culture and education. Who today amongst intellectuals in their fifties could deny the contribution of Azbakeyya Park to their extracurricular education? Translations of world literature, Marxist works, art books, architectural magazines, rare books, were all affordable on modest budgets in this perpetual and cheap book fair. (El Kadi 2012: 126)

There was once a time when the quarter of Doqi emerged as a residential area with spacious greenery, wonderful stylish villas, and architecturally appealing buildings. Perhaps what made the charm of Doqi was that it had a residential flair but with a much less pretentious aura than Zamalek, as it was near Cairo University, the marvellous Giza Zoo, and the Orman Garden, which were part of the larger complex of the Giza gardens. The Zoo and Orman gardens (both originally conceived in 1873 as botanical gardens) were constructed under the reign of Khedive Ismail, as a testimony to both his fantasy of Europeanising the public spaces of Cairo and his abiding obsession with the imaginary of replicating innumerable *Bois de Boulogne*. Since the reign of Mohamed Ali (1805–44), the practice of introducing sophisticated horticulture imported from all corners of the world, and the creation of magnificent gardens, was maintained by a number of his descendants. If Mohamed Ali initiated the first garden in Cairo at Abu Zaabal, near the Khanka, and then established one more sixty-acre garden in the vicinity of his palace in Shubra, it was thanks to Ibrahim Pasha that over five million ornamental and fruit trees were planted all over the country (Hamdy *et al.* 2007: 612). We are told that Khedive Ismail conceived six memorable gardens, amongst which is the still-existing Orman Garden. It originally included some 95.2 feddans (now shrunk to about 28 feddans) that were meant for providing the palace with its supply of fruits and vegetables imported from Sicily. The Orman Garden is famous for being the richest and most diversified garden remaining in Cairo; it organises a well-visited and popular annual horticulture fair. It is also famous for its mesmerising scenic landscapes and for its romantic pond, crowned by a small wooden bridge. Prince Hussein Kamel, Sultan of Egypt (1914–17), had a striking palace in the Orman Garden, which was apparently demolished in 1955.[13] The majestic iron gate at its entrance is a reminder of the royal and yet colonial past, and its endless greenhouses preserve a unique and rich variety of cactuses. The following description of the garden might convey the aesthetic ideals of the nineteenth-century *Belle Epoque* architecture, housing a significant colonial archive:

Among the major and conspicuous landmarks of this garden are the rocky garden (1.5 Feddans) containing 200 species of *Cactus* and succulents belonging

to 11 families, the rose garden (2 Feddans), the water pond containing water
plants such as: *Cyperus papyrus, Nelumbo nucifera, Nymphaea caerulea* and
*Aeschynomene elaphroxylon.* It also includes a herbarium containing King Farouk
I's private collections of wild and medicinal plants, fifteen green houses and
seed exchange unit. The plants are cultivated in the garden in 12 sections, e.g.:
*Strelitzia, Ficus* and Roses. (Hamdy *et al.* 2007: 618)

The trees and plants that were imported from the most unusual regions
remain a testimony to the incredible transfer of technologies, goods, flora,
and fauna under colonial empires.[14]

The complex comprising the spaces for the Zoo and the Orman Garden,
followed by the creation of the spacious grounds of Cairo University, made
Doqi/Giza one of the most pleasant and agreeable quarters, embellished by
unique exotic trees and rare birds. For one former resident of Doqi, Dalal
Gamal al-Din Beheiry, daughter of a distinguished medical doctor, who grew
up in a spacious upper-middle-class building that shares the corner of Harun
Street opposite the Orman Garden, the late 1960s were the best times. Her
daily wandering through the alleys of the Orman Garden to reach Cairo
University was simply a magical delight. Dalal recalls that during the time
she was a student of English literature at Cairo University (from 1968 to
1972), the wonderful abundant red Poinciana trees, shading the spacious
and pleasant streets of Doqi, formed a unique landscape. Dalal went to Cairo
University every day with a female friend who lived on Harun Street, and
walking, if not strolling, was one of those pleasures that are no longer possible
today. Even more, up until the late 1960s or early 1970s, Dalal enjoyed the
privilege of going by bicycle to the nearby Shooting Club. She also recalls
how much she enjoyed listening as a ritual to the sound of the bongs of
Cairo University's clock, since noise pollution was not as overwhelming as
it is today. There were memorable landmarks in the quarter, like the most
famous and popular coiffeur called Lambo, who was frequented even by
upper-class Zamalekites. Fruits and vegetables were available at the corner
of their house. That part of Doqi had the best stationery shop, crucial for
each new school year, the best small groceries, the nicest fruit juices, and
the best-stocked sweet shops. In other words, up to the early 1970s, the
middle and upper middle classes of Doqi seem to have enjoyed the most
pleasant and pleasurable urbanity.[15] Above all, Doqi has been famed since
the 1950s for the incredibly large number of well-reputed, efficient hospitals
and clinics, like the al-Kaateb, the Ali Pasha Ibrahim, and the Dr Mohamed
Chabrawichi hospitals. There are today over thirty hospitals listed in the
neighbourhood (Due-Gundersen 2018).

Final verdicts. Egyptian court issued a final verdict on 262 members of the
Muslim Brotherhood, with a lifelong prison sentence. (EREM News 2019)

During the summer of 2013, after the ouster of former president Mohamed
Mursi by the army on 30 June, the pro-Mursi Muslim Brotherhood squatted

in al-Nahda Square, followed by their occupation of the Orman Garden. The sit-in, which lasted roughly forty-five days, resulted in extensive damage, if not the destruction, of a large number of trees and plants, such as the century-old bamboo trees that the demonstrators used to erect their makeshift tents (Samih 2013).

The apparently violent squatters were evacuated equally violently by the police forces. These incidents were followed by anonymous 'thugs' who looted the Herbarium, while many valuable artefacts and objects belonging to the period of Khedive Ismail, as well as the private collection of King Farouq's medicinal plants, were also recklessly removed.[16] This valuable component of the colonial archive will appear overseas sooner rather than later, in places like Sotheby's and Christie's auctions. The same thing has happened to some of the archives of the Museum of Cotton, which caught fire a few years ago; to some valuable paintings stolen in 2018; and to a large quantity of Islamic art that has disappeared since 2011.

The sit-in ended dramatically, with the sentencing of 23 followers of the Muslim Brotherhood to life in prison, 213 others to 15 years, and 22 people to 3 years (Youssef 2018). I paid several visits to these gardens during the month of May 2018, just after the early flower exhibition. To my dismay, the amount of rubbish and plastic waste, spread everywhere in the garden and around the pond by recent visitors, is a spectacularly distressing scene – so much so that one wonders whether day visitors are more destructive to these surroundings than the Islamist protesters who squatted there.

For those who nostalgically believe in an imagined, beautified, and clean vintage Egypt, the appropriation of the public space of the Zoo (and of other public gardens) by the poor and popular (thus 'uncontrollable') masses is often perceived as the main reason for its decline or 'degradation' (Battesti 2006: 504). This class-biased perception is oblivious to the fact that the 'change of hands' and of 'public' with respect to a public space does not necessarily translate into a failure. The question, then, is failure for whom, and for which classes? On the contrary, if today's uses of the Zoo garden are so remote from its original inception, they still do not reject what the anthropologist Vincent Battesti – who has closely observed the practices of the visitors – called 'the popular passion for the zoo' (Battesti 2006: 491), a lively passion of 'excited crowds' that, during feast days and holidays, such as the feast days after Ramadan, can reach up to 500,000 visitors a day (Battesti 2006: 492). The same logic could be applied to the informal practices of occupying the street.

One often hears that even today Doqi enjoys the privilege of having numerous entrances and wider streets, in contradistinction to insular Zamalek. Doqi also enjoys a multiplicity of popular food markets like the Soliman Gohar market, large, well-stocked supermarkets like Metro and Saudi, numerous banks, Vodafone shops, pharmacies, bakeries, and fresh juice shops, testifying to well-equipped consumer outlets and facilities. Doqi hosted in the 1960s a large middle class consisting of the intelligentsia, university professors, journalists, judges, and professionals. It contains a number of marvellous villas belonging to the pre-1952 bourgeoisie. Many of these were appropriated by the Government to be turned into now-decrepit public schools. The few remaining villas are rapidly disappearing, even more so since 2011. Those that have survived this onslaught have ironically been taken as embassies and foreign cultural centres, and continue to exist and function as such.

In Harun Street, where I live, the large, charming villas that house the Pakistani and Yemeni embassies still exist. The Saudi Embassy maintains two annex buildings in my street, together with the Iranian Embassy. A few metres from Harun Street, on Hussein Wassef Street, the old villa of the Goethe-Institut has been fashionably renovated by the Worschech Architects Society to marry an older, colonial-style villa with a newly built addition in postmodern architecture, ornamented by a wonderful oriental garden with palm trees. In fact, these three properties originally belonged to the embassy of the former GDR (East Germany), and were appropriated by the German republic after Germany's unification (Thiele, n.d.). The remarkable design managed to create three separate entities that are connected in an imaginative style. Many people I have talked to in the neighbourhood have expressed optimism that the magnificent Goethe headquarters, renovated at a cost of some 10.4 million euros,[17] would eventually gentrify, or at least upgrade, the neighbourhood from its current depressing, declining condition. In fact, the building complex looks like bunkered space in the midst of a crumbling area. Not far away in the direction of Tahrir Street, one more magnificent villa hosts the Russian Cultural Centre. Ironically, Harun Street starts with the *mudiriyyat al-amn* (the Central Security Office) and ends with the police station (*qism al-buliis*). This means that after 2011, both ends of the street were barricaded with cement walls and the entrances blocked, with armoured cars and hordes of policemen standing across from the buildings, resulting in horrific traffic jams and impossible traffic detours.

Harun Street is bursting with awe-inspiring, tall, mature trees. The description would be idyllic had not the street been turned into a completely chaotic scene with endless heaps of rubbish, car parks, public schools (no fewer than six in the immediate area) booming with amplifiers, and permanent squatters in the space of the street. *Madrassat al-Hurriyya li-l-Lughaat* occupies several buildings around Harun Street. The main building, a magnificent European-style palace, which must have been appropriated by the Nasser government and converted into a school, is located on Charles de Gaulle Street opposite the Mahmud Khalil Museum. But that is not the only one to have been annexed in this way. At the corner of my building is another school, *'Abdul Moneim Riad li-l Banin* (a boys' school), which twice a day produces herds of uncontrolled, aggressive kids spouting testosterone, running wild in the street. It competes with yet another language school, located near the *mudiriyyat al-amn*. Hordes of kids buy sweets and drinks after school, endlessly littering the streets. A large number of them often end up playing football in the entrance hall of our building. Why our entrance hall? It's still a puzzle. Quite often, many mothers are jostling at the entrance door of the school opposite to my building, while waiting in the street to collect their children as they come out. When the students leave the school, the street descends into panic, even paralysis, between traffic jams, the desperate mothers, the roving peddlers, the state employees of the numerous banks and government offices, and the double or triple parking on those roads.

Worst of all are the hideous and poorly maintained apartment towers erected in the 1980s and 1990s. Almost all of them have on the first and second floors an assortment of small shops, groceries, boutiques, popular cafés, and stalls selling cheap *fuul* and *ta'miyya* sandwiches, and both *baladi* and Western cafés offer *shisha*. The roving street vendors also cater to the poorer patrons of many of these popular cafés and shops.

The obvious disorder and mounting dirt of the public space must surely be perceived by the middle classes as degeneration, and yet these popular cafés and stalls seem to be doing quite well financially, as they cater to such a large population occupying the street almost round the clock. It would be misleading to conclude that the neighbourhood is disappearing, since it is bursting with a colourful street life that never sleeps. My observations lead me to conclude that the quarter is simply changing hands. The rich, and the better-off middle classes, have started to move out to suburbia over the past decade or more. Some of the newcomers are moneyed, while others originate from the aspiring lower and the rising middle classes. Numerous Gulf investors[18] and refugees of Arab origin who hear about the sale of recent flats in the area are now occupants in this quarter.[19] The new inhabitants reshape and renovate the public space and the entrance halls of buildings in line with their contrasting tastes and lifestyles. No one would be astonished that on each single floor, a myriad of cacophonic designs, colours, and doors have to coexist simultaneously as expressions of excessive individualism.

The depopulation of entire quarters by their former residents is definitely no news. The phenomenon is even more acute in the centre of Downtown than elsewhere in Cairo. Architects have expressed alarm at the rapid pace of the depopulation taking place at the centre (El Kadi 2000, 2012; Abaza 2011b). This departure was naturally followed by an entirely new repopulation, dominated by a colourful and more popular street life. For instance, in her work on the centre of Downtown Cairo, Galila El Kadi writes the following about her conscious decision to become a resident of Downtown in the 1980s, a decision that unfortunately was never really followed by the elites.

> I would at last be able to live here, and to wake up happily each morning, hardly able to believe that I was a resident of Wasat al-Balad, literally the city centre. By choosing to live in a district deserted by its inhabitants and in social decline, I once again surprised my family and circle of acquaintances. I thought I was spearheading a movement to take back the centre by those who had

deserted it, but I was rapidly disabused of this notion, for it was rather the opposite that took place: I witnessed the city centre still emptying out and with it the departure of the more prestigious public services, a phenomenon that was beginning to pose questions for the researcher in me. (El Kadi 2012: 10)

The history of Cairo teaches us that its changing elites have often moved from decaying districts into new areas, leaving behind them run-down, derelict spaces. Former residential quarters such as Azbakeyya, Isma'ilyaa, Tewfiqeyya, 'Abdin, Kasr al-'Aini (where the administration was located in colonial times), al-Hilmeyya, Shubra and Munira, and Garden City, which in the past hosted the elites, embassies, hotels, and prosperous department stores of the time, reveal that gone are the glamorous days of mansions and palaces, which today remain in ruins as a reminder of a nostalgic past. These districts have been turned into densely populated lower-middle-class areas. The architects Galila El-Kadi[20] and Ahmad Hamad have called this phenomenon the 'nomadism of the rich', suggesting that the elites have failed to establish spaces with which they could identify in the long term. El-Kadi[21] insists that there is no clear understanding of a '*vieille ville*'. There are only new quarters, which become fashionable locations, but for how long? They soon become overpopulated and uncontrollable, leading the rich to move elsewhere. It is as if, in the modern history of Cairo, the rich have become powerless to defend their own territories and spaces. For example, Mohandessin and the satellite Nasr City districts (created in the late 1950s and early 1960s) were trendy locations in the 1970s and 1980s, but the new satellite cities and gated communities took over in the 1990s and reversed these aspirations. The shift led countless villas in Mohandessin to be torn down and replaced by towers, and once again a large number of its residents moved out, leaving behind them a congested and chaotic neighbourhood.[22] Conversely, Mohandessin, like Doqi, has not witnessed an increase in real-estate prices in recent years, compared to New Cairo and Sixth of October, which suggests that the two older districts have become a secondary market for the second-tier middle classes.

Reading El Kadi's work on the centre of the city led me to conclude that the origins of the 'Desert Dreams'[23] imaginaries could be traced back as early as Mohamed Ali's constant relocation from one palace to another. El Kadi provides lively examples from the Egyptian literary sources to how the perpetual migration or nomadism of the elites became a constant pattern, reaching a peak in the 1940s. It was during that period that the old quarters have been portrayed in the popular imagination and in Arabic literature as decaying and dirty spaces with narrow alleys, unhealthy and miasmic. These were often juxtaposed to the newer, cleaner, more modern districts like Heliopolis, Maadi, and even Zamalek and Garden City. The pressing question remains: where, in today's nomadism, is there place for both continuity and change in relation to the Eastern and Western Desert cities? Even though the satellite 'desert dreams' are sold today as clean, sanitised, quiet, modern spaces, free from street vendors and beggars, their creation as material construction is considerably less sound than 'Abbaseyya, Heliopolis, or Maadi were when they were first built, because no public transport system or other proper infrastructure has been installed to service these new desert cities. Their logic lies solely in the domain of neo-liberal privatisation, giving rise to such amenities as private security guards and the personal car and driver, considered necessary measures to safeguard their elitist status.

### *Abraag*: Gobbling up villas

One important concept we invoke is the notion of *re-description*. How can particular spaces, built environments or ways of living be re-described, not as elements or evidence of particular principles, macro forces or structural arrangements, but as aspects of what Celia Lury (2012) refers to as n-dimension spaces, states of existence that *might be*? This is not *only* a matter of imagination, fantasy or forward visualization. The task also entails re-describing existent conditions as components of a process that might be taking place *right now*, but which is opaque, occluded or rendered inoperative. It is rendered inoperative simply because we are seeing and engaging the realities examined in a particular way. So there is a *doubleness* here that involves a sense of aspiration, of making things different, but also of seeing in what exists something other than what we think we are seeing. (Simone and Pieterse 2017: 10–11)

The disappearance of romantic, decaying villas in my part of Doqi accelerated after the January 2011 revolution.[24] These were replaced by the huge, ugly, frightening, so-called modern towers (*abraag*, sing. *burg*). The only signs of the past as an era remain anchored in the villas currently occupied by the foreign embassies, which seem, paradoxically, to be the unintentional but genuine preservers of the vanishing *Belle Epoque* architecture, thanks to their long-term leases. The question is whether this type of preservation will continue, as the Government is urging embassies to move out of central Cairo to the new capital city.

The landscape of the monstrous towers immediately evokes a free association with the recent series of scandals involving collapsing buildings and the leaning Pisa-like building that threatened to collapse in the Azarita quarter of Alexandria in May 2017.[25] The numerous disasters of collapsing towers since about 2005, resulting in many deaths, due to escalating corruption in the construction sector, bear witness to these monstrous, overbearing misconstructions. These are becoming the 'natural' predicament of Egyptian urban life. As an Al Jazeera documentary[26] has demonstrated, no Alexandrian is a fool. These *abraag* are perceived by the majority of lower-middle-class Alexandrians as collective graveyards. Nonetheless, even though these buildings are in danger of collapsing into piles of rubble, they remain the only housing available for the economically declining middle classes.

In Alexandria alone, after the 2011 revolution, 9,700 such buildings (called in Arabic *mukhaalif*, 'not conforming to the rules', or illegal) were constructed, in addition to the 14,500 that already existed ('al-Kahuul', 2013). It is no coincidence that numerous architects and urban planners speak of the city's change as a 'massacre', as if it were a conscious massive destruction of Alexandria as a port.

Back in Doqi, my fifth-floor balcony faces one of those towers, which must have been erected more than fifteen years earlier. It has been deserted for more than a decade, a not uncommon phenomenon in Cairo. It looks like an unpainted, windowless ruin, as if it had been devastated by war. It is easy to speculate that either it has a serious architectural defect, or there are problems with the owners. Although this brown twelve-storey monstrosity blocks my view, its emptiness works in my favour. Had it been occupied, I would have no privacy at all; I would have been forced to keep all my shutters down, as almost all Cairenes are inclined to do these days.

At the beginning of the street, the *Mudiriyyat al-Amn* (the main district police station), bunkered by huge concave walls erected after the revolution, make the already congested traffic even worse, if not impossible, during school time. The street was converted into a one-way street when the walls were added. It looks like a war zone, a cut-open belly with an exploded intestine, spitting endless electrical wires and pipelines into the street and over all the cafés that have turned the street into a sleepless zone.

Even on Fridays, the only day when traffic slows down, my street serves as a main thoroughfare, since the security measures block almost all the streets around the police station. The construction of an underground tunnel began in 2016. The aim is to create an underground passageway between Charles de Gaulle Street and the street leading to Cairo University. After noon prayer, traffic jams fill long, narrow Harun Street, making it even more inaccessible to the public. The *Majlis al-Dawla* (Council of State) is located on the major street, Charles de Gaulle, an extension of Murad Street, which runs parallel to Harun Street and attracts numerous state employees and their customers. Besides the innumerable schools, there are numerous banks and offices in the quarter. In Refa'a Street, on working days, long queues of people stand in the street in front of the bank *al-ta'amiir wa-l-iskaan* (Housing Construction Bank) to apply for cheap government housing projects.

Messaha Square, a few minutes away from Harun Street, with its greenery and trees, was in the past a place of respite, where the well-to-do classes spent their leisure time in outings to restaurants and cafés. Today, like many other areas, this square has become overpopulated with decaying, run-down shops, small, cheap supermarkets, popular bakeries, countless offices, high-rise buildings, numerous banks, and one international hotel that has looked quite deserted since 2011. This density of occupation makes traffic hellish from nine o'clock in the morning until four or five in the afternoon. Like the majority of the old districts in Cairo, Doqi has degenerated into chaos because of the invasion of unregulated commercial activities and shops, which occupy almost all the ground floors of most of the buildings and some that have taken over the street.

In 2016, for a short interval, Messaha Square was transformed into an alternative to Tahrir. It became a scene for demonstrations and its space was tactically used by activists, since Tahrir Square had become filled with army tanks and police forces, making any kind of gathering difficult as a result of new security measures that threaten arrests and violent confrontations with the State. Just such an event took place on 25 April 2016, when a large number of demonstrators, shouting 'Down, down with the military', protested against the decision of the Government to give away the sovereignty of the two islands Tiran and Sanafir to Saudi Arabia. These demonstrations resulted in prison sentences of two to five years for some 150 people ('More than 150', 2016). Since 2011, all the demonstrations and marches that departed from the Mustafa Mahmud Mosque in the nearby quarter of Mohandessin have passed along the central thoroughfare Tahrir Street, which crosses the Galla' Bridge to Zamalek and continues to Tahrir Square. Thus, during the first three years of the revolution, Doqi witnessed numerous marches and violent confrontations, even after the downfall of Morsi when followers of the Muslim Brothers were squatting in the area of the Orman Garden near Cairo University. My daughter, who was staying with friends living at the end of Harun Street at the time, remembers taking to the streets with her friends on 25 January when the demonstrators marching from Tahrir Street and the extension of Giza Street called upon those watching from the balconies to join them.

## Notes

1 This section on the elevator was written in 2016.
2 See 'Between the Sky and Earth'.
3 See, for example, 'Attorney general orders imprisonment', 2018; Fadel 2018; al-Guindi 2018a, 2018b; Kamel 2018; Khalil 2018; Mounir 2018.
4 This is, in fact, the tune of the newly replaced elevator in my building.
5 Elevators either trapped between floors or collapsing have become a highly frequent phenomenon that one hears of constantly in Cairo. Paradoxically, such cathartic incidents have turned out to be the only way to unite the residents of a building and force them to pay for replacing the elevator, as has been the case amongst several of my acquaintances.
6 This section was written in 2016.
7 The late Amina Rizq was a famous Egyptian actress in the genre of melodrama. She was the eternal mortified victim in Egyptian films of the 1950s and 1960s.
8 The film adaptation of 'Alaa Al-Aswany's *The Yacoubian Building* by Waheed Hamid, directed by Marwan Hamed, presents an outstanding and humorous scene around the elevator. The main character, Zaki Bey Dessouki (played by 'Adel Imam), stands in the entrance hall in front of the elevator, screaming about the elevator being stuck on one of the upper floors because the doors were not properly closed. The homosexual resident Hatem Rasheed (Khaled al-Saawi), chief editor of a prominent francophone newspaper, then enters. Rasheed is accompanied by an Upper Egyptian conscript (Bassem Samra) picked up from the street, Rasheed's future lover. Zaki Bey orders the obviously lower-class young

man to climb the stairs to fetch the elevator for him. The bemused, helpless young man answers that he will only climb the stairs if Mr Rasheed orders him to do so. Zaki Bey then makes an avalanche of implicit sexual jokes about the young man's physical fitness and strength, after which Mr Rasheed orders him to climb the stairs. This ironic scene is heavy with class connotations.

9   See the Zamalek Association page on Facebook. The association states that it was created in 1991 by some fifteen residents, whose main mission is to maintain and regenerate the quarter with respect to cleanliness, sanitation, and the maintenance of trees, while campaigning for conserving the old 'heritage' constructions that have been demolished or remodelled out of their original character.

10  That Zamalek will possibly be invaded by 'beggars' has been often mentioned by complaining Zamalekites. This argument, however, is class biased, as almost all the streets of Cairo, with the exception of the gated communities, are equally occupied by popular life ('Traffic diverted in Zamalek', 2017). This argument implies that the island has hitherto been spared from beggars, which is a complete denial of the ubiquity of child street vending, the increasing number of beggars especially during the month of Ramadan, and the control of on-street parking space by *munaadis* (car parkers).

11  Regarding the controversy related to the Zamalek Association, see El-Khawaga 2014.

12  There is an obvious problem in classifying who belongs to the middle class(es) in Egypt; the term is itself confusing. It could be argued that both the older generation and the new residents of my building belong to the broad 'middle class' since they are or were doctors, engineers, and state employees, with a university education. It might even be that the newly arrived residents of the past decade dispose of more wealth than the old residents, but they lack the status of belonging to the intellectual and professional class, which enjoyed a certain cultural expertise – for example, owning a personal library. In the two flats of newcomers that I have visited, I was struck by the complete absence of books.

13  See 'Vintage photo of the palace of H. H. Prince Hussein Kamel'.

14  The list of gardens created during the reign of Khedive Ismail is impressive. But the current disappearance, if not intentional destruction, of these historical gardens through the undertakings of greedy and corrupt officials, more quickly than ever after 2011, requires further research, which to my knowledge has caught the attention of some architects like Galila El Kadi. To his credit, Khedive Ismail will be remembered for the creation of most beautiful gardens, such as the Fish Garden Aquarium in 1871, the Horeya Garden in Zamalek, the Azbakeyya Gardens in 1876, the Zohriyya Garden on Zamalek Island in 1870, and the River Garden in 1878. See Ministry of Agriculture and Land Reclamation 2009.

15  Personal communication with Dalal Gamal al-Din al-Beheiry (Doqi, 22 March 2018).

16  Personal communication with an anonymous state employee at the Orman Garden Herbarium (May 2018).

17  See 'Goethe-Institut und Deutscher Akademischer Austauschdienst in Kairo'.

18  One flat in our building was sold in January or February 2017 to a Saudi investor who plans to transform it into an office for training Egyptian teachers to work in Saudi Arabia.

19 There is, for example, a popular Yemeni restaurant just opposite Saudi Supermarket at the corner of Messaha Square and al-Salwli Street, attracting a large Yemeni émigré population.

20 Personal communication with architect Ahmad Hamad (interviews December 2008, January and February 2009); Galila El Kadi, personal communication, 7 June 2009.

21 El Kadi also uses the term 'nomadism of the centre of power', describing the way in which the modernist rulers of Egypt, like Mohamed Ali and his son 'Abbas I, constantly moved outwards and changed palaces. Mohamed Ali did this mainly for security reasons, continually fearing for his life, while 'Abbas and Said dreamed of expanding into newly created districts. See El Kadi (2012: 43, 46).

22 But the exodus of the bourgeoisie and the middle classes towards the desert cities had already started to occur by the second half of the 1980s, as argued by Galila El Kadi. The quarter of Mohandessin, for example, witnessed a frightening transmutation between 1980 and 1992 when one-third of the villas and small buildings were demolished (500 disappeared out of 1,500 buildings), to be replaced by towers, while over 200 buildings were raised by adding further storeys. The number of spaces transformed into commercial use tripled between 1976 and 1986, rocketing from 1,232 to 5,197 (El Kadi 2000: 111).

23 *Egypt's Desert Dreams* is the title of David Sims's book analysing the history and expansion of Cairo's desert satellite cities.

24 The phenomenon of disappearing villas dates to before 2011. However, after 2011, it seems that increased corruption allowed even further destruction of historic buildings, mostly in Alexandria.

25 On this point, see Alexandrani 2016.

26 See the Al Jazeera documentary 'al-Kahuul', 2013.

# 4
# My flat: Nostalgia and *al-zaman al-gamiil* (the 'beautiful old times')

Noura Hassan's tiny top-floor flat in the central Cairo neighborhood of Bulaq contains barely any furniture; instead, her belongings have been packed into dozens of cardboard boxes.

In the bedroom, rolled carpets and bed slats lean against the walls, while a sheet laid on the tiled floor marks the place where Noura and her husband have been sleeping for the past few weeks.

Stepping out of the front door of the two-storey building where the 56-year-old mother-of-two lives, the rubble from the demolitions of other buildings in the street is visible; her building is scheduled to meet the same fate in a matter of days.

Hassan is one of thousands of residents of a tiny section of central Cairo who have for decades fought off efforts by the government to demolish their homes, to make way for redevelopment.

The conflict in the Maspero Triangle, where almost 80 percent of properties have had their residents evicted, reveals the underside to the government's attempts to modernise the Nile-adjacent area, which officials say is the most highly-valued land in the capital. (Al Tawy 2018)

How many times have I in my reveries imagined I was flying away (running off) with my entire flat, to transplant it ... far away ... elsewhere ... but where would that be in Cairo? Day-dreaming in my flat ...

According to Laila Bahaa Eddin, the former owner from whom I purchased my Doqi flat, the building was constructed by the architect Ramzy 'Omar.[1] There is a glaring modernist 1950s flair to this building that can also be traced in the numerous gigantic architectural works of Ramzy 'Omar, including his distinctive design of the Ministry of Foreign Affairs, which was constructed at a later stage of his career. My spacious flat consists of some 160 square metres, with three large living rooms, two bedrooms, a large kitchen, two bathrooms, well-conceived corridors, and one storage room. It has been marvellously designed by a fashionable interior decorator who enjoyed wide fame and recognition in the 1970s and 1980s, commissioned by Laila's mother. The lovely layout testifies to a pleasant, *bon vivant* lifestyle. It must have been an idyllic space in past times. Today, it is an entirely different story.

At present, only three residents (out of fifteen flats) belonging to the older generation who moved in in the 1950s and 1960s have survived the massive exodus of the building. In total, until 2017, there were seven flats (excluding the Palestinian women's hostel) that were occupied by residents. The remaining seven have either been transformed into commercial spaces (categorised as *tugaari*) or have been deserted and are kept closed. By the late 1990s, one resident after another had moved out to better-off areas like Zamalek or the Sixth of October satellite city. The sons and daughters of several residents I have spoken to and personally know have all moved to the gated-community life of the satellite compounds. Two of the three old residents (a medical doctor and an engineer), who are in their sixties, have inherited the rent contracts of their flats from their parents and are thus regarded as the only second-generation residents entitled to these apartments. The third and longest resident, my next-door neighbour, Mrs Mars., who is in her mid-eighties, moved into her flat in 1957 with her late husband, who was an officer/medical doctor. Mrs Mars. has managed to transfer her lease to her daughter's name, thus securing the succession of the family to the flat.

Some of the current residents would recall with immense nostalgia the grandeur and beauty of the edifice when it was possible to meditate on the view of the Pyramids from the higher floors. I often meet in the stairs ninety-three-year-old Madam Sha., whose flat is on the second floor. She often states with great pride that she is amongst the few remaining old-school residents to take the stairs, with the aid of a walking stick. She is endlessly eager to talk about *al-zaman al-gamiil* (the 'beautiful old times'),[2] in a nostalgic tone, while descending the stairs. Mrs Sha.'s discourse reveals a collective nostalgic mood, which idealises the past precisely because of the harshness of the depraved present. While the January revolution has also generated a nostalgia for Mubarak's time compared to the harshness of the military regime, Mrs Sha.'s beautiful past consists of the pre-1952 royal era.

I imagine that Mrs Sha. makes a statement out of taking the stairs, even as she complains about the countless young men and women who have made a habit of misusing our elevator and littering the building. Her words often take you back in time, reminding anyone that she belongs to a generation that harboured different ideals. Madam Sha. was a renowned school director who fought to promote mixed-gender schooling and introduce progressive methods in education. In the 1960s, she must have been regarded as an enlightened feminist. I was told that she had encountered much resistance from the regime, which perceived her ideas as dangerous and morally threatening at the time. It seems, too, that she was slandered in the press for her opinions and her courage to speak out and stand up. Madam Sha. is proud to state that in her youth, she once worked as an employee in the state administration, which required climbing many stairs on a daily basis since the elevators were often malfunctioning. It did not hinder her from doing her job. Madam Sha. is the only resident I have known in the building who makes a statement out of the act of taking the stairs. The debate of stairs versus elevator had been a central issue of divisive wars amongst the residents of our building for years.

Whenever I encounter Madam Sha. on the stairs, it is difficult to stop her lamenting thoughts of how the world has been turned upside down. She cannot refrain from recounting and recalling her nostalgic memories when the building was a true building and not the *'ashwaa'iyya* it has become. These recollections evoke the details of the factors that kept it in pristine condition, such as the 'wonderful and clean Nubian *bawaab*' (*zay al-full*, 'clean as jasmine'), praised for his hard work and good habits.[3] Those were the good old days, when plants ornamented the entrance hall[4] and when 'respectable' residents were polite to each other. Of course, the 'beautiful' past *has* to be romanticised, considering the depraved present state of not only our building, but almost all aspects of Cairene daily life. Madam Sha. tells me every time she meets me that she is lucky to have lived such good days, which compensate for the ugly and decadent current reality. How she pities these crowds of youngsters who frequent our building for their ignorance, as their aesthetics encompass nothing else but filth. But the character of Madam Sha. is looked upon today as a charming relic belonging to another age. Respected, certainly, but perceived as overpowered and lost.

The spectacular view of the Pyramids that was once visible from my living room has now disappeared behind monstrous high-rise buildings that came later. My building was believed to be amongst the first in the neighbourhood to have an 'intercom' (as the residents called it) that locked and unlocked the main entrance. Last but not least, a red carpet adorned the entrance. Like the plants, both of these items have disappeared. Its wide marble staircases retain a particular nostalgic charm of a lost era, but some pieces of marble flooring in the entrance have turned into bumps as groundwater threatens to eat up the foundations. Another neighbour from the older generation, a medical doctor, narrated the following story: When the former owner of the building passed away, his son inherited five of the flats, and his sister inherited the other half of the building. The son took the liberty of helping himself and removing the marble of the entrance and the original fancy gate that protected the building, to be installed in his newly constructed villa in Sixth of October City. This must have been in the late 1980s or 1990s. Once again, according to my neighbour, no resident dared protest against such abominable damage to the building. My neighbour the doctor was then working in the Gulf countries. Upon his return, he was shocked at the theft of the entrance-hall marble. Signboards for the ground-floor shops were added later, right on the two sides of the entrance door. A third signboard, which keeps collapsing, was added at the entrance gate about two years ago, when my next-door flat on the fifth floor was converted into a commercial space, making the entrance hall appear even more chaotic. However, in the midst of this disheartening disorder, on 6 November 2017 the *Lagnat al-tanssiq al-hadaari* (National Organisation for Urban Harmony [NOUH], affiliated with the

Ministry of Culture) nailed a memorial plaque at the entrance door of the building stating that 'The journalist Ahmed Bahaa Eldin lived here. Born 11 February 1927 – Died 24 August 1996'. The magical spell of this plaque seems to have instilled a great sense of pride in the *bawaab*, who carefully drew my attention to it. The downstairs shopkeepers say repeatedly that this plaque testifies to the good old days, of which they were part as long-time indigenous residents of the quarter.

Bicycles are often parked in the entrance hall. Y., the *bawaab*, is constantly moving items such as ovens, cupboards, shelves, toys, and sofas, which can be parked and stored for weeks in the entrance hall, subject to removal when the residents become more vocal and complain collectively about the 'mess'. The entrance hall remained gateless until January 2011, when the residents became anxious about rumours, which were later confirmed, of incidents of shootings and confrontations taking place in the main arterial streets (Tahrir Street and Charles de Gaulle Street). They opted for the least expensive solution, consisting of portable black iron gates of shoddy material that are moved in and out on a daily basis. In the season preceding the start of school, these gates are littered by a massive display of school bags from the two shops downstairs, called New Robina and 'Alaa Eldin, which often blocks the entire entrance and hinders movement in and out of the building. Still, no resident of our building would dare express indignation against the shop owners, because they are friendly and helpful to all the residents. For example, I often leave cash for the electricity bills when I travel for long periods, to be collected at the 'Alaa Eldin shop. I also often leave the monthly salary of the rubbish collector with Umm Tam., the garage keeper. All these payments are monitored via my long list of mobile phone numbers, which includes the collectors for the water, electricity, and rubbish services.

I visited Laila so often in my youth when we were studying together at the American University. Alas, my wonderful memories of this space clash sharply with today's degeneration of the neighbourhood. The Bahaa Eddins moved into the building in the 1960s as tenants and purchased the flat in the 1990s when the owner started to sell bits and pieces of the building, resulting in the division of the entrance hall into the tiny shops that exist now. The front façade consists of six small shops: two of them are retailers of clothes, two sell school bags, and one specialises in a variety of sport items. The sixth and largest, which opened about two years ago, is owned by a well-to-do Upper Egyptian who owns a perfume company. He first purchased two flats on the third floor of our building, and his office took up, on an informal basis, the task of administrator on behalf of the residents, which includes collecting the necessary payments for water and for the electricity used in the stairs and elevator areas. The right side of the building was once occupied by a small grocery and a café that was shut down in 2016 after a violent confrontation between the owner and the person renting it. In February 2017, the coffee shop was once again rented out to new tenants,

**Figure 16**    Coffee shop chairs parked at the garage, 27 May 2017.

creating two different cafés right near each other and turning all of Hussein Wassef Street into an open, movable, and expandable café with plastic chairs that vanished into the garage in the morning and reappeared in the evening.

> In December 2009, forced evictions were carried out by security forces in Al-Nour Alley in a narrow extension of Batn Al-Baqara near the area of Kom Ghorab. The buildings stood on a narrow strip on the verge of a steep slope parallel to Ein El-Sirra Road, an area categorized as "unsafe' by the ISDF (Informal Settlements Developments Facilities). Around 46 buildings were demolished within 15–20 days, according to residents interviewed by Amnesty International. The area had been informally settled in the 1970s and residents had connected their buildings officially to electricity supplies, each having a meter, and informally to water pipes and sewerage systems. (Amnesty International 2011: 42)

During Ramadan 2017, the street cafés grew like a long snake all along the walls of the school across from our building, almost reaching the main street of Charles de Gaulle. These cafés, filled mostly with men, remain open until dawn, filling the entire street with backgammon players and *shisha* smokers and, of course, with excessive noise and music. Quarrels amongst the customers can lead to police interference at dawn. Most recently, young women have started to sit around and share this public space. Finally, opposite these two cafés on Harun Street, another Western-style coffee shop opened a while ago, attracting wealthier customers who can afford more expensive cappuccinos and espressos. It occupies the pavement as if it were engaging in a dialogue with the two other *baladi*-style cafés.

Since my return from a sabbatical in Berlin in September 2017, the street has taken a new turn, becoming a highly entertaining space for youngsters. It evokes a lively circus. At night the street is extremely noisy. Football fans spend the entire night screaming at television sets playing football matches. Less often, the police mount attacks against so-called drug dealers in the street at around four o'clock in the morning, resulting in youngsters running noisily away from the police. Most recently (in 2018), gangs of young boys, both residents of the neighbourhood and students of the *Huriyya* school, planted themselves in the street for long hours. Some would bring cars, which they used to play loud *mahraganaat*[5] music. It gave the impression that the music was coming from amplifiers in the *baladi* cafés, but this was not the case. The young men would then block the intersection of Harun and Hussein Wassef streets with their dancing performances. They would be carrying whips with which they hit the floor while dancing. The performance would continue until perhaps ten o'clock in the evening. At that point, probably, an angry neighbour would phone the police, as I am told by Mr Al., my neighbour, which explains why the large crowd of youngsters would suddenly disappear from the street. But they would reappear the next day as if nothing had happened and the music would resume to penetrate the life of the neighbourhood.

'Like cat and mouse' is the expression I often heard in the neighbourhood to describe the relationship between the *baladiyya* (local officials of the quarter) and the café and shop owners. It is as if the street is constantly witnessing a theatrical stage consisting of *al-karr wa farr* (attack and retreat), with young people appearing, disappearing, and reappearing at various times of the day to interact in the street, and with the forced removal of plastic chairs from the street – a process that the *baladiyya* has nicknamed 'musical chairs'. Some café owners along the Nile manage to hide the chairs by plunging them into the Nile when the officials stage attacks on the cafés, closing down their small refrigerators and clearing out their small spaces that infringe on the street. After a few hours or days, the cafés reopen. It has become a normal sight to see the *baladiyya* truck pick up the plastic chairs of the cafés that are on the street, probably after some neighbour has made a complaint. But time and again, the café is barely affected, as it is only a matter of time before the chairs reappear.

An identical scenario is also played out regularly in the small shop in the building next door to mine that specialises in newspapers and stationery. Their refrigerator, located on the pavement of the street, is repeatedly shut (or locked up) by the *ra'is al-hay* (district chief), but never actually confiscated to cease business from resuming its activities once normalcy is established.

My next-door neighbours have often expressed concern about the glaring dirty looks that men systematically give any woman going into or out of our building, creating so much discomfort, they say, that the women have refrained from going out in the evening. This report of sexual harassment might be a little exaggerated, as young women are often seen smoking *shisha* in the cafés on the street. The same female neighbour eventually confessed that her husband does spend a lot of time in the café – as if, over time, we residents have all gotten used to the lively café street life.

According to hearsay, the cafés have suffered several police raids for their illegal status, for infringing upon the public space of the street, and allegedly for hashish deals. But they were never closed down for long periods of time. Umm Tam., expressing fear of these street opponents for the first time, told me that the café owners are aggressive street bullies from the Sayyeda Zeinab quarter. They seem to have connections with the local officials, which explains why they are prepared for any violent encounter that might ensue. In 2018, my neighbour Mr Al. informed me that the continuously fluctuating associates of the café owners are more than thirty in number, as a testimony to their disputed reputation. In addition, so far, the café owners have refused to pay their water bills – even though they and the garage are amongst the most substantial consumers – causing numerous problems to the collectivity of the building.

My building consists of fifteen flats, three flats on each floor. With the exception of the Palestinian female hostel occupying the entire top floor, only six other flats are occupied by residents. More accurately, only half of the building is occupied by residents, while the other half is rented out as offices for unregistered commercial activities. A couple of these so-called offices on the first and second floors seem to maintain rather fictive activities, since no customers are ever seen frequenting them. I was told by the *bawaab* that the company on the first floor ceased to pay the rent, and that the owner of the flat was helpless, as suing the company would take years without any guarantee of winning the case.[6]

My spacious and well-designed flat is witness to a rich history, since Laila's father was none other than the prominent journalist and intellectual, the late Ahmed Bahaa Eddin. The flat was designed his wife, Daisy. Ahmed Bahaa Eddin is remembered as a well-travelled, widely read, erudite pan-Arabist and nationalist thinker who developed a keen interest in national liberation movements, in particular Indian independence. He maintained close relations to Kuwait since he worked for many years as the chief editor of the then famed *al-'Arabi* magazine, which had a reputation for its outstanding articles on culture in the Arab world. The Bahaa Eddins moved between London and Cairo for many years. Accordingly, in the late 1960s and 1970s this flat hosted glamorous intellectual and social gatherings, uniting highly placed ministers and politicians with opposition intellectuals, painters, and poets. When the celebrated Palestinian poet Mahmud Darwish was exiled from Palestine, he began visiting Cairo more frequently, so that the Bahaa Eddins' flat became a place he visited often. Other famous visitors included the

Palestinian writer Ghassan Kanafi, the famed journalist Hassanein Haykal, and numerous artists and painters, as Laila Bahaa explains in a memorial article about her father's intellectual milieu (Bahaa El-Din 2016).

I spent some exceptional moments with Laila in this flat as a young university student in the late 1970s and early 1980s. I clearly recall the moment when President Sadat was assassinated on 6 October 1981, a strained period when a large number of intellectuals and public figures had been put in jail prior to the assassination, causing massive public resentment. During that year, Laila's parents were living in Kuwait, so we could enjoy the entire flat on our own, and Laila was generous in organising gatherings and meals for all her friends. After the dramatic event of the assassination of Sadat, Laila and I spent long days watching television, walking around the neighbour-hood, and contemplating the magical view of the Pyramids from the large windows. The endlessly repeated television footage of the assassination, followed by the funeral, held our attention. But most striking was the stillness of the empty streets, which made us appreciate the beauty and peace of that part of Doqi that was caused by Sadat's assassination – ironically, a dramatic moment that was also magical in other ways.

This event turned out to mark a watershed moment, as by the mid-1990s the district had changed radically, and even more so after January 2011, as if chaos had become the natural but uncontrollable force that shaped the city.

Rubbish piled up, a situation that was brought on by the long absence of the rubbish collector in my street, and grew to epidemic levels after January 2011. The uncollected heap of filth in the two back stairwells of the building attracted an army of stray cats with an active life of their own. The stray cats of Cairo appear and reappear as a theme in many novels, as the silent heroes of Cairene streets. An example is Sonallah Ibrahim's vivid descriptions in *Dhat* of the fights between neighbours in the stairwells occasioned by the presence of cats. It is quite typical in Cairene spaces that one neighbour takes on the task of feeding the cats, while some other mysterious neighbour – we are all certain we know the culprit – secretly poisons them, causing intense fights and electric atmospheres amongst the residents. The mating season is certainly the worst as the cats' obscene screams torture the entire building, but we all know, at the expense of sounding cynical, that someone will take the easy solution of removing the cats in a lethal way the next day.

## Public schools, microphones, and belly dancing

The public primary school, *Madrassat al-Hurriya*, which starts at about eight o'clock[7] and ends around two o'clock, plays extremely loud amplified music every school day. Class after class of children belly dance for almost six hours every day at the tiny entrance court of the school. The court is so tiny because the larger part was probably sold off to a private investor, and the space of the school playground is distorted because it was taken away from the court of the huge unfinished building opposite mine.

Several of the residents, myself included, have noticed that the dosage of loud music doubled in 2017, as the time spent in taking up dancing with the children turns out to be a convenient way for teachers to evade doing their teaching work in classrooms. The mesmerising, cacophonic flow of so many languages and music genres defies any logic. It also fascinates me, as I think it could well be the subject of a superb anthropological work on Cairo's unique and disturbing soundscapes as an expression of the increasing 'disjunctures' (to borrow from Appadurai) of globalisation (Appadurai 1990: 295) as well as the specificity of the 'glocalisation' processes. But practically speaking, one has to wonder whether the multilingual songs – German lullabies, high Arabic or colloquial Sufi *zikr* and other religious music, famous Arabic film songs, or Egyptian belly dances – really have any educational significance for these small children.

Every day, we hear many of Suad Hosny's film songs (quite erotic, funnily enough), such as '*Ya wad ya tekiil*' (You Heartbreaker), followed by some eccentric English songs by a Muslim American convert about how glorious Islam is, which the children have to repeat by screaming behind the amplifiers.[8] In 2016, Indian Bollywood music was added to the list, since it is an excellent accompaniment for belly dancing.

As time went by, I noticed a slight change in the choice of songs chanted in the morning in the courtyard. This may have been due to the arrival of a different team of teachers in 2017, which led to the demise of belly dancing and the disappearance of Suad Hosny's film songs. For example, during the months of September, October, and November 2017, after singing the morning national anthem, the dose of nationalist songs (*aghaani wataniyya*) significantly increased, which might perhaps reflect the growing omnipresence of the military-style urbanisation encroaching in everyday life. More precisely, the songs that are known as *aghaani al nasr* (the 1973 victory songs), such as the song '*Bism Illah, Allah akbar, bism Illah*',[9] with text by 'Abdel Rehim Mansur and music by Baliigh Hamdy,[10] are played constantly on certain days of the week.

I cannot help associating all these nationalist songs with the atmosphere of war I grew up with in the 1960s. The fear I felt as a child overtakes me now every early morning in my bedroom. The *aghaani wataniyya* – the songs composed for the 1973 victory and the ones that were broadcast before and after 1967 – never fail to evoke in me the worrisome atmosphere of war, the blue-painted glass of all the houses surrounding us, the sandbags in front of the entrance halls of the buildings as a precaution against bombs, the regular evacuation preparations for potential Israeli air raids, and the collective tragedy of collapse and humiliation that followed the 1967 defeat. The repetitive nationalist songs from the school every morning only add to the crippling feeling of melancholy that makes me decide to escape my flat before 7.30 in the morning.

There are predictable repertoires and rituals in the morning salute of the flag, as well as improvised variations in the music played, that strike my ear as a chaotic and yet ritualistic sound track. The routine starts around 7.30, and lasts twenty minutes to half an hour. On certain days, some German exercise in dancing (or perhaps a modernised lullaby?) begins the exercises of saluting the flag. Since no one speaks German in the Arabic public school, the words cannot mean much in these surroundings. However, the German song is often replaced by the popular romantic hit released in 2017, '*Talaath daquaat*' (Three Heartbeats), by Yussra. The '*Talaath daquaat*' video clip went viral on social media, spreading the message of how great it is to enjoy the lavish lifestyle of the elite. In the second half of the clip, Yussra appears in a long, sexy, yellow dress with a large entourage of famous actors and actresses, singing and dancing at the al-Gouna beach resort. The video clip/song became the official advertisement of the international al-Gouna film festival that took place in September 2017, in which the tycoon Naguib Sawiris is given credit for his public support to the event. The song was written by Tamer Habib and the video clip directed by Mariam Abu 'Ouf.[11] The video clip included innumerable young, cool, and good-looking actors and actresses in fashionable bathing suits, shorts, and sexy skirts, almost all the actresses with silky long hair – an insipid Hollywood mimicry of Egyptian-style glamour. Good-looking men wearing long ponytails and shorts present an updated image of current well-to-do Egyptians. It was a successful advertisement for the image of Western, 'modern-looking', trendy, and promising stars, who rose with the success of the 2016–17 Ramadan *musalsalaat.* The clip succeeded in promoting al-Gouna as a safe paradise for the beautiful and exuberant rich, who are seen to enjoy a leisurely lifestyle on yachts and the sea, sipping drinks under the glowing sunshine. Visually, Yussra's '*Talaath daquaat*' clip commodified al-Gouna's glamour and Egyptianised Hollywood dreams of stardom.

Yussra's clip, along with the multiple variations of *aghaani wataniyya* songs, are broadcast loudly and incessantly all day long, piercing everybody's ears and exhausting the entire neighbourhood en masse. The jarring contrast between the dream of beach life visually triggered by the video clip, the shabby schoolyard, the littered street filled with depressed, desperate, shabby, aimlessly wandering state civil servants, the *munaadis* (car parkers) all competing for a few centimetres of much-disputed space, and the terrifying female school teachers constantly shouting in harsh authoritarian tones, is simply staggering. '*Talaath daquaat*' produces a traumatic effect in me, magnifying my state of melancholy. I would even speculate that commodifying dreams in this way is the best recipe for escalating the class tensions and anger engendered by the current economic depression and the soaring prices that resulted from the flotation of the pound in 2016.

Another repertoire song, advertised in a second video clip and endlessly diffused on television, is *'Masr betsallem 'aleikum'* (Egypt is greeting you).[12] It could be viewed as one of the more recent propaganda songs by the regime. It came out in 2015, as an advertisement for the Egypt Economic Development Conference in which Sisi announced the founding of the new Egyptian capital city. The song claims its cosmopolitanism by combining Arabic, French, and English in its repertoire, but in reality its entrapment in the realm of military state propaganda adds to a bitter taste and poor command of foreign languages, making it even more bizarre to constantly hear it after Yussra's lavish al-Gouna images. There are several video clips that diffuse this particular song. They include numerous photographs of Sisi posing as the modern nation builder, with the Pyramids, the Sphinx, and the Suez Canal behind him, modern-appearing women dressed in white coats as doctors/scientists (and thus 'progressive'), together with numerous images of industrial and construction sites. The video clip advertises a modern Egypt that is in a state of constant movement.[13] It is as if the regime has borrowed the exact icons, language, and symbols of the Soviet socialist realism era, but by this time, after the lapse of a century, the theme lends itself heavily to kitsch. In short, the remarkable absence of irony in this footage is profoundly disturbing.

This brings me to my next point, namely, how the state propaganda has recently invested in video clips for purposes of self-promotion, selling the image of a so-called open-minded and modern military establishment, as in the case of the World Youth Forum launched by Sisi on 5 November 2017 in Sharm al-Sheikh.[14] It was sumptuously inaugurated with a large number of foreign young men and women from the global South swinging and singing in front of Sisi, in different languages including Brazilian Portuguese, Hindi, Spanish, and English. This all took place against a background of continuous human rights violations and abuses, including the incarceration of activist 'Alaa 'Abdel Fattah, who was entering his fourth year in prison at that time, and the recurrent arrests of other young activists, such as Mahinur al-Masry. The World Youth Forum, with its slogan 'We Need to Talk', was highly criticised on social media as a mere window-dressing strategy that obfuscates the harsh truth in today's Egypt (Ryder and Rizk 2017).

Having made this detour, let me come back to the morning ritual of the flag salutation. The music is abruptly interrupted by the female teacher, who screams 'Good morning' into the microphone in heavily accented English in order to draw the attention of the students. She begins with a systematic avalanche of orders and scolding, in Arabic, directed at the sloppy children standing in line across from her. Then she screams once again in English, 'Ready-steady-go'. Here the students jump and exercise, while they all scream in English '1-2-3-4-5-6-7-8'. Next comes the singing of the classic nursery rhyme 'Frère Jacques', which has been altered into an Arabised *'Frero Jako'* version. Then the students all shout back in unison, in English, a long sentence that I have failed to understand, even though I hear it every day. It starts with 'Welcome to our school ...', followed by some incomprehensible sentences which the children repeat every day. This is followed by reading the opening sura of the Quran, the *fatiha*. On some days of the week, the *fatiha* is followed by the Prophet's sayings. After that, the students sing in Arabic one more song that starts with '*Ya madrassti, ya madrassti*' (My beautiful school). Finally comes the singing of the national anthem, '*Belaadi, belaadi*' (My nation, my nation).

In November 2017, I noticed that the Suad Hosny film songs that were sung around 9.30 were replaced by modernised Sufi music, sung in modern melodies and starting with *La ilaah illa allah* (There is no god but Allah) and *Allah akbar* (God is great). The teachers replaced belly dancing with a kind of imitation of the *zikr* dance. Recently, the children have been equipped with small drums while they dance in the courtyard. Once more, the most frequently repeated songs, besides Yussra's new hit, are the Sufi *zikr* songs and the song '*Masr betsallem 'aleikum*'. On some days, Spanish Zumba dancing, instead of the Sufi *zikr* dance, takes over for hours on end.

My conclusion, after listening daily for almost three years, to this changing assortment of school assembly songs is that, even though the music is never the same, there is no coherent logic to what purpose the music is used for, apart from the dancing that takes place during the 9.30 music session.

Actually, this incessant, highly vigorous belly-dancing trend could be rich material for a surrealist film, which could be nicely shot from my fifth-floor living room. However, it also means that I cannot possibly sit or work in any part of my flat during the school day, and I reschedule my work for the evening. But work is impossible then as well, because of my upstairs neighbour, a hostel for Palestinian girls on the upper floor (some fourteen female students, almost all registered at Cairo University), who also have developed a penchant for belly dancing until early dawn. In fact, the director of the hostel, Madam Mun., an elderly, well-intentioned Palestinian woman, seems to be quite strict in not allowing the young ladies to go out in the evening. Nor are they allowed to receive male relatives in the hostel, which means that they stand outside in the corridor of my floor when they receive visits from their male cousins. And last but not least, since the television is one of their main forms of entertainment, this has resulted into escalating fights over the volume of the sound, which not only myself, but also my next-door neighbour, suffer from. Furthermore, some of the students took a liking to jogging at midnight on the balcony, resulting in sleepless nights for my neighbours and me who are just a floor beneath them.

Problems with the hostel, though, have been lingering for a while. Some three years ago, a significant fire occurred in the hostel due to the apparent negligence of some of the students living there. Of course, tons of water were poured to control the hazardous incident, destroying my entire ceiling. The repairs were not properly done. I had commissioned an entrepreneur who took an absurd sum of cash to 'fix' my ceiling, causing deeper cracks in the building just over a month after the repair job was completed. When I consulted an architect, it was clear that I had been ripped off. Thus the ceilings in my living room and bedrooms are still susceptible to collapsing. I was never able to obtain any indemnity from the administration of the hostel, which is funded by the Palestinian Embassy. In order to be reimbursed for repairs, I needed to obtain approval and a report from an employee of the *baladiyya* (the town council), who never showed up at my flat. After endless signatures and many exhausting trips to the *baladiyya* and the surreal police station in Doqi, faced with a line of exhausted but quite aggressive officers (mainly against the poor) to make a *mahdar* (a police report) with my lawyer, I finally gave up my claims, as I completely lost faith in the process.

My first visit to the terrible public school opposite my building was in March 2016, when a devastating sand and rain storm uprooted one of the satellite dishes on our roof. It remained swinging upside down for two days, threatening to fall down and destroy the upper balcony of my neighbours, the Palestinian female students' hostel. During that frightening night, Madam Mun. came to me in panic when the huge swinging dish was about to land on her balcony. Only then did we discover that the school had secretly installed two dishes on our roof that were connected with numerous wires that crossed the street to land on the roof of the school. It is true that I had already noticed these wires between the two buildings. Before this incident, I had even asked our *bawaab* about these countless white wires passing through my balcony, and why they landed on the roof of the school, but he played the fool and I received no answer to these queries.

It soon became obvious that our *bawaab* had received quite awesome sums as bribes from several neighbouring private companies and residents, including the school, to install the countless dishes on our roof and let the wires pass through our building. It is as if our building has become the focal point through which all the satellite wires of some five or six other neighbouring buildings pass, to be connected to a few more buildings opposite ours. We then discovered that several buildings behind us also used ours as a corridor, passing the wires through the top of the roof. After paying several visits to the headmistress of the school, imploring her to remove the dish and wires, her ritual answer was hypocritical laughter that she would do whatever I wanted, but possibly thinking I was a deranged woman. There was never a follow-up to this conversation. It was then clear to me that the situation would continue as if nothing had happened. The headmistress was simply trained to smile at me and reply like an automaton with a long, ironic '*haaader*' (yeees).

After consulting with several neighbours, I decided to climb to the roof and cut the wires myself. It had to be done on a quiet Friday so that they would not hurt an innocent bystander. The result was spectacular. In less than an hour I had one female and one male teacher knocking at my door, begging me, determined not to leave before I consented to retain at least one of the dishes because 'the children need internet for learning ... and also the night guard needs to watch satellite channels'. The encounter turned into an incredible scene of a power struggle, as the two young teachers felt that they were dealing with someone from an entirely different planet (class-wise, too). They adopted the status of the powerless (the *masaakiin*) and downtrodden but they kept on nagging and nagging, almost blackmailing me that they would not leave my floor until they obtained my consent to reinstall the dish. I refused and made fun instead of their devastating, amplified Suad Hosny songs that are a threat to one's sanity. My behaviour bewildered them. The deadlocked encounter went on for perhaps twenty minutes. I was determined not to give up and remained firmly at my door, reacting exactly in the same way they did, by replying with no and no and no. Their persistence was eventually defeated by my stubbornness. I had finally won. But who knows whether they might have found an alternative route to hijack our building again by installing another covert dish elsewhere during the summer?

On 13 July 2010, with no prior warning, central security forces and Dar El Salam police arrived with a bulldozer to demolish buildings under a dangerous cliff called Gabal Khayrallah. So began a wave of forced evictions in one of the 'unsafe areas' of Establ Antar and Ezbet Khayrallah – in Al-Mahgar street in Dar El Salam neighbourhood – that left at least 21 families homeless, apparently because of corruption during the enumeration process.

The police and security forces ordered and in some cases forced the 21 families to remove their possessions. They told the families that they would be given alternative housing in 6 October City, so the families loaded their possessions onto lorries provided by Cairo governorate, each paying 200 Egyptian pounds to the drivers. However, as soon as the demolitions began, those overseeing the evictions ordered the lorries to be unloaded, saying, according to the NGO Network for the Defence of vulnerable groups, that they suspected that the 21 families were trying to cheat their way into alternative housing. Only a day earlier, an enumeration committee had counted the residents, guided by a man who was a local resident. After the 21 families were made homeless, the man allegedly said he could get their names on the enumeration list for 5,000 Egyptian pounds (US$841), as he was said to have done for his two brothers who were apparently 'outsiders'. (Amnesty International 2011: 94)

### Garage wars

Lawlessness prevails on all levels amongst the neighbours and between the *bawaabs* and the garage keepers, and constant fights lead to anonymous parties puncturing car tyres, or to the garage keepers stealing objects from other cars. However, they mainly focus on those they regard as 'enemies', since they have never stolen, for example, from my old next-door neighbours, whom they respect. But no one dares to confront the family of the garage keepers because of their power in running the show, which can degenerate into violence. Umm Tam., the garage keeper, a strong, stout *baladi* woman in a black *gallabeyya* (long robe), has squatted in four empty rooms over the garage, which were meant to be storage rooms for the owners of the building. Two of these rooms contain two beds and a sofa in which Umm Tam. spends quite a lot of time. No resident dares confront her about her squatting.

The topic of evicting Umm Tam. has often been brought up in the residents' meetings. However, no one has so far summoned the courage to undertake any action against her and her sons. One neighbour asserted that Umm Tam. uses the garage merely for her own profit, renting it out to various members of embassies for thousands of pounds per month. Apparently, too, Umm Tam.'s two sons use the water of the building to conduct a private car wash business, running up water bills that they refuse to cover. Again, no one dares stage a confrontation with her or her family out of fear of retaliation.

Umm Tam., now a grandmother, has raised four boys on her own, two of whom spent quite some time in jail for taking part in violent beatings and street fights at the corner of our building. This has definitely given her not only material but symbolic power in her almost total control of the street as her private fiefdom.

Umm Tam. decided to like me because I immediately understood that I would be better off having her as a friend than a foe. I keep a warm relationship with her sons, who have been socially stigmatised by the middle-class residents of the building. There is a Robin-Hoodish element about her in the way she defends the rubbish collector and the sons of the *bawaab*, i.e. the weakest protagonists of our neighbourhood. Sometimes, too, skirmishes over car parking occur between the *bawaab*'s brother, who controls the car park on Refa'a Street, and Umm Tam.'s family members, resulting in long-term boycotts between the two families.

Umm Tam. does not live in the building because she owns an entire building elsewhere, but she can be seen every morning occupying a chair right in front of the entrance of the garage, dictating who can and cannot park in the entire street – which is filled, in any case, with school buses and double-parked cars. It goes without saying that Umm Tam. truly controls the street through her networks and her ties of friendship with the shop owners in my building. I am fortunate not to own a car, but I am an eyewitness to the constant loud banter and skirmishes in the street and on our stairs between Umm Tam. and her circle of numerous enemies amongst the new residents who have purchased flats since 2008.

The other half of the building has been turned into substandard offices and commercial spaces (*tugaari*), which means that numerous employees come and go constantly at all hours of the day, even as late as ten o'clock in the evening on certain days of the month, particularly the residents on the third floor. Once a month, the numerous female employees come to pick up their salary, which means that, after their departure, the entire entrance is littered with rubbish and chewing gum. It is quite normal to find coffee and tea spilled, and cigarettes butts thrown, on the fine-looking but quite old marble stairs. While the *bawaab* and his two sons are constantly repri- manded for not cleaning the entrance and stairs as often as they should, no resident is prepared to pay him a proper salary that could get him to do a thorough job.

On the third floor, two flats have been turned into a franchise for a French perfume and cosmetics company. These are owned by a well-to-do *Saa'iidi* (Upper Egyptian) businessman. This flat was owned in the 1960s by the prominent lawyer Ahmed al-Khawaga, who had purchased it in 1957. His daughters sold it in 1998 after both parents had passed away. As one enters the flat, one is struck by a library that does not conform with the employees or the activities of the franchise headquarters of a French perfume and cosmetics company. This is, in fact, a bit of Ahmed al-Khawaga's library, left behind, and it stands as a remnant of a vanished era. The owner of the company, a truly honest person, has committed himself to collect money from each resident for the collective electricity and water bills, since he owns three flats. His secretary, Madam M. M., an astute and thorough accountant, who has been constantly chasing every single resident to pay his dues of 120 L.E. per month (which would also include the *bawaab*'s salary), has lost the stamina needed for the job after several skirmishes with some of the tenants. After all, this was not her job, as she often reminded me. She is only doing us residents a favour. She does not see why she should be insulted or humiliated on a daily basis by the residents for the sake of a few pounds. Furthermore, the owner of the company was kind enough to allow the many meetings of the residents to take place at his office. However, over time, he too became disillusioned by the tenacity of the neighbours in refusing to pay the collective water and electricity bills for the elevator and the entrance door. So he has decided to pull out of the association, avoiding the residents' meetings under the pretext that he is constantly out of town.

Meanwhile, the owner of the company and his numerous employees sustain an open and fierce war with the *bawaab* and Umm Tam. Umm Tam. is a master of the art of blocking the cars of the perfume company owner, his son, and the employees. The employees have thus learned to park some distance away to avoid her fierce reactions. But these tactics work both ways: some of the employees and the owner's son have learned to replicate Umm Tam.'s tricks and block the other cars, in order to make Umm Tam.'s life with her parking clients even more difficult. Through these progressively more sophisticated blockades and tit-for-tat tactics, my harmless and extremely well-mannered next-door neighbours have ended up having their cars blockaded too. How futile it is to see them involved in ongoing fights and losing their temper every other day. The fights escalated in November 2016, when the son of the perfume owner started going down in his pyjamas every morning to purposely blockade the car of my upstairs neighbours. This now happens almost every single morning when Mrs A., the daughter of Mrs Fati., is taking her children to school and ends up immobilised inside the garage. When I paid my neighbours a visit on 18 November 2016, Mrs A. was all tears wondering where to go and whether our building might soon be deserted. But then matters calmed down between February and May 2017, when I was away, after Mrs A.'s husband had a serious talk with the owner of the perfume company, leading to a de-escalation of the matter. Since no one wanted a crescendo of violence, I found upon my return in June 2017 that a reconciliation had taken place and relations had become more conciliatory. After all, dislikes are quite normal amongst neighbours, but the garage wars did not hinder anyone from attending the meetings of the association.

The perfume company owner stopped paying any wages or communicating with the *bawaab* after a huge fight for a reason I failed to grasp. 'Our *bawaab* and the rubbish collector are richer than you and me ... the rubbish man makes money with rubbish so why pay him? ... Besides, we have no real rubbish and our maids take it downstairs and dispose of it without his assistance.' This is what I heard from one of my newly arrived neighbours who refused my proposal to raise the salary of the rubbish collector from 5 L.E. (not even half a dollar per month) to 20 L.E. Bear in mind that this neighbour is a retired businessman, who owns a car and employs a chauffeur and various other servants.

Two sides of the garage and the entire entrance façade have been trans-formed into numerous small shops selling clothes, school bags, shoes, and sportswear, a small supermarket, and an extremely filthy and abominable café that closed down in 2016 (and was replaced by two other cafés in 2017). The first café closed after its owner, another *Saa'iidi* millionaire, had a violent fight with the tenant who failed to come up with the rent. We are told that the millionaire theatrically pulled a gun and shot him in the leg in view of everybody in the street. This melodramatic Hollywood scene apparently frightened all the residents. This millionaire owns about four flats in the building and never pays any public utilities, elevator maintenance, or electricity or water bills, which accumulate in the thousands per month. Strangely enough, nobody brought up the subject of any police interference and the culprit was never punished because the owner is obviously influential. This also explains why there is so much fear of confronting him by creating a legalised residents' association – as some of the residents suggested in the meeting, its legality would be a lost cause.

The shopkeepers hang around in the street the entire day and do not seem to be doing well or selling anything, as the shops are almost devoid of custom-ers, except for the shop selling school bags just before the opening of the schools in September. There is one tiny clothes shop that seems to me to be a cover-up for some probably illicit business, although I am not sure what this enterprise involves. But the shopkeepers excel at registering every single movement on the street. They have their chairs all lined up in front of the entrance door of the building and they often inform me gently who has come into or out of the building (the postman, the collector of electricity bills, or my own friends who have lost their way) and when. I often chat with them on a daily basis. They are kind enough to provide me with small change when I am returning in a taxi.

These tiny and apparently useless shops produce an endless supply of cartons and boxes that are profitable for the rubbish collector, but this waste would certainly not make anyone glowingly rich. During the first years after the revolution the rubbish collector almost stopped coming altogether. Only last year, when I struck a deal with him to pay him 50 L.E. per month provided he regularly cleans all the stairs, did he start turning up every second or third day. The reason for his infrequency was not only because he was not properly paid by the residents, but because he needed to rent a truck and usually lacks the cash, unless he can be sure of collecting the cartons and boxes of the shops, which would make up for the trouble of collecting the other residents' waste.

Would one define my neighbours' reaction towards the rubbish collector as a pure form of class discrimination? Not only that, the rubbish collector is a Copt, which makes me wonder if it is not typical Muslim middle-class religious prejudice. Only three residents followed my initiative of paying the rubbish collector more money after the pile of rubbish reached gargantuan dimensions. I ended up hiring a small truck with professional rubbish removers who took away some thirty large sacks of accumulated rubbish from the back stairs; it cost me 500 L.E. plus an entire day away from work. But none of the other residents wanted to pull their weight and contribute to the payment of the removers.

The problem with the commercial offices of the building is their misuse of elevators, which they appear to carry out as a form of vendetta. The countless numbers of boxes that are moved through the elevator almost seem like a collective endeavour to destroy this poor antiquated moving wooden box. If a terrible accident were to occur, perhaps that would be enough of a reason for the residents to take more concrete action. Most fascinating is how, if you enter the building and some person is ahead of you waiting for the elevator to come, she or he pretends not to notice you and rushes into the elevator to quickly slam the door, even if you are screaming that you also need to use the lift.

### The fifth-floor co-working space

An internet café – no, let us be precise, a 'co-working space'[15] – for young people opened a year ago on the fifth floor, across from my flat. Some seventy visitors or more come on a daily basis and remain until midnight. It goes without saying that they all need to use the elevator.

They socialise and hang around in the corridors, with extremely loud laughter, chatting, and constant mobile phone calls. They are so loud that I can no longer relax in my living room without hearing clearly everything being said. The visitors not only do their best to further destroy the poor elevator, but they strew the stairs regularly with an astonishing amount of litter. I should be tolerant towards youth, since we had a revolution that I support, but to be frank, these crowds are loud and inconsiderate. The stairs are made of old, beautiful marble, but it seems that anything antique-looking is worthless, not modern enough, and can be abused.

My floor has turned into a constant power struggle over space, with young girls and men hanging around in the corridors. They love to leave hand and shoe prints everywhere on the walls of the corridor, which I have painted twice. The poor plants I have put in the corridor have been ruined, too, and some have disappeared, not to mention the rubbish I pick up daily from between the poor sick plant pots. But Madam Mun. (the director of the Palestinian hostel), who thinks that I am a bit of a lunatic, has often ironically told me that the fault is mine. 'No sane person would leave anything in the corridors here, be it plants, pots, or decorations.'

Time and again, I wonder whether Cairo is unique in having become a place where it is an acceptable pastime to spit, to throw litter, and to leave scribbles inside elevators. No one believes the elevator could soon break down, and no one really cares. 'Be optimistic and it will not collapse,' says Mr Mus., the director of the co-working space, who apparently has been trained by an NGO in dialogue and tolerance and how to speak softly to people. But he, too, seemed reluctant to pay the *bawaab* the salary I had proposed after a long struggle with the various residents.[16] This so-called decent salary is 100 L.E. (less than nine dollars) a month, while a cappuccino at the Cilantro café across from my building costs 25 L.E., or one-fourth of the would-be 'decent salary'. As I keep reminding my neighbour when the abandoned plastic cups from these expensive cappuccinos are constantly found in the antiquated moving wooden box, it is logical that the *bawaab*'s son could be tempted to steal a PlayStation from their office when they employed him as a cleaner.

Meanwhile, living in this building for less than a year has turned me into a melodramatic theatrical character. When the *bawaab*'s son cleans the staircase and it is immediately littered in less than an hour, I take the liberty of shouting with all my strength, playing with the powerful acoustics of the stairs, that the times of slavery are over. Often, too, I would stick a paper on the entrance door of the co-working space, stating that the *bawaab*'s son is 'NOT AN ABYSSINIAN SLAVE', or I would collect the cigarette butts from the stairs and throw them on their desks. But to no avail. They think I must be a lunatic since I clean the public stairs by myself, while I have never seen any of those youngsters picking up a broom. No cleaning, because physical work is a humiliating task fit only for maids. After each fight with my smiling-trained neighbour Mr Mus., he always ends up denying that this constant noise and littering is a violation of my own space. After almost six months of negotiations about the urgency of putting out and emptying wastebaskets, Mr Mus. still finds it more practical to litter the stairs. He complains that his 'bellboys' – a term he is proud to use since he seems to have just learned it – keep on disappearing, one after the other. Mr Mus.'s soft and trained voice, on the subject of bellboys amongst other things, became one of the main reasons why my aggressive instincts are kept on red alert, until I completely lost my temper and started screaming like mad in the stairs on a regular basis. I am now ready to call in the police to shut the place down. Gone are the days when I cared whether I would be counted amongst the *feloul* (the supporters of the old regime) if I took any action against the disruptive youth. But their presence is becoming unbearable.

### Chewing gum everywhere

After all, it's all in our heads. 'If you don't notice the chewing gum sticking to the stairs, it doesn't exist, but if you keep on noticing it too much, it is because you have lived too long in Germany, Madam. You tend to focus on details which we never see,' Mr Mus. keeps on telling me laughingly. This is why no one else sees the accumulated black mud in between the stairs. After having spent days with the *bawaab*'s son removing the sticky blackened gum from the floor, and having pinned so many written warning notes on the walls of the entrance hall about the horrid gum, the inventive youth started sticking their gum on the iron bars on top of the stairs. It is cleaner this way, right?

If you tell the people to take the stairs, because the elevator is about to fail, they take it as an affront to their masculinity, femininity, or chastity. How dare you humiliate them with the task of exerting physical effort such as going down the stairs when there is an elevator available? When they noticed that I was threatening them, some customers started to take the elevator to the fourth floor and then the stairs to the fifth, knowing that I was watching them at the entrance of the co-working space. When the electricity bill for the building's public spaces was raised to 2,000 L.E., Mr M. refused to pay his share, for how could we, the residents, prove that his customers are the main culprits?

On 17 November 2016, finally, the elevator fell down, with two employees from the perfume company in it. Mercifully, no one died, although the two employees remained in shock for a while, but the cabin of the elevator was broken as a result. The incident turned out to be a blessing in disguise. The traumatic fall resulted in the company forbidding all its employees to use the elevator. For me, this meant a significant reduction of noise. I declared to the residents that I would *not* contribute to repairing the elevator as long as the flats listed as companies contributed nothing to the building's

maintenance or to the payment of the exorbitant electricity bills. I decided
to take a chance: while I was on my way to make a *mahdar* at the police
station against the Shefs Company, I phoned my lawyer. He told me to
return home, as these *mahdar*s are futile.

Am Sayyed the wonder man, the elevator repairman, fixed it and said that
'everything is fine'. And the Shefs Company, as if to challenge everyone,
continued to use and abuse the elevator as if nothing had happened. In
fact, a few neighbours remained in complete denial of the collapse. Some
of them said, no, '*Kheir kulluh kheir*' (Everything is going well), it did
not collapse. It was the *bawaab* who pulled out the *sikkina* ('the knife',
meaning the key) again. This version of the story was debated by various
neighbours for a long time after the incident, resulting in metaphysical
meditations about the truth of the incident: some said that it might be
pure imagination since the elevator was now in good health and functioning, except that some of the wooden parts of the box had mysteriously
disappeared.

After so many complaints from several neighbours about the impossibility
of tolerating an internet/co-working space with so many customers going
and coming in our building, and after my own threats to resort to lawyers,
Mr Mus. announced to Mr Al. and the other residents that he was going to
search for another place and depart in March 2017.

However, March arrived, then April and May, and Mr Mus. did not leave.
We were then told that because the rents in Doqi were soaring, Mr Mus.
had decided to remain in our building for the next five years. The result was
that he changed his strategy, which will be revealed in the coming
passages.

Meanwhile, Mr Mus. finally started to close the entrance door of his flat.
This reduced the noise significantly, and I no longer screamed at his customers
on a daily basis or threatened to resort to the police. His clientele reduced
their presence in the corridor; my many messages on the wall, and my
terrorising attitude, finally met with some success. He also started to remove
the daily rubbish from the stairs, although the chewing gum remained an
uncontrollable epidemic.

## The *itihaad al-shaagheliin* (building residents' association) that failed to take shape

> The elevator has a history of at least 2000 years. Rome's colosseum even had
> a system of 12 winch-powered elevators operated by slaves to lift wild animals
> and gladiators straight into the bloody action of the arena. (Graham 2014: 243)

As the building's problems and disasters kept growing, several residents came
up with a proposal for collective action. Exchange of information amongst
the residents usually takes place in the entrance hall, the street opposite our

building, the stairs, or the elevator. These are crucial spaces for greeting each other, gossiping, and exchanging information for a few minutes about the latest news and incidents occurring in the building, information about the shop owners and their infringing on the entrance hall with the school bags,[17] the rubbish, the sewer leaks, the changing ownership of the cafés, or the latest soaring (or not) purchase and rental prices of the flats in the neighbouring buildings. For example, it seems that everyone in our building is well informed that my next-floor flat has been rented out for 7,000 L.E. per month after it was transformed into a commercial space, and that the first-floor flats will similarly be transformed into more commercial outlets.[18] The exchange of knowledge about real-estate rents and sales becomes a crucial collective barometer at the heart of the grapevine amongst neighbours.

Norbert Elias and John Scotson's study on two working-class communities in England, one older and more established and another consisting of newcomers, reveals how important gossip is as a communal mechanism that serves various functions. It can range from a form of entertainment to status enhancement, at the expense, on the one hand, of debasing and humiliating others who are socially inferior, or conversely as a form of praise to arouse charity and concern in the community.[19] Their study reveals how gossip can be a pervasive mechanism in stigmatising entire communities and perpetrating stereotypes rather than revealing the truth about this community. Within the miniature cosmos of our building, it is important to note that the information exchanged about who is who, and who said what about whom, has generally been an important prelude to the fights that occurred at residents' meetings at a later stage, and the ways in which each neighbour would situate himself vis-à-vis the others. Indeed, gossip has been a central mechanism in creating bonds, enmities, likes, and dislikes that would reach a peak in subsequent meetings. Gossip about taste and lifestyles, the décor of salons, and other differences amongst neighbours comes up in conversations as a barometer marking class boundaries, even though not all neighbours really know what the living rooms of some of the neighbours they dislike actually look like. But the real purpose of this kind of gossip is to spread subjective impressions that 'so and so is not really of our taste or class', so as to express distance and form a basis for disagreement later on.

The starting point was to get together to form an official body that could act in the name of the residents as a collective. We obtained the list of telephone numbers from Mrs M. M., the secretary of the cosmetics and perfume company, who then helped in fixing dates when all residents could be made available. I myself spent long hours on the phone to coordinate the meetings amongst neighbours with clashing schedules and commitments. I knocked at the door of the fourth-floor neighbours to ask them if they were willing to contribute financially to the repairs. They all said yes, but not all were willing to attend meetings.

During 2015 and 2016 we had quite a few endless and extremely tiring meetings, in a large meeting room in the office of the cosmetics and perfume company. These meetings were supposedly in preparation for forming an *itihaad al-shaagheliin* (building residents' association). The urge to found a formal organisation was related chiefly to the unresolved problem of the elevator. We started the first meeting with seven enthusiastic residents, which grew to eight after the third meeting.

I volunteered to obtain the proper document from the Doqi property district, as an official requirement for founding the association. The document in question is called the *'awaa'ed*. It is an officially stamped paper that presents the history of all the proprietors of the building, the successive sales of the flats, and the long list of the contracts of the permanent tenants. This document was to be sent later to the district office of the quarter, accompanied by the ownership and tenancy contracts of all the founding members of the residents' association, together with their IDs. The bureaucracy to obtain this small piece of paper took me an entire morning, a sport I undertook as part and parcel of doing ethnographic fieldwork. Visiting this falling-apart administrative building in Doqi, with its endless tiny rooms packed with employees, roaming customers, and antiquated files, gave me an invaluable look at the level of misery and wretchedness of the helpless state employees. The employees became cooperative the moment I adopted a smiling face and started chatting with them. But the process took, as usual, a magnificent collection of stamps, together with comings and goings to several offices. The two employees who helped me most with the paperwork categorically refused to be given any *bakshish*, insisting that not all state employees are corrupt. I was decidedly moved by their sincerity and brought them sweets as a token of human appreciation. Once I obtained the document, I gave it to Mrs M. M., who distributed it to all the residents.

Residents' meetings were long and tedious, sometimes lasting for as long as three or four hours, during which no one could agree on anything. These meetings were often marked by unspoken, hidden hostilities and struggles, such as the simmering one between Mr Al., Dr F., and Mr O. on how to organise the association in three categories: first, the owners of flats; second, the permanent tenants (who do not enjoy the same status and privileges as owners); and finally, the commercial companies. The largest (and absent) owner of several of the flats was our main adversary, since his negligence is the reason the building has collapsed. Simply put, he has never paid any utilities, electricity, or water bills. The association would have been the only legal body that could force him to deal with the acute, unresolved issue of the elevator.

Mr Al. and Dr F. seemed to have been arguing about the elevator endlessly for more than a decade, well before my arrival in the building. But there was more to the situation than simply arguments and disagreements. Mr Al. could hardly sympathise with Dr F.'s way of handling payments and the repairs of the building. It is true that Dr F. volunteered to repair one marble pillar at the entrance hall, to which we all contributed a share. However, the way it was restored left a lot to be desired, as it looked much worse than it had when the upper marble part was detached. Nor did Dr F. seem to be particularly bothered by the decaying entrance hall, not even by the broken glass and the missing doors of the stairwells. He seemed to be even less concerned about the garage ceiling that looked about to collapse, a health and safety hazard to the parked cars.

Most of the meetings were contaminated by a rivalry between these two gentlemen (Mr Al. and Dr F.). The gentlemen were in an open competition as to who knew the technical details better, since both claimed to command some sort of scientific knowledge of how best to conduct the affairs under discussion. Dr F. was a well-known and well-to-do medical doctor, specialising in venereal and skin diseases; Mr Al. was a retired engineer. The latter's constant complaint was that Dr F. claimed to be busy around the clock, thus impossible to reach, while Dr F. presented his neighbour Mr Al. as an early-retired, leisurely character who spent most of his time at the Gezira Club. The two of them had never-ending arguments on how to handle the disobedient Y., the *bawaab*.

Once the word *bawaab* was uttered, an avalanche of comments from competing voices surfaced to take over the floor, throwing light on the degree of hostility towards him. He was attacked for his careless behaviour and his targeting of the garage keeper as his enemy. This was mainly the stand of the newcomers to the building, whereas the old residents seemed to interpret the behaviour of Y., the *bawaab*, and Umm Tam. as part of the natural canvas of the latest 'organic' tapestry of life, in which transformations and unavoidable degeneration had become part of our life and our street.

Both gentlemen had known Y. for decades. In the meetings they seemed to compete by exposing the details of the *bawaab*'s life, his multiple informal, if not dubious, jobs that led to the sale of the entrance-hall space to small shops, and his spicy marital life. Meanwhile, the seventy-four-year-old Mr O., the third rival, a former director of a state-owned company (who is much enamoured with maintaining a bureaucratic habitus and adopts a more formal high Arabic language in his address to others), insisted on meticulously drafting the constitution of the association. Whenever the gentle and soft-spoken Mrs Fati. (the niece of my next-door neighbour Mrs Mars.) or I tried to put in a word, Mr O. would immediately shut us down, for no obvious reason except perhaps that women should not have much of a say in such meetings. The main obsession of Mrs Mun., the director of the Palestinian female students' hostel, was the constant worry about soaring prices every-where, which made her repeat time and again that the hostel might not be able to make ends meet. Her strategy for saving money was to bargain constantly over what the hostel's share of the expenses should be, since they occupy an entire floor and have over fifteen women residing there.

In the end, the countless hours spent on drafting the constitution of the association turned out to be a waste of time. Alas, to our disappointment, or rather relief, Mr Al. found out that the rules and regulations for such an association could be easily downloaded from the internet, and Mr O.'s draft, according to Mr Al., was packed with legal errors. Perhaps it was simply their proximity to one another that led these three gentlemen to their increasing mutual dislike. The fourth rival, Mr Mus., had only one concern: how to maximise his profit by making the elevator available to his large cohort of customers, with no concern for the inconveniences this imposition posed to the building residents.

In retrospect, the association turned to be a pure waste of time and effort, since the entire mission was futile. I went so far as to organise a meeting with my astute and shrewd lawyer and Mr Al. at Mr O.'s flat – a meeting that they requested, and that lasted a couple of hours, in which both gentlemen bombarded my lawyer with endless queries. Alas, as my intelligent lawyer predicted, all these talks would end in nothing concrete. He strongly advised me not to act on anything, or volunteer to deal with Egyptian bureaucracy, before a collective agreement on the payment of his fees was settled. He warned me that my good intentions could be perceived as naivety by the other neighbours, who would always promise payment and never deliver.

Since we had all agreed on the urgency of creating some sort of governing body, we had one more meeting in my flat with only my upstairs neighbours – Mrs Fati., the niece of Mrs Mars. (my next-door neighbour), and her son-in-law, Mr Ahm., who seemed to be quite well informed on legal issues, together with Mr Al. It was Mr Al.'s wish not to include all the neighbours, in order to avoid further clashes and to create a 'clan' apart, with the three of us who got along well. The meeting lasted for four hours. This time Mr Al. did everything to hinder the founding of the association. He was extremely negative, arguing that we as residents would never be able to counteract the absent owner who owns the majority of the flats. Besides that, Mr Al. expressed his disagreement with the other neighbours' attitude toward numerous points. He brought up the entire history of the management of the building, emphasising that problems had always been solved in an amiable way without resorting to any institutional framework, which was doomed to fail in any event. However, his interpretation turned out to be completely misleading, as two of the residents who had been committed to taking the initiative in fixing the problems became bitter and disappointed because of the nonchalance and carelessness of the other residents. But they remained powerless to come up with a collective consensus. Shortly thereafter, one of these residents passed away, and the other left the building for the compound life. Would not the former neighbour who moved out to a gated community be the best evidence of the failure of amiability? Then Mr Al. insisted that no one would be willing to take up the responsibility of the treasurer, since the accounts constituted the most strenuous and dangerous responsibility in the association. He stated repeatedly that he himself would not want to be the treasurer, nor would he want to take any responsibility in the association because this building has made him sick. In a theatrical manner, Mr Al. said that he risked a heart attack if we continued with the association.

Finally, Mr Al. openly said that he mistrusted all the other 'ageing' male residents because they were petty and mainly concerned with fighting each other. Mrs Fati., Mr Ahm., and I were puzzled. Had Mr Al. retreated because his and his mother's flat has a contract of permanent tenancy with the powerful absent landowner? Had he realised that opening a war on the owner through the association would cause him trouble? No one can answer this question. But all the participants left my flat after midnight in a depressed mood. The chapter of the association was without a doubt closed indefinitely.

## Notes

1 The late Mohamed Ramzy 'Omar (1944–94) was a prominent architect who designed the current Ministry of Foreign Affairs building, which opened in the early 1990s (Hassan 1999). Ramzy 'Omar also designed modernist buildings like the former Sheraton Hotel in Giza, the Sheraton Hotel in Hurgada, the logo of the current Egyptian flag, and the Czech Embassy in Doqi (not far away from Harun Street). Ramzy 'Omar was a popular architect, a favourite of both the Nasser and Sadat regimes, and carried out many projects for the army, like the military hospital in Ma'adi (Mohamed Ramzy 'Omar).

2 The expression *al-zaman al-gamiil* has become a nostalgic cliché expressing longing for colonial and royal Egypt. It is often accompanied by a display of vintage photographs of old colonial Cairo, when the streets looked cleaner and emptier, when women looked Westernised and finely dressed, and when no veil was seen in the streets. This is certainly only one facet of the story. It is equally manifested in living rooms decorated with photographs and emblems of the former royal family, the former Egyptian flag, and Ottoman artefacts. Interestingly, this nostalgic trend is turning into a collective phenomenon. A good example is the Facebook group that calls itself *al-Zaman al-gamiil Facebook* الزمن الجميل. It posts mostly old Egyptian films from the 1940s, 1950s, and 1960s, Arabic music, and orientalist photographs (including an endless display of Lehnert and Landrock photographs), as well as pictures of famous actors and politicians from these earlier eras.

3 The Nubians are often stereotyped as hard-working, mostly honest, rather obedient building keepers. This stereotyping certainly expresses a superiority complex that Egyptians hold with respect to the black Africans.

4 I have tried twice to put plants in the entrance hall, but they disappeared.

5 *Mahraganaat* or *Electro Shaabi* music originated in poor districts. It features electronic music, highly ironic and loose language, and homoerotic dancing. It is a new and eclectic youth style in dance, borrowing from Latin American dance, Bollywood, and numerous other musical traditions.

6 During early 2018 the owner managed to expel the bankrupt company and the flat was rented to another design company.

7 In 2017 the starting time of the school changed to 7.30. On some days the saluting of the flag can take half an hour.

8 This was observed in 2016.

9 بسم الله ... الله أكبر بسم الله بسم الله
كلمات:
بسم الله ...الله أكبر بسم الله بسم الله
بسم الله ...أذن وكبر بسم الله بسم الله

10 A different version of this song was sung by the late iconic singer 'Abdel Halim Hafez.

11 See '3 Daqat – Abu Ft. Yousra'.

12 The Arabic-English-French song by Hesham 'Abbas; see 'Masr Bitnadikom – Hesham Abbas'.

13 *Masr betsallem aleikum, bit nadiikum we bitnaaku*
*Edna fi edeiku naamil musgizaat*
*Masr fathlkum eideiha*
*Kullu itraahin aleiha*
*Masr taani hatibni al ahramaat*

It's the land of inspiration and the cradle of civilization.
Egypt is the great gift of the Nile.
With more work and dedication
And with the people's love and devotion
Egypt will be rising once again.

*Pour l'Egypte de nos jours,*
*Peuple uni et plein d'amour,*
*Traçons tous ensemble le bon chemin.*
*Ecrire une glorieuse histoire*
*D'une vie prospère et pleine d'espoir,*
*C'est ainsi que nous voyons demain.*

14 The Youth Conference organised by Sisi, 5 November 2017; see 'World Youth Forum – the official song'.

15 The co-working space is advertised on its website as offering a space for 'meeting and lecture venues, trips, sound studio, consultation, partnerships with student activities, monthly campaigns and events, workshops, library, entertainment and fun'.

16 However, as time went by, and after endless meetings, controversies, and discussions, Mr Mus. agreed to pay the *bawaab* the salary that a number of residents agreed upon by the end of 2017, and that amounts to 100 L.E. a month.

17 In contrast to the fierce café owners, all the shopkeepers are quite considerate and affable to the residents. The amount of space they occupy in the entrance of our building is constantly negotiable. In fact, the front shopkeepers do not hide their utter dislike of the customers of the cafés for being loud and disturbing.

18 Y., the *bawaab*, keeps the residents informed about the sales and rents of flats in the neighbourhood. This information is then widely exchanged amongst neighbours, since the few remaining residents keep toying with the idea of selling their flats and moving out to the compound life. This idea is expressed in talks with the neighbours when they complain about the degraded state of the building. In these conversations, estimates and speculations about the price of one's own flat are often offered.

19 See in particular chapter 7 of Elias and Scotson (1994: 101).

# 5

# The elevator saga: The degeneration of everyday material conditions

City building is predominantly an organic and quasi-state affair, hinting at vast systems of social organization, exchange, oversight, regulation, violence, reciprocity and continual deliberation – aspects of sociality. (Simone and Pieterse 2017: 39)

The much-venerated, ninety-three-year-old Mrs Sha. shares her flat with her son Mr Al., who, despite his resistance to the founding of the residents' association, is still one of the few residents one can rely on when catastrophes hit the building. He willingly comes up with advice on water pumps, on electrical devices that need to be purchased, and how these can be repaired. And last but not least, Mr Al. was kind enough, when I moved into the flat, to provide me with the telephone numbers of the pharmacies, electricians, groceries, and other services in the neighbourhood. He even volunteered to install my satellite dish in my flat after a long consultation about the path of the wires. The long-term residents consider Mrs Sha., Mr Al., and my next-door neighbour, eighty-three-year-old Mrs Mars., the knowledgeable residents, who hold a symbolic power not only because of their mature age, but precisely because they are amongst the few remaining 'old guards' of the building. Their extended contacts in the area, their acquaintance with the small shopkeepers of our street, allows them to sift out the efficient from the mass of unprofessional workers. They became a major support when I first moved into the flat, as we seem to speak a similar language, especially in times of crisis.

Mrs Sha. and her son constitute the living memory of this building. They can trace the history, the moves, the stories, and the personal biographies of almost all the residents of the building, including those who have left or passed away. Mr Al. recalls to this day all the skirmishes and controversies that occurred between the owners of the building and the tenants when the owners started to sell off flats and spaces in the building bit by bit, resulting in its dismantling, if not its gradual decomposition, and thus rendering any collective decision-making a practically impossible mission. This may explain why, as time went by, Mr Al. became so unenthusiastic, increasingly lamenting the impossibility of undertaking any collective action, let alone creating an association. Having said that, Mr Al.'s hard work and effort in circulating to the residents, every now and then, letters updating the state of affairs in the building reveal a major personal concern in maintaining the building's good name.

Here is one good example from amongst the numerous letters sent to all residents, dated 24 October 2016:

> On 31.12.2015 I informed you that the unpaid water bills have been accumulating for the past five years. 71,000 L.E. have been paid. Also, on 26.12.2015, a new water meter replaced the old one that had been dysfunctional for the past six years. It was replaced 300 days after having signed a contract with the company and after seven months of tracking down the employee. However, the water company continued to issue unjustified [*guzafiyya*] bills that continued from January to May 2016, amounting to 100,000 L.E. They then stopped issuing bills from October to June, since they are issuing more bills *guzafiyya* for the garage and the restaurant.
>
> One more point to be added:
>
> During that time the [water] motor [*laff*] broke down and some spare parts had to be replaced.
>
> Electricity: an electric mess took place in the *bawaab*'s room, in the wires that feed into the elevator and the water pumps. The breakdown was temporarily solved, but the electrical cable and the electric box need to be changed and this would cost 3,500 L.E.
>
> One more observation:
>
> 1. The electricity bills increased during the two last months.
>
> 2. The elevator. The problem of the elevator can be summarised as follows: a tender, or proposal, was offered to change all the doors [for the five floors], the key panel, and the light, amounting to 16,500 L.E., but this offer is no longer valid because of inflation; it has increased to 20,000 L.E.
>
> 3. The brakes, the oil for the motors, and the locks [*maqbad*] on the fifth floor have been fixed.

This letter was written after Mr Al. had gone to the water company several times, after I gave him the contacts I had made following my own numerous visits to install the water meter. Mr Al. ended up negotiating the unresolved and horrendously high water bills with the employees.

When I had the plumber renovate the antiquated plumbing system of my flat, he was horrified by the state of the stairwells. He warned me about the imminent threat of a fire, with so many uncovered electrical wires passing near the leaking sewage and water pipelines. Not to mention the peculiar location of the numerous air conditioners belonging to the various shops, which had all been installed on top of the ground floor of the back stairs, without any water protection. The city of Cairo has been blessed by a typical absence of rain in winter. However, any change in this climate pattern could spell disaster. Mr Al. took the initiative to bring in an electrician to check the wires; this electrician began to remove a large number of useless connections. Then the iron door leading to one of the stairwells and to the garage was removed by Mr Al., and cut into several squares. These were placed on top of the first-floor air conditioners to protect them from water leaks, rain, and leaking sewage that could drop onto the hundreds of uncovered, chaotic electrical wires. This proved not to be a great solution, however, since anyone can now enter the building from the backyard.

Meanwhile, the problem of rubbish remains unresolved. Some of the residents, instead of bringing their rubbish to the ground floor, throw it directly from their windows. Some of it lands on top of the iron protections, which cannot be accessed from the ground floor, as they are perched high on top of the walls, where the rubbish collector cannot reach them.

Mr Al. has also been active in the past in collecting for the communal electricity (for the entrance hall and elevator) and the water bills. Sadly, and as stated before, as time went by, Mr Al.'s stamina failed him, often leading him to erupt into fits of bad temper when the problems mounted. The water tank on the roof once collapsed because of a huge leak. Replacing it required a collective contribution from all the residents. Not all residents paid their contribution, but at least Mr Al. politely but firmly knocked on all the doors and pressured people to pay their share.

### Never-ending bids for the elevator

Dr F. presented several offers from local elevator companies in Cairo during the meetings we had at the perfume/cosmetics company. At one of the last meetings, a representative from one of the companies gave us a long and detailed lecture on his proposal. However, Mr Al. and Dr F. could never agree on any offer, as all of these proposals seemed to have some sort of problem, quite apart from the personal dislikes and differing ideas about what a new elevator should look like. In the meetings, both Mr Al. and Dr F. endlessly picked on several problems: the companies had either a dubious history or poor-quality products; they relied on the imported Chinese spare parts that plague the market; the products were known to present certain risks after installation. Compared to all of these, our existing, decaying, antiquated elevator turned out to be the best of the choices available. As time went by, between 2014 and 2016 prices soared, reaching a 50 per cent increase, which meant an unavoidable renegotiating process with all residents regarding their monetary contribution to this project. In the meetings, there was a constant argument about whether to replace the entire elevator, including the cables (which seemed to be quite solid) and the motor, or to replace just the box and the doors. Several architects warned us that the companies specialising in replacing elevators in Egypt all have dubious reputations for causing more damage, particularly when installed in older buildings. One of the companies, for example, proposed to Mr Al. to install a larger box, which would have required digging in the foundations of our exhausted building. Luckily, Mr Al., in his choleric manner, sharply rejected the proposal, which was probably not the wrong thing to do.

Another issue arose in these meetings that particularly affected Mr Mus. as the director of the co-working/internet space: should the elevator require a key? All the residents agreed that it should except Mr Mus., whose fifty to seventy daily visitors could not function with a keyed elevator. And even if the commercial tenants contributed a double share compared to the residents, how would the use and abuse of the elevator be controlled, and who would be responsible for the maintenance when the residents' use is minimal compared to the commercial establishments?

After incessant complaints from me about the dangers of collapse, I proposed shutting down the elevator for a few hours a day, an idea that was welcomed by Mr Al. and the residents but abhorred by the co-working-space crowd. After a couple of months, the closing of the elevator was discontinued, as the customers were constantly pestering the *bawaab* to make it work. The co-working space director complained that customers could not use the stairs during the fasting month of Ramadan.

I left for my sabbatical to Germany for a few months in 2017. Upon my return to Cairo in May 2017, Mr Al. decided to take firm action, because all the residents were completely fed up with the clientele of the co-working space, who had doubled in number and produced even more noise and nuisance for the entire building. Mr Al. had had a plastic key installed in the elevator in January 2017 for 1,000 L.E. (the cost to be shared by all residents), to limit the number of trips the elevator had to make. Each resident had received one plastic key, which was quite simple to copy. The endeavour was certainly welcomed by the residents, but Mr Mus. kept on knocking on the residents' doors, arguing that the key should not be required during Ramadan, because his customers were fasting and could not take the stairs. No one listened to him, since all the residents rallied behind Mr Al.'s initiative and prevented the commercial enterprise from using the elevator. However, Mr Mus.'s customers invented a solid set of ingenious tricks to continue using the elevator, such as telephoning the people already upstairs to call the elevator up to the fifth floor, with their friends inside the cabin, thus revealing how easy it was to get around the key.

Then the following disgraceful incident happened, leading to an increase in collective tensions. On 30 May 2017, one of the workers at Shefs, the co-working space, inserted glue into the elevator's keyhole. This act of vandalism broke the wooden box that contained the buttons to all the floors of the building. The residents reacted with indignation and fury. When I went to speak to the workers at Shefs, one of them replied in an aggressive tone that the key was introduced without their consent. They shouted again that their customers could not take the stairs during Ramadan. Already, a couple of times earlier, the entire box containing the buttons had been pulled out when someone had inserted the key into the box too violently.

**Figure 17**   Inserted key to the elevator, 11 June 2017.

I immediately went to Mr Mus.'s office. Fearing my encounter, he first gave the excuse of not being available because he was praying. When I returned, the young employee pretended that he was in a meeting as an attempt to avoid me. When I knocked at their door for the third time, another employee, who had been recurrently impolite with me during the past year, said defiantly that he had destroyed the keyhole since Mr Al. had installed it without asking them, which was certainly a lie. I blew up at him, screaming with all my strength that this was *'ashwaa'iyyaat* (lower-class) behaviour.

What I literally told him was that this was a *zeriba* mentality (*zeriba* means 'barn', implying animal behaviour – uncouth and lowly), to bring out into the open the difficulties residents experienced from the mounting problems of his business.

After hearing my thunderous screams in his office, Mr Mus. tried twice to reach me on my mobile. From these threats, he understood that this time I would not let the incident go without taking some action. In effect, this step appeared to terrify him. I unleashed a torrent of reproach, rebuking him for his hypocrisy in maintaining a soft voice when speaking to me while his employees and clientele came across as abusive, vandalising the building not only by their treatment of the building and its amenities, including the elevator, but by turning a blind eye to the accumulating dirt, the cigarette butts on the stairs, and the endless discarded gum. After screaming at him on the phone for a while, I decided to go to the Doqi police station to make a *mahdar* about the unauthorised conversion of residential space and its implications of its transformation for commercial use. The officers were ready to lend a hand, as my physical appearance, with my short grey hair and obvious class affiliation, renders me quite exotic, if not downright odd. A young and good-looking officer, Mr Ahmed, was directed to help me by his superior officer, the *hadret al-baasha* (the 'pasha', a title given to officers and other higher-status persons), who kept on authoritatively giving him orders. This superior kept shouting in a theatrical manner, urging him to be more efficient and hurry up in serving me. The helpless Officer Ahmed, on the other hand, was pleasant and rather cheerful as he listened to what I had to say. He seemed fairly familiar with my narrative of the disruptive neighbours. It seemed that he received hundreds of complaints daily from the Doqi district about poorly regulated commercial activities. Officer Ahmed was skilled at drafting petitions where the specifics of an official language are required to make the complaints plausible in official circles dealing with injunctions related to infringements of the law. Indeed, he was well trained in writing the specialised language required to convey my complaint in the *mahdar*. However, it was clear that all he really wanted was to finish his job as soon as possible and go home, as it was an unbearably hot summer day, reaching over forty degrees, and above all, it was Ramadan. When I urged Mr Ahmed to make an appearance at our building to threaten my neighbour, he smiled approvingly, but as far as he was concerned, my demand was only wishful thinking. Good-looking and smiling Officer Ahmed told me that I should take the *mahdar* to the *ra'is al-hay* (district chief) of Doqi to file a complaint about the infringement of the commercial spaces on the residential flats. I returned home, stopping at the perfume and cosmetics company. They photocopied the *mahdar*, and Mrs M. M. promised to distribute it to all the residents. When I passed by two days later, the *mahdar* was still on the desk on the pretext that their bellboy had not shown up. It was once more a waste of time, as no one was really interested in confrontations or fights, and Mrs M. M. was not impressed by my efforts to take the matter forwards.

On 10 June 2017, Mr Mus. brought in a new elevator repairman – certainly not Amm Sayyed – and reinstalled a key identical to the previous one. Mr Mus. apologised to Mr Al. when he realised that a collective anger was building against his actions.

Immediately after the key incident, I informed Mr Al. that I was pulling out of the meetings and discussions about the elevator and boycotting any talk with Mr Mus. Before I left for the summer holidays, Mr Al. informed me that one more meeting took place at the perfume and cosmetics company, and a final agreement was reached on the replacement of the elevator. The Shefs co-working space agreed to take over the renovation and contribute a higher share of the repair costs. My reply to Mr Al. was that I would only pay my due share for the renovation after one year, depending on how the usage and maintenance went. However, my feeling was that Mr Mus. had finally managed to dictate his own agenda to all the residents in the building.

By now it had become clear to me that I needed to get out of Doqi soon, as the deterioration of the building continued at an alarming speed, with more flats turning into commercial outlets. The first-floor flat, recently sold to a rich Saudi investor, was meant to be transformed into an office for training teachers for export to Saudi Arabia. The Egyptian consultant to the Saudi investor informed me that they intended to increase the flat's capacity to receive over 300 customers daily. The Saudi investor soon expanded his entrance onto the staircase, thus appropriating a large part of the corridor leading to the common areas of the stairs. The renovation made it necessary to remove the old Carrara marble of the stairs, to be replaced with a cheaper stone that looks like toilet tiles, creating an incredible aesthetic discordance with the older features that gave the building its character.

The renovations of the first-floor flat started in January 2017 and continued until November. The owner decided to tear down all the internal walls, in the process removing a significant number of iron bars, causing considerable worry to Mr Al., whose flat is directly above it. For months, the entrance door of the devastated flat was left open, leaking water all over the stairs. On 6–9 June 2017, during Ramadan, an unbearable heat wave hit Cairo, but it did not hinder further renovations made to the fourth-floor flat belonging to a well-to-do woman from the Gulf. The workers would start to work around 9 p.m. after the *iftaar*, loading sacks of sand and stones, and finish around 3 a.m., just before dawn. The digging and unbearable noise on the first and fourth floors drove me to phone the police twice.

Mr Al., for his part, resorted to the police station nine times because of the renovation schedule that went on after midnight, day after day. In the building, the news circulated about the unfortunate ninety-three-year-old Mrs Sha., who could not sleep at all because of the unremitting hammering coming out of these renovations. The demolition of the walls and the removal of the iron bars drove Mr Al. to complain to the *baladiyya* or the *hay* (the administration of the district). They sent an expert to check if any breach of regulations had been committed. All the older residents, including me, were seriously afraid that the building might collapse at any time. Apparently, according to the administration, no breach of regulations had occurred. But who really knows whether bribery was used in order to create documents to protect someone's dubious economic interests?

By now, our neighbourhood police officer who was best acquainted with the situation seemed to have arrived at an entente with the Saudi owner of the first-floor flat and the son of the *bawaab*. Once a complaint was filed by telephone, he would unfailingly turn up for half an hour, to tell us that the noise would soon cease. I recall that one night, upon returning home at eleven o'clock, I found a man with a donkey cart at the entrance, removing from the first floor a number of heavy iron bars, which were probably sold at the *sabtiyya* second-hand iron market. Meanwhile, the street cafés often remained open until the early morning, producing such unbearable levels of noise that one was compelled to sleep with closed windows. Sleep might as well have been an outlawed act in our quarter, and sleep deprivation more the norm. Life during the Ramadan summer of 2017 became truly unbearable.

## Who has no quandary with water?

No old building in Cairo escapes the numerous tribulations related to water shortages due to the antiquated system of water mains. No one would be astonished at the recurrent water shortages in our quarter, particularly in summer, and yet 'respectable' Doqi is far from being a slum.

On top of our building, similar to countless Cairene buildings, a tank for water storage was installed, obviously long ago. Despite the fact that ever since I moved into this building, everyone has complained that the tank was forever filthy, no action was ever taken. Traditionally, Y., the *bawaab*, used to clean the tank on a regular basis: in times when the 'building was still respectable' and the residents were 'beks' (*bahawaat*) and 'upper class', as Y. puts it in a nostalgic, yet ironic tone. During these 'beautiful times', according to Y., he climbed the roof and cleaned the tank at least twice a year, since he was remunerated for it. This was a dangerous and tough job, as it required climbing the roof. In more recent years, Y. has refused to clean the water tank, as he increasingly felt that he was unjustly treated by the residents. For Y., the feeling of 'respectability' is associated with the previous residents who departed a long time ago, in contrast to today's 'disrespectable', but still wealthy, residents. In fact, Y. has often harshly (and perhaps hypocritically) made fun of these more recent arrivals in my presence, when I invested more cash from my personal purse to clean the stairwells, or overpaid (according to the rest of the residents) the rubbish collector. How often has

Y. commented that some of my neighbours are certainly richer than me, but stingy with money and nasty when communal spending for the building is required? Also, Y. would insist that he was never hit or bullied by any of the previous residents, or insulted, as has been the case with more recent arrivals. Umm Tam., too, often refers to the nostalgic past using exactly the same expression of 'during the earlier times when the building was respectable and the people better educated', in contrast to today's more vulgar residents, according to her point of view. Here the reference to education translates to a form of civility and politeness that has disappeared from view. It is not that today the residents are less educated, but obviously in the popular imagination, while they are certainly better off economically than the previous residents, they definitely lack manners and the credibility associated with them. This means that mistreatment goes both ways. So, when Y. was once hit by one of my neighbours, his revenge was to disappear for a while, immobilise the elevator, and cease to clean the entrance hall and stairs.

Returning to the water problem, luckily the container finally collapsed last year, because of two tremendous leaks that brought a finale to its functionality. Two neighbours (Mr Al. being one of them) took the initiative of replacing it with a new one in March 2016, after an intense, powerful, and frightening waterfall cascaded down one stairwell to form an instant swimming pool, terrifying all the residents with the possibility of causing a fire by coming into contact with the exposed, antiquated, and falling-apart electric meters.

The low water pressure on the higher floors is an additional problem that is often solved by installing small private (or individual) pumps. This always weakens the water pressure on the lower floors, as the shares of water for the upper floors are, in a sense, hijacked from the lower floors. This is why, in theory, individual pumps should be installed only after consulting the entire building. However, this has never been the case, as by now we all know that each resident acts automatically as he pleases. In almost all the older buildings of Cairo, there usually exists one main water pipeline that feeds the whole building. The water bills are charged collectively to the entire building, to be divided according to the number of flats. A collective electrical water pump operates for the entire building. Ours has been subject to numerous breakdowns, causing recurrent water cuts. Since the transformation of some units of the building into commercial areas, the problem of collecting bills has not been totally resolved, because in principle, the commercial units are charged much higher rates for water than the residential units. The next problem is that most of the shops, as well as the largest owner, who owns four flats, refuse to pay their share of the collective water and electricity bills. In fact, the water company has several times cut the water due to unpaid bills, which mainly harmed the residents; the shop owners are less concerned because, in case of water cuts, they can obtain water from the public tap at the end of the street.

Meanwhile, for some unknown reason the collective water bills end up amounting to thousands of pounds. These are often not paid on time because there is never enough cash remaining with the treasurer, Mrs M. M., the secretary from the cosmetics and perfume company. Mrs M. M. actually advised me to disconnect my water from the communal water pipeline, as their company did. When I started the bureaucratic procedure of installing independent pipelines and a water meter, Mr Al. protested vehemently in one of the association meetings, arguing that such a step would be disastrous if each of the fifteen flats installed its own pipelines. The stairwells would become even more dangerous with masses of pipelines, individual electrical pumps, and wires competing for space with the electric meters. He was perhaps right, as it turned out that there was no space to place the water meter except at the entrance of the collapsing garage (its ceiling almost falling down), with lengthy pipelines extending to the fifth floor. Since no resident was able to put pressure on the water consumption of the garage keepers, who earn their living by washing countless cars in the neighbourhood, and since we have often been threatened with water cuts, I was followed by the third-floor neighbour, and a total of three residents ended up installing our own pipelines with independent meters. In fact, we jammed the garage and the building itself with even more do-it-yourself pipelines, piercing even more holes and further destroying the back stairwells. As a result, the entrance of the garage now contains three water meters, plus two extra water pumps. In fact, if you are keen on spotting details of Cairene life, you will notice that many buildings today are overwhelmed with these water meters, often located on the back or side of the ground floor of the building.

### As if water meters do count

The process of obtaining the water meter was another long and torturous path that took me almost four months to complete. Here is the detailed description of the long course to be followed, leading to the external visual chaos described earlier.

The main hero of our story at this point is Mr Mohamed, the most expensive plumber I have ever had in Cairo. Before fixing the water, one month earlier, Mr Mohamed had replaced all the sewage pipelines on my entire side of the building, after we found out that they were leaking near the electrical wires, which might have caused any number of electrocutions. When I asked my neighbours to share Mr Mohamed's bill for this assignment, three of them consented. However, after the work was complete, almost all the neighbours refused to come up with their share, claiming that Mr Mohamed charged unreasonable rates (8,000 L.E.). One person insisted that I had been cheated because, according to him, the imported German brand of plastic pipeline that Mr Mohamed had proudly installed had a flaw. He also claimed their own plumber was certainly better (and more superior) than Mr Mohamed.

**Figure 18**   Water meters, 15 September 2016.

**Figure 19**   Water meters, 6 January 2017.

**Figure 20**  Water meters and pumps, 6 January 2017.

Two other neighbours insisted that the pipeline had never leaked, that it was just Mr Mohamed's unprofessional assessment and imagination, that my endeavour was useless and a waste of time, and that they had changed their minds and would not reimburse me. These were the same neighbours who also refused to increase their payments to the rubbish collector, claiming that they did not produce rubbish, and if they did, their servants would go down to throw the rubbish in the stairwells, as if this would be a valid reason to *not* pay the rubbish collector. However, Mr Mohamed expected this reaction, and had accordingly insisted that a significant amount be paid in advance before he took on his job.

Mr Mohamed's specialization is pipeline work in a style he calls *bil habl* (with a rope). It involves hanging dangerously from the top floor, sitting on a slim piece of wood supported by two ropes. Working from top to bottom, he replaces, bit by bit, all the pipelines of the building, with the help of a crew of four workers. This is fascinating to watch, and is an extremely laborious task, which goes some way to explaining the high rates he charges his customers.

The procedure of applying for a water meter (*'addaad*) is quite an intricate process. It requires patience and perseverance with the Egyptian bureaucracy. The water company serving the Doqi district is located in Giza, in so-called modernised offices overlooking the Nile. Astonishingly, upon my first visit, I encountered young, good-looking, pleasant women willing to assist the clients, while remaining quite distant or sometimes even hostile towards their male colleagues. On the other hand, the male employees looked all worn out, and some of them were quite unpleasant with their customers.

Here are the instructions they issued. First, one needs to go to the water company with the contract proving ownership of the property, to pay the unpaid water bills. But since no bills have ever been issued for my flat, a sort of arbitrary calculation was made by a worn-out male employee, who looked like a heavy hashish addict and who pretended to ponder my file at length – a fictive file, which obviously lacked any documentation regarding the water consumption of my flat. As this worn-out employee took a thick packet of money out of his pocket, he concluded spontaneously (or so it seemed to me) that I should pay some 1,400 L.E. for the months that were not paid by the administration of our building – i.e. the collective monthly bill sent to Mrs M. M. of the cosmetics and perfume company. My impression was that the employee calculated that sum based on my appearance and my apparent class affiliation – obviously, I belonged to the better-off residents, as my title of *doktoorah* would suggest. Later on, my neighbour Mr Al tried to subtract what I paid from the overall unpaid bills of the building and the sum did not make much sense. Never mind: let us consider it a kind of *ettaawah* (the tax collected during Mamluk times) to the State. Then a request is written and filed at the water company. One can then purchase the water meter, but its installation requires a few more months. One is instructed that the next step consists of the owner (me) installing 'special' thin pipelines that have to be connected to the main pipeline.

Mr Mohamed, the plumber, who is highly experienced in this kind of work, purchased the longest 'special' thin pipelines I have seen in my entire life (as I recall, over fifty metres of pipeline). These were installed on the outer wall of the garage, for lack of space elsewhere, then extended upwards through five floors and down again. This acrobatic operation cost me some 10,000 L.E. While Mr Mohamed was installing the pipelines, numerous fights erupted with the neighbours, who claimed that the pipes could be hit by cars entering and leaving the garage. Endless problems then arose with my newly installed water pump, as well as with the location of the new water meter, which was right next to the water meter of the perfume company and their newly installed electrical water pump that blew up a couple of times, causing another inundation to the garage. But that was not the whole story. One of the main sewage pipelines leaked recurrently from the bottom into the garage, threatening to flood the place while producing unpleasant miasmas. The plumber hired by one of my neighbours fixed only one part of the pipeline, while he let it leak on the other side. Mr Mohamed then fixed it, leading to more endless controversies with the neighbours about payment.

After the installation of the water pipelines, an employee from the water company has to inspect the work and approve it. This inspector first disapproved of the width of the pipelines, which were the wrong size according to the company's standards. Mr Mohamed insisted that this was not the case. After long phone calls, begging, insisting, and nagging, the employee finally approved the pipelines. My file was then sent to an entirely different administration in the Kit-Kat neighbourhood, so that their employees would now in be in a position to install the water meter. This step alone took two more months, as the employees came while I was away and then would not install the meter without some extra cash. After almost two months of chasing the employees, Mr Mohamed agreed to go to the water company, paid the instalment required (the *bakshish*), and the job was done.

But then more fights ensued between the neighbours and Mr Mohamẹd about the location of my meter, as the neighbours' meter was attached to the main pipeline. These fights went on for some time, each blaming the other for the repeated leakages and other small disasters that occurred on a daily basis. Then an iron box was installed around the pump, supposedly kept locked to protect the pump from theft, but the lock was useless and this part of the job was never really completed. Mr Mohamed acknowledged that the work was sloppy, but he seemed to have become fed up with the constant skirmishes with the neighbours. He then installed two electrical pumps, to be controlled from the kitchen (for which the electrician, installing wiring cables from the ground floor to the fifth floor, charged some 5,000 L.E.). This was meant to increase my water pressure since the water was being drawn from two sources: the upper tank as well as the main pipeline. But this made the water pressure too strong, so that it was no real solution. Finally, the water that came out had a red-brown colour. Mr Mohamed insisted that this is a characteristic of the Chinese pumps he installed. After all that work, the colour of the tap water remains muddy and brown to this day.

The fights between Mr Mohamed and Mrs M. M. from the perfume company escalated as the small water-pump disasters continued to multiply. As time passed, Mr Mohamed ended up conducting several wars on different fronts in the building. One was against the *bawaab*, who apparently asked him to pay extra money for access to the building to complete the plumbing work. Another war was against some of the neighbours, who protested the holes he was making in the walls to fix the sewage pipeline. Then came the explosion with Mrs M. M. on the placement of the water meter that led to water cuts at the perfume company, and the reappearance of muddy red tap water for longer periods.

Mr Mohamed was truly disgusted at the despicable state of the stairwell, which looked like a wounded belly spouting deracinated wires, dilapidated electricity meters, and the numerous air conditioners of all the first-floor shops. But how truly shocked could he be when so many of the stairwells in Cairo probably look that way?

Mr Mohamed never really finished the job in my flat. I am convinced that he was simply fed up after long months of endless work. He predicted even more unforeseen problems, because when one problem was nearly done, another appeared in a never-ending cycle. The last time I saw him, he told me seriously, 'You should sell your flat. What I experienced in this building, I have never seen elsewhere ... this is a horrible place ... with horrible residents, and they are all liars.' He even proposed to me two possible flats for sale in Mohandessin as he urged me to find a way to move out of the building. Apparently he was not the only worker who was disgusted with the entire setting. Since I installed the water meter in 2016, the employee has come only once to read it. I am still not really sure that he charged me the correct price for the meter, and I might not ever sort that out.

**Figure 21**    Stairwells and rubbish, 24 September 2016.

## The surreal stairwells and the *bawaab*'s space

> Almost every wealthy person in Cairo has a 'bowwab', or door-keeper, always at
> the door of his home, and several other male servants. Most of these are natives
> of Egypt; but many Nubians are also employed as servants in Cairo and other
> Egyptian towns. The latter are mostly bowwabs, and are generally esteemed
> more honest than the Egyptian servants; but I am inclined to think, from the
> opinion of several of my friends, and from my own experience, that they have
> acquired this reputation only by superior cunning. (Lane 2005 [1836]: 158)[1]

Aside from being styled as a 'classical' orientalist text,[2] and therefore subjected
to critical scrutiny after the positive reception of Edward Said's *Orientalism*,
E. W. Lane's observations remain intriguing and certainly worth consulting,
especially those pertaining to questions of continuity and transformation in
the current customs of Cairenes. Yet, what makes it so deranging is rather
the continuity of certain habits over a time span of almost 200 years, and
yet this continuity can never be identical to the past.

There is nothing unique about the *bawaab*'s dwelling in my building. All
Cairene buildings seem to share one identical trait: namely, the most depressing living space is that of the *bawaab*, the doorkeeper of the building, who
is treated like a half-slave by most of the residents. Yet the slave's 'hidden
rule' should never be ignored, as in some respects he can become an enslaver
of his master. The so-called slaves have the power to stop elevators whenever
they please, and claim that they cannot be repaired. They can also lock
entrance doors and ruin both locks and keys. They can unintentionally or
intentionally spoil water pumps and motors. Or they can simply disappear
for long periods of time, leaving the entire building to sink into neglect.
Their sons might work as cleaners in some of the flats, providing them with
irresistible access to knowledge about each resident's privacy, secrets, habits,
and vices. They are often sent to purchase food and pay telephone bills.
Physically living on the level of the ground floor makes them a literal 'lower
caste'. One can only wonder why so many residents remain in constant
denial of the despicable living conditions of those living just underneath
their flats. Why is it that no resident dares to gaze even briefly at the sight
of the frighteningly filthy stairwells?

It is as if, by nature or providence, *bawaab*s don't really deserve to have
any privacy. In most Egyptian buildings, the *bawaab*'s family ends up living
in just one tiny, creepy pseudo-room. Our *bawaab* basically claimed a space
from one of the rear stairwells that he turned into two tiny, dark rooms; five
persons lived in this shared space until a few years ago. The living room
includes an oven, chairs, and beds. Privacy is practically impossible to maintain
in such a space. The only window through which some meagre light can
penetrate has been forged from the entrance hall of the building, facing the
elevator. Thus, the people who come and go can hear everything in the
*bawaab*'s living-cum-sleeping room while waiting for the elevator. When the

electricity employee comes each month to read the meter, he has to go through the *bawaab*'s private space, as the counters are just a few metres away from the living room. If any problem arises in the rear stairs, or if the rubbish collector wants to clean the stairs, he has to go through the *bawaab*'s 'flat'. (The rubbish collector's only other option is to go up the opposite rear stairs and come down from the roof.)

As long as the beautiful H., the former wife of Y., the *bawaab*, lived in the building, she kept this tiny space impeccably clean and tidy in spite of its creepiness. H. was a hard-working and sincere woman who eventually took over her husband's responsibilities for the entire building, especially in later years when Y. started working elsewhere as a taxi driver, vanishing from the building for long periods. Things deteriorated, however, when H. got cancer and was seriously ill. We then heard that Y. repudiated and divorced the beautiful H. and once again vanished from our building. Her sons told me that she now lives on her own in the Bulaq quarter. Not much later, Y. brought into the building a younger and apparently inexperienced second wife.

I often heard from my neighbours a sort of a repertoire about our *bawaab*'s contested life story. Y., the *bawaab*, is one more *Saa'iidi* (Upper Egyptian) who arrived to take up residence in Cairo. He is remembered by many as having been, in his younger days, a pleasant, hard-working, and honest man. During his early years in Cairo he married his first wife, H., after a passionate and romantic love story, as both families were against their marriage – in particular because H. was an exceptionally fine-looking, intelligent, and remarkable woman. H. ran away from her strict and conservative Upper Egyptian family after serious threats about what would happen if she married Y., which she did. The fervent love story ended happily with a secret marriage, after which the couple had to hide for several months in the villa of an influential upper-class family in Zamalek who protected them.

When young Y. had freshly arrived from Upper Egypt to work in the building, he was much loved and respected. As time went by, however, it seems that Y. lost this initial innocence, recalled by numerous neighbours as if they were all reading from an identical script. The kind and naive Y. apparently underwent a personality transmutation, or at least this is the constructed narrative with which the residents would like to paint Y.'s portrait. Certainly, Y. realised that the meagre salary he was earning would get him nowhere, so he started to moonlight doing wheeling and dealing jobs on the side. One of these drew on his astuteness as a real-estate middleman, spreading the word about rents and sales of flats in the area. Apparently, it was also Y. who managed to bring in all the downstairs shops by extracting a percentage from both parties to finalise the commercial transaction.[3] As the years went by, Y. completely lost interest in the building, making it clear that the cash he was earning elsewhere through other informal activities had redirected his ambitions, as we heard he had purchased a small plot of agricultural land around Giza. This allowed him to move into another residence with his second wife, who keeps a foot in each. In practical terms, his two elder sons are the ones who take care of the building, since for the past two years, I have never seen Y. clean or do anything else in the building. Y. probably also lost the sympathy of many of the neighbours when he divorced his sick wife and began to appear more utilitarian in his principles.

The circulating gossip was that Y. won the custody of the children in the divorce settlement, with the result that his then five-year-old youngest son was left in the sole care of his two brothers (ages fourteen and nineteen) in the building. The youngest son must have suffered from the adverse effect of being brought up by his siblings, and there is suspicion that this might be the cause of what many believe are autistic symptoms. Immediately after Y. married his second wife, he had a daughter who won all the family's attention at the expense of this youngest son.

The three sons have remained in the two rooms under the back stairs of the building. But since H. left, their living space has also witnessed an obvious degeneration. Recently, miasmas coming out of Y.'s rooms have extended to the elevator. The younger wife appears to ignore these issues related to hygiene. But her extended family, her mother and numerous male cousins, also originating from Upper Egypt, often colonise the entrance hall and the back stairs of the building leading to the garage, so that, upon entering the building, one is often confronted by a large gathering of people occupying the back entrance door and the stairs, which are transformed into an open-air living room. Y.'s relationship to many of the residents deteriorated to the point that in 2013 one resident slapped him; he felt that Y. had failed to show sufficient respect in a conversation after he forgot to lock the rear door leading to the garage. Y. had developed in recent years an aggressive way of speaking to almost all the residents of the building, sometimes including me (even though I pay him correctly and give extra money to his sons for cleaning the stairs). This attitude suggests a certain carelessness, if not defiance, towards the humble job he is doing. A subjective reading of Y. could be that he turned bipolar, causing him to be extremely helpful and show that he is protecting my interests one day, while turning quite nasty the next day. Along the years, Y. started to accumulate enemies. Even though he had misbehaved a couple of times, he came to me twice asking for help. He was complaining that his wallet was once stolen from his flat, and then his motorcycle. I told him to ask around amongst his close friends in the neighbourhood who knew what they were doing and were probably taking vengeance for some unknown issue, which I refused to know about or listen to. Instead, I gave him some cash he might need to cover his immediate needs.

## Major transformations – '*Tout est bien qui fini bien*': A happy ending with the elevator? Not really

A significant transformation occurred in the life of our little universe, a quasi-miracle, coinciding with my return on 7 October 2017 after my sabbatical absence. A new elevator had finally been installed. I was kept informed about

**Figure 22**  New resident altering entrance and floor of my building, 5 May 2018.

the progress of the work during the entire summer via emails and telephone calls from the daughter of Mrs Mars., my next-door neighbour. Mrs Mars, who can barely walk, decided to take a long break away from the building by staying on the North Coast, clearly in order to avoid taking the stairs, because the building was deprived of its elevator for nearly four months. The fact that I, too, took a four-month break from my building allowed me to calm down and distance myself from the mounting tensions with my other neighbours.

Upon my arrival, I was informed that all the residents had finally contributed financially to the replacement of the elevator. The work on the new elevator took three months, from the end of June to the end of September 2017. Numerous meetings took place during my absence, as I was informed by my neighbours. While it was Mr Mus. who was the main instigator of the replacement, the contract was signed under the umbrella of the director of the perfume company because of his informal status as treasurer of the building. Besides that, he has come to earn the confidence of the residents and a sound reputation for financial honesty in our building. Luckily, and after so many years of negotiation, talks, fights, and disagreement, all the partners of our building (excluding me, since I was away and had already decided to move out of the building) had agreed on a specific company.

The story, as told to me by Mr Al., went as follows: it just so happened that the director of the perfume company had an acquaintance who is the director of a reputable elevator company, and he accordingly struck a deal with him based on trust and friendship. Naturally, as is so often the case with trade workers in Egypt, the elevator company promised to finish the work in a couple of months, but instead took four months. The new elevator was estimated to cost around 100,000 L.E. Each flat's share amounted to 8,000 L.E., plus 500 L.E. for an additional backup system for electricity cuts.

The contract was signed on 21 June 2017 with a company called the Arab Lift Company. The contract was circulated to all residents and was signed on behalf of all residents by the director of the perfume company as the main partner with the elevator company. The contract stated that the elevator would be installed at the cost of 105,000 L.E. The work was to begin on 1 July 2017, and the date of delivery of the finished elevator was to be 15 August 2017. As a main condition, the first instalment, payable in advance, was 52,500 L.E., or 50 per cent of the total value. The next 25 per cent was to be paid after installing the outer door, the cabin, and the motor, then the final 25 per cent after installing the elevator and putting it into operation. Monthly maintenance check-ups would be free for the first full year. In case of late delivery, 1,000 L.E. for each week of delay would be deducted from the total amount. The monthly payment to the company for the elevator's maintenance after the one-year guarantee is 250 L.E.

In the end, the company was five weeks late in delivering the elevator, which meant that 5,000 pounds were deducted from the sum, reducing it to 100,000 L.E. It was agreed that the perfume company would pay 30,000 L.E. of the total and the Shefs co-working space the amount of 20,000 L.E., since as commercial enterprises they were the heaviest users of the elevator. The shares for me and my neighbour on the fifth floor amounted to 8,000 L.E. each, plus 800 L.E. for additional work on the security system of the elevator.

The Palestinian women's hostel also had to pay a higher share, as the number of residents was fifteen and sometimes even more. It was also agreed that the co-working space would pay 1,000 L.E. per month for maintenance, which would include the higher electricity bills. It was further agreed to raise the general maintenance fee of the building from 130 L.E. per month to 180 L.E.

After the new elevator was installed, it was decided that anyone should have free access to it for going up, while a magnetic key (distributed only to the residents who paid their share) would be used for getting down. This was a concession made to the co-working space. Meanwhile, it seems that many people have managed to reproduce the plastic magnetic key, allowing a heavier load of passengers going up and down than had been anticipated. Small skirmishes occurred, as the son of the perfume company director made a deal with the elevator company to open the elevator for going down without a key from the third floor only, and did not inform the residents.

The new elevator has no character at all, and its design is representative of the current taste found everywhere. The charming old wooden cabin has been replaced by an ugly, but functional (as some would believe) metal one, with a mirror and a fake, locally produced yellow marble floor ornamented with unappealing oriental patterns and flowers, while the musical theme from the *Love Story* movie is lightly heard upon arrival at the selected floor. Very ugly iron doors replaced the stylish old wooden ones. These were installed without undertaking the final painting and repairs, leaving the entrance hall and the hallway areas of all five floors in a devastated state. But who really cares about aesthetics or outer appearances at this point? It is as if the building's belly has had one more scar added after a long and difficult surgery.

Six months after its installation, the new, modern elevator started to turn erratic. It often suffers unexplained paralyses that can last for a couple of days. Above all, it started to emulate the old elevator by again pausing mysteriously between floors. This means that the modernised system of locked doors can be even more dangerous and frightening than the old elevator. In such a scenario, no *bawaab* can come to the rescue as was the case before. The residents obtained an answer that silenced all of them. This is a highly sophisticated, digital system that functions with a laser touch, which is why it gets easily interrupted.

Tensions eased a bit – only for a short time, unfortunately – leading me to reconcile with Mr Mus. I decided to contribute half of my share of the elevator, and promised to pay the other half within a year on the condition that the elevator was kept clean and well maintained. He and his newly hired young female employees, who are all students from Cairo University, became friendlier to me and seemed to be more receptive to my comments and criticism. This time I used the argument that it has been two years now that I have been repeating identical comments about noise and the dirt in the elevator. Since the problem of the elevator had been partially solved, surely we could find a solution for the common good of the building being kept clean. On 28 October 2017, less than a month after the new elevator came into service, the first chewing gum appeared on my floor. This led to further negotiations about cleaning the stairs. After several visits to Mr Mus.'s office, repeatedly trying to convince them that it is to everyone's benefit to have a clean floor, they finally removed the chewing gum. Meanwhile, Mr Mus. decided to change the concept of the co-working space by raising his fee and becoming, so to speak, more 'elitist', leading to a decrease in customers. This was accompanied by one more renovation of his flat, which included cleaning the marble of the stairs.

Then I suggested that Mr Mus. purchase a simple mechanism that would automatically close the front door of his space. On 21 November 2017, the gentle, smiling female student proudly came to inform me that the door would finally close automatically, which made such a difference. I promised I would purchase a plant for their balcony once they finished the renovation. Then Mr Mus. came up with the idea of painting the entrance of the building. He asked me to sign up for his idea, since my signature would encourage all the other neighbours to pay.

Unfortunately, this productive truce did not last long. The co-working space began leaving their door open again, with no regard to our deal about keeping the door closed to reduce the noise, resulting in continuous fights stemming from my complaints. All the conversations in their flat can still be heard in my entrance halls, kitchen, and living room all day along. I spent almost two years shouting and complaining on a daily basis. It became a sort of a ritual for me that whenever I went out of my door, I automatically entered the co-working space and told them to shut their door. Countless times, I lost control. Finally, I started to renegotiate the main issue: cleanliness can only be beneficial to all.

The 'bellboy' has in the meanwhile been replaced by an elderly cleaning woman who takes away the litter from our floor and the one downstairs every day. To be fair, a certain improvement on our floor is evident.

### Virtual disappearance of the *bawaab*

A rather less cheerful and dramatic event occurred in September 2017. Our *bawaab* and his entire family practically evacuated the building. His flat was deserted and remains so until today. Many of us thought that something must have happened to him. In fact, he re-emerges only every Friday around seven o'clock in the morning, when everyone is sleeping, to silently clean the stairs with his son. And since I am the only early riser in the building, my guess is that Y. seems to want to avoid the residents.

I was later informed by the running gossip that Y.'s life has been completely altered. His ex-wife filed a lawsuit against him for *nafaqah* (child support according to Islamic law), and apparently won. The court ruled that her ex-husband should pay the amount of 29,000 L.E. for the arrears of child support. I was told by one of my neighbours that our *bawaab* had avoided paying child support, which carries a prison sentence. Thus he is awaiting the court proceedings and the sentence of imprisonment. He seemed more inclined towards the idea of going to prison for a few months rather than making amends with his ex-wife and paying for his children. His strategy is thus to hide in his second and probably undeclared house in the Saft al-Laban popular quarter. Apparently, too, his former wife had 'kidnapped' the youngest child from school, as the neighbours informed me. Numerous residents in our building commented upon her act as rational and humane, since it had been noticed that the child was mostly left alone and neglected by his stepmother. He was often seen playing on his own in the entrance hall of the building for entire days, with no care or supervision. My suspicion was that he was developing autistic behaviour to shelter himself after his stepmother delivered a daughter immediately after the wedding who was treated like a little princess. Meanwhile, the second son from the first marriage left his father's residence and chose to live with his mother after failing school, apparently because he didn't get along with his stepmother. Our *bawaab* justified his physical disappearance by the fact that less than half of the residents pay him a monthly salary, and many had fallen out with him and were boycotting him. Recently, Y. informed my neighbour that nothing would really compel him to work for the building.

In earlier times I tried to engage with his sons by assigning them small extra tasks like watering my plants on the stairs, cleaning up the chewing gum (which is a tedious task, as it has to be done with a knife), or carrying some heavy luggage, giving them a generous tip. Unfortunately, this did not really work out for them in the long run. I then turned to giving a small monthly salary to the middle son, who was then sixteen and whom I liked. At the start, he was always enthusiastic. Alas, as time went by, his stamina to keep up the work failed him. Half of my plants disappeared and the other half died. He has often been seen working at the bag shop, but he was soon dismissed for apparently the same reason. Recently, he moved to a job in the small bookshop in the next building, but once again, he did not last more than a couple of months.[4] Unfortunately, he was also dismissed from school. Neighbours have often made vile comments about his lack of intelligence, accusations that merely reproduced simplistic class biases, as if he naturally deserved a life of servitude. Contrary to what had circulated about this young boy's character, I found him highly intelligent, but distracted and lacking basic attention skills, by the sheer fact of his limited opportunities and the deplorable conditions and accommodation. It would have required some impossibly Herculean efforts on his part not to reproduce the stereotypes into which he has been moulded.

Would Y., the *bawaab*, leave our building on his own accord? Any attempt to evict him from his two-room pseudo-flat would be practically impossible. It would be even more difficult to fire him, since no unified and formal body representing the interests of the residents has been created. The effective disappearance of Y. coincides with the theft, or rather the vandalising, of the iron bars on top of the stairs on 17 October 2017, and the constant invasion of a number of beggars knocking at all of the doors simultaneously.

Ironically, on 25 January 2018, a significant burglary took place in the office of the perfume company, a worrying incident that had no precedent in our building. Apparently, two men climbed the stairwells, broke the windows, and managed to steal some 800,000 L.E. and consumer items (perfumes and cosmetics) worth 100,000 L.E. This was actually the fourth time that the office was broken into. However, it was by far the most serious theft. At first, the company owner refused to contact the police, because he wanted to avoid any useless nuisance. He was no doubt convinced of the inefficiency of the police in such cases. Then the *bawaab* convinced the company owner to let the police interfere. As soon as the police arrived, the *bawaab* was dramatically taken from the building in handcuffs. He was kept at the police station for some six hours. There was no physical abuse, but mostly insults and despicable treatment. Furthermore, the *bawaab*'s brother and cousins, who live in the neighbourhood, were also arrested and investigated. The police finally resorted to the surveillance cameras located in front of the school across the street. We were told that two unidentified men (clearly not our *bawaab*) were seen loading the merchandise into a taxi. Apparently this theft was one of a large number of robberies of villas in gated communities by professional criminals. The *bawaab* was resentful and angry because he was the one who persuaded the perfume company director to contact the police, but had ended up being mistreated by the police. He later communicated to me his belief that the thieves must have been in close contact with someone within the company, as it could not have been a coincidence that such a large sum of money was in the office at the time unless some inside information had been leaked. None of the residential flats have ever been robbed, but since most of the building has been transformed into commercial enterprises, the *bawaab* asserts that it is practically impossible to control the number of people coming into the building.

Beginning in February 2018 (well after I moved out of the flat), the brand-new elevator started to have unexplainable electric breakdowns quite dissimilar to the previous interruptions. Then, in April 2018, the breakdowns occurred every second day. The maintenance employee from the elevator company discovered to his dismay that some mobster had been continuously removing some spare parts incorporating an arrangement of nails from the front doors (called a 'fork' in colloquial Arabic), resulting in the frequent paralysis of the elevator. As a matter of fact, these acts of hooliganism had been going on for nearly a month and a half without the residents or the *bawaab* being able to find out why this was happening and who was responsible. According to Mr Al. once again, several parts of the various doors on different floors had been dismantled, amounting to some seven serious failures. He reported that these despicable acts happened about four times at the door of the ground floor and three times on the fourth floor, explainable by the fact that there are practically no residents living on the fourth floor.

One possible explanation for this act of hooliganism (once again according to both Mr Al. and Mr Mus., who by now are on good terms) is that the secret enemy of Y., the *bawaab*, has been taking his revenge by constantly fiddling around in our building. But who could the mobster be? And why is it that he repeatedly paralyses the elevator in such a manner as to make it so dangerous?

Mr Al.'s suspicion is that Umm Tam.'s son, the garage keeper, might be the culprit, since a violent fight had recently taken place between him and Y.'s brother, resulting in a grave head injury to Umm Tam.'s son. However, Mr Al. was not fully prepared to accuse Umm Tam.'s son. It is a fact that Umm Tam.'s son has been known for many years in the quarter as a drug addict; nonetheless, he has always displayed affable manners towards most of the residents. Nevertheless, as the repetitive intentional disruptions kept on occurring, and as the spare parts of the doors kept disappearing, Umm Tam.'s son was sent away to a clinic for rehabilitation.

What came next as the proposed solution from both Mr Al. and Mr Mus. was to install surveillance cameras on all five floors. Video and surveillance security cameras companies seem to be in high demand in the cities of New Cairo, Sheikh Zayed, and the Sixth of October. They have become fashionable gadgets in the gated communities and secluded compounds, so why not emulate the surveillance lifestyle? This idea seemed to have won the consent of the majority of the residents. It turned out that the perfume company had been robbed not once but four times, according to the news circulating in our building – one more reason why video camera surveillance seemed necessary. However, no one had so far raised the observation that none of the flats of the absent residents have ever been robbed; instead, only the commercial spaces have been targeted. The newly opened Saudi labour contractor on the first floor had already installed one camera on its floor. Mr Al.'s suggestion was to install a total of eight cameras, three at the entrance hall and one on each floor. This did not seem to me to be a practical solution, considering the fact that a complete blackout reigns on some floors during the night, as light bulbs have been stolen too; nor was I sure how the twenty-four-hour video recordings would be monitored and archived. Mr Mus. communicated later to me that he was willing to keep and control the recording equipment and the PC network in his office. 'Almost every second night, violent fights erupt in the street because of the cafés. The street has become dangerous,' said Mr Mus., expressing serious concern about the security of his own business. I only nodded at Mr Mus. The privileged posture of the distanced observer, which I have adopted, allows me to conclude that the lively street life and the entertaining street fights are a completely different story from flat robberies. It is fascinating, though, how the imagined culture of the guarded compounds has stained my neighbours. Nevertheless, this

kind of mimicry lacks any of the alleged privileges that come with the segregated, gated life.

I moved out of my flat by the end of November 2017, convinced that even
if improvements were to be felt with the new elevator and the more measured
control of the neighbours' noise, the cacophonous public schools and the
quite entertaining but certainly deafening circus life of the street would still
be enough reason to move out. But at least the negotiations over space on
my floor, and the problem of the elevator, were partially solved. Having said
that, the moment my neighbours heard that I was moving out, their doors
were reopened and the noise resumed. I promised my neighbours that I
would pay for the downstairs renovations and still planned to help the co-
working space with plants and other practical solutions to keep the place
clean. But since I paid my share for the elevator, we are back to square one.
Mr Mus. removed the automatic closer on his door, and fights over the open
door and the noise arose time and again. Seriously, I have no regrets whatsoever
about leaving Doqi.

There were equally long negotiations over renovating the entrance hall,
which led to more disagreements and fights between Mr Al. and his neighbours
about the amount to be paid. In January 2018 one more new design company
opened on the first floor in the building, while one more resident moved
out. Another flat owner, who no longer lives in the building, advertised the
sale of one parking space in the garage for 180,000 L.E. This was discovered
by coincidence by Mr Al., who reprimanded him, asserting that the garage
is not private, but communal property. Mr Al. threatened to sue him if
he persisted in trying to sell his garage space. Then, in March 2018, my
next-door neighbour Mrs Fati. took over the responsibility of treasurer of
the building. It seems that the official treasurer, Mrs M. M., stepped down
from the job after the robbery of the perfume company's offices, during
which the fund for the building's utilities was also stolen. Since this was
the fourth robbery of the company's headquarters, the remaining residents
took the collective decision to transfer the treasury to a safer place. However,
two unexpected 'miracles' occurred in May 2018. The entrance hall was
renovated, and the holes in the wall were fixed and repainted, which significantly improved the appearance of the building. It turned out that Mrs Fati.
discovered a surplus amount in the treasury, which was rightly invested in the
entrance hall.

The second miracle was even more surprising: the co-working space finally
installed a soundproof glass door, resulting in the permanent closure of their
main door. Noise was significantly reduced. Mr Mus. felt so proud when he
phoned to specifically announce the installation of the glass door. This was
a sign that he was much concerned about my opinion of him. The plants I
promised as a gift to decorate his office were to arrive soon. However, these
improvements, so to say, did occur after I and a few of the other remaining
residents had already left the building.

If there is a lesson to be learned from the experience of the building, it is that collective action and communal negotiations proved not to be a lost cause. A number of neighbours told me that they perceived my actions of removing the rubbish from the stairwells, fixing the entire sewage system, and negotiating about the elevator as the trigger that incited the residents to collective work. And yet, was it too late, since many residents had already left?

I have to confess that I was extremely privileged to have the financial option of leaving my exhausted building and its disturbing soundscape. The process was not, however, without complications. As some of my older-generation neighbours learned about my decision to depart, they expressed a certain resentment and dismay about the obvious collective exodus of residents. For the past two decades, the older neighbours have seen so many residents, with whom they got along so well, move out for quieter places. Besides that, I have created solidarities and ententes with almost all of the older neighbours. Now that I have left the quarter, I can enjoy the privilege of observing and documenting it from an ethnographer's distance. The lively circus life of my former street is actually quite interesting, as new and fashionable cafés have opened at the head of the street, hosting large crowds of young women and men who are probably all Cairo University students. For them, the street life of the quarter must have attractions.

Moving out has certainly calmed me down. I can finally enjoy the undisturbed sleep that I have missed for so long. For the majority of middle-class Cairenes, my chronicle sounds pretty banal, perhaps a déjà vu soap-opera saga. It simply highlights the pattern of the growing, but logical, escapism of the middle classes towards the fringes of the city, and the characteristics of the city that conspire to displace people. I wonder whether Sisi's grandiose project of the new Egyptian capital will attract the rich as much as it has been advertised.

In retrospect, the experience I went through in Doqi was a continuous and uninterrupted assault on my senses and a violent and yet obscure abuse of my body – an abuse that could hardly be handled psychologically. Self-reflection, or rather, self-analysis, through the process of writing this book, turned out to be an exercise in a mental and humoristic exit. I could already sense that a serious ailment was imminent. At a certain point, my concern was focused on how to trigger the move forwards and find a solution; how to transcend the melodramatic theatrical persona I was unconsciously being moulded into by my interactions in the building. At a certain point, too, the rising tensions prompted me to question my social position as a divorced female academic, living on my own. I began to wonder about the growing sensation of frailty and insecurity from which I suffered after 2011, a feeling that had hardly ever occurred to me when I had previously lived in Zamalek. Why was I ceaselessly battling and fighting? Why was I constantly on the defensive? In particular, why should this be happening after 2011, when the powerful public visibility of protesting women in the streets had mesmerised the world? I wondered whether the degeneration of everyday material conditions, which has shaken even relatively privileged middle-class women like me, had systematically led to a surge in public misogyny.

A number of active feminist groups like *harassmap*, which are highly involved in taking action against sexual assault, continue to work ('HarassMap'). During 2011 and 2012, a number of women spoke up on television about the violence and sexual harassment they underwent in the square. Feminist groups have worked to increase awareness of sexual assault. Other ongoing endeavours towards empowering women include the Nazra Association for Feminist Studies (unfortunately banned recently), the continuous efforts of the Women and Memory group, the significant role of human rights activists like Aida Seif al-Dawla, the publicising of the problem of violence, the growing public visibility of gifted and intelligent female singers, modern dancers, film directors, musicians, and actors. It seems to me that all these endeavours constitute distinct evidence that women's demands have led to a certain improvement.

Ironically, it might also be that since 2011 the heightened gender awareness has been paired with a growing tendency to inflict hardship on women (and men too). My personal observations suggest that blatant misogyny and overt aggression – from which, perhaps, middle- and upper-class women might have been partly sheltered in earlier times – is today overtly in the air. This brings me to the next point. If the counter-revolution has won a first battle, it was not only through shutting down and jailing opponents, destroying the burgeoning civil society, and forced disappearances; more fundamentally, it triumphed by making everyday life even more Kafkaesque and alienating for the large majority. Everyday life has turned into a permanent battle against irrationally soaring prices and unliveable, inhumane housing conditions that touch not only the poor but extend to the declining middle classes at large. The heroism of the silent majority was not experienced only in the images of the protests in the squares; their heroism today can be seen in the art of surviving, circumventing quotidian injustices and humiliations and trying to navigate a harsh daily life as wisely as possible, while being aware that there will be little, if any, improvement in the future. But above all, my speculation is that a collective staggering feeling of loneliness and alienation is the thing that most strongly overburdens daily life under the military.

Having said that, the case of the Doqi building taught all the residents that collective efforts on a small scale can work. After all, a number of issues (the elevator, the dirty entrance hall, the noise issues on my floor)[5] have been partially solved, precisely because of the growing public awareness of the non-existence of government interference. With the return of the warrior to the secluded bubble island of Zamalek, '*la boucle est bouclée*' (the circle is closed). It seems that I remain a prisoner of my bourgeois aesthetics and perhaps my traumatised childhood, which may explain why my move out of Doqi resulted in my living just across from my grandparents' residence, in which I was born. Given the soaring prices of Zamalek's real estate, I ended up purchasing a flat in a 1960s Bauhaus building that was apparently specifically constructed to house the members of the Czechoslovakian embassy during Nasser's time. The building was probably sold or given away to the rising elites in the early 1970s who could afford living in Zamalek. I recall quite well that, when I lived in the villa as a child in the late 1960s, certain family members held a conceited view of the then new petit bourgeois who were pouring into the newly built high-rise buildings, across from our big and beautiful garden. It is into one of those 'petit bourgeois' buildings that I have moved. Although certainly smaller than my Doqi flat, my Zamalek flat has turned out to be my oasis of peace, where I can simply sleep without being woken up by an upstairs neighbour jogging on the balcony at two o'clock in the morning, causing my flat to quake, or by the police harassing the youth in cafés. I finally understand the luxury of being able to live on the residential island of Zamalek, where the outer gates of the building remain locked with an intercom, and where a *bawaab* whose salary is more than double Y.'s is responsible for paying electricity and gas bills and taking the rubbish downstairs.

## Notes

1 Edward William Lane (1801–76) resided in Cairo in 1825. He spent three years there, and returned in 1828 to complete his *Description of Egypt*. Leaving aside Lane's well-known orientalist outlook, and his ever-recurring tone of immutable continuity and changelessness, this observation still fits in twenty-first-century Cairo.

2 This statement is certainly made by Edward Said in his posthumous work, *Orientalism* (Said 1979: 15).

3 In fact, before I purchased my flat from my friend Laila Bahaa Eddin, Y., under Laila's instructions, had already found another buyer, with whom he had made a deal. However, after I showed interest in purchasing her flat, Laila gave me the priority to purchase it, on the condition of paying Y. a commission for having found the previous buyer. His commission amounted to 50,000 L.E.

4 Some two years earlier, he had been given cleaning jobs at the co-working space, but ended up stealing a PlayStation, thus escalating the tensions between the *bawaab*'s family and the office. He was finally dismissed.

5 The problems of the accumulating rubbish, the collective water bills that are never reimbursed by the street cafés, and the street noise still remain to be solved.

# 6

# Tale IV: Order

In the renewed assault on the island (of Qursaya in 2012), some homes were damaged, and angry residents showed a group of reporters doors that were clearly kicked in.

Soldiers were crying out 'God is great' as they charged, firing guns in the process, many residents said. One compared the invocation to 'fighting a holy war against Israel'. (Al-Jaberi 2012)

It has been argued that the current dominant discourses about the cities of the global South seem destined to be entrapped in the predicament of both 'neo-liberalism' and the 'war on terror' as insurmountable paradigms that were imposed by US hegemony (Kanna 2012). In the aftermath of 2011, the optimists like me believed that the empowering effect of the occupation of public space during the Arab revolutions could have challenged these scenarios by proposing possible alternatives. After 2014, it became clear that the discourse of the 'war on terror' gave even further legitimacy to the supremacy of the army.

Many people believe that a restoration was set in motion when General Sisi became president. For these people, the army's occupation of the streets, after the rule of the Islamists, means 'restoring order', which seems to be synonymous with the reinstatement of the political figures and financial tycoons of the ancien régime. After January 2011, the street witnessed the rule of thugs (even though these were the thugs of the ancien régime), together with an increase of criminality and violence. For the middle classes, the thousands of street vendors conquering all possible and unimaginable spaces, occupying entire streets, corners under and on bridges, passages, and alleys of the entire city, hindering traffic, symbolised the 'disorder' of the city. The public visibility of the street vendors says a great deal about the consequences of the long years of failed neo-liberal policies – policies that pauperised millions, including university graduates, to whom nothing was left but street vending.

Contrary to what some Western pundits believe, Sisi had won considerable popularity with his discourse of restoring 'order' and stability in the country before he became president. One sign of this appeared when the regime proposed to collect funds from the citizens in the form of shares and bonds for the Suez Canal project: the banks were invaded by flocking customers. In just a few weeks, some US$8.5 billion were raised. Evidently, Sisi touched a chord of nationalist sentiments that was highly effective (Oakford 2014). The question is how long can the army bet on popularity? Hasn't it already been scarred by the steep deregulation of the currency under the World Bank measures, the soaring prices, and the ongoing harsh political repression?

David Harvey reminds us that the process of Louis Napoleon Bonaparte's restoration was a matter of extracting surplus value through capitalist appropriation of the city. The Haussmanisation of Paris that occurred under that same Bonaparte went hand in hand with further despotism and suppression of rights (Harvey 2008). Reading David Harvey with the Egyptian landscape in mind is compelling in view of the striking analogy between Sisi and Louis Napoleon Bonaparte. Both authoritarian regimes of order were enamoured with grandiose infrastructure projects. Napoleon, for example, extended his Cairo infrastructure plan to Europe. Both resorted to supporting or enlarging the Suez Canal – Napoleon financed the original digging of the Suez Canal and Sisi is currently working on enlarging it.[1] The two 'restoration cases' bear similarities: in both cases, the expansion in infrastructure is essential for appropriating the capitalist resources of the city. For example, the Egyptian army has recently been extremely busy constructing highways, roads, and bridges at nodal points to provincial towns and all around Cairo. The *Belle Epoque* Downtown underwent a face-lift in March 2015, consisting of a massive whitening of the façades of all the buildings surrounding Talaat Harb Square, exactly as it was previously done under Mubarak, while the authorities continue to rigidly close down almost all the popular cafés in the pedestrian zone of Sherifein Street. Once again, this could be interpreted as a populist move, uplifting the nation with a sentiment of grandeur and, above all, 'order' in the street.

This restoration in the city is occurring precisely simultaneously with the massive campaign led by the Sisi regime to 'clean up' Downtown by the forcible eviction of the large number of street vendors. At stake here are the vested interests in revamping the *Belle Epoque* Downtown, whose historic buildings have attracted the capitalists and tycoons who dominated the scene well before 2011, with the intention of appropriating the centre and its surplus value. Al-Ismaelia Real Estate Company has been acquiring a significant number of historic buildings in Downtown, such as the Art Deco Gharib Morcos Building, constructed in 1916; the Kodak Buildings, constructed in 1924; the Davis Bryan Buildings; the 22 'Abd al-Khalek Tharwat Building, constructed in the 1920s; and Cinema Radio, built in the 1930s (Al-Ismaelia, n.d.). Al-Ismaelia has been hosting art installations and exhibitions, which certainly strengthened the image of a unique metropolitan flavour. Several trendy cafés, catering to the youth, opened around that area. In a way, this space is becoming a window to the nostalgia of Cairo's colonial grandeur. The aim is obviously a neo-liberal form of gentrification of the Downtown centre, whereby art and culture (including revolutionary art) have already been instrumentalised in the process of further appropriation of the historic buildings.

### Harsher comeback of police forces

The Nasserite journalist 'Abdallah al-Sennawi commented in the *al-Shurouk* newspaper in August 2015 (al-Sennawi 2015) on the mutiny of a group of low-ranking officers, identified as the *umanaa' al-shurtha* in Sharquia, which he saw as representing the cry of the unheard, deprived police forces. Because they are poorly paid, these low-ranking officers have gained a reputation for pettiness and corruption. During the past few years, myriad jokes have circulated about them. They are recruited as officers precisely because of their poor education and low status. But al-Sennawi rightly insists that they are perceived as both the evil victimisers and the victims of the corrupt and vindictive state apparatus, because of their position at the bottom of the hierarchy. Their protests were a response to the killing of three officers and the wounding of several others in a terrorist attack (which have significantly multiplied against police forces in the past years) on the road between Damanhour and Rashid. Al-Sennawi draws an analogy with the violent 1987 rebellion of the police forces, warning that their ambiguous position and violent behaviour towards innocent citizens, together with their reputation for corruption, are highly revealing of the escalating tensions that led to the army's intervention.

This bring us to the next point. Although the Ministry of Interior has been reinforced and its budget and personnel significantly consolidated after 2011, it remains far from being a homogeneous and consistent apparatus. Its hierarchical structure comprises vast class and economic disparities, with the result that it speaks with multiple interests and 'voices', as Maha Abdel Rahman has argued (Abdel Rahman 2017). Clearly the poorly paid, often rural-origin conscripts who were posted on the front lines with barely any shelter or proper food, squatting for endless days in the streets behind the concrete buffer walls erected around Tahrir by the army in 2011 and 2012, confronting demonstrators, represent an entirely different world from that of the highly placed officers and generals who gave the orders to fire on the protesters.

### New Capital Cairo, the army's grandiose dream

CAIRO (Reuters) – Impoverished residents of red brick homes on an island in the Nile look nervously across the river at another Cairo slum, bulldozed this summer into a wasteland of rubble.

Both areas are earmarked for tourism or business developments, part of efforts by President Abdel Fattah al-Sisi to attract investment and boost an economy still reeling after Egypt's Arab Spring upheaval of 2011.

Since taking office in 2014, Sisi has sought to transform Cairo, building a new administrative capital on its outskirts and aiming to turn the city center into an investor's dream. Glossy magazine adverts make Cairo look more like Dubai, with glitzy tower blocks on the banks of the Nile.

But there is an obstacle to that vision: people living there. Many say they do not want to leave, and have not been told what will happen to the districts they have called home for generations.

The plan for the Nile island, Warraq, is being overseen by the army and a government housing body. Areas scheduled for development include slums where authorities say residents have built illegally on state or privately owned land for decades, such as Warraq and the nearby area razed this summer, Maspero.

Under pressure from former general Sisi to transform those areas, authorities have either attempted forced evictions or offered compensation in money or property.

Officials say the thousands evacuated are making way for projects that will bring prosperity to all Egyptians, and that some residents will return when development is completed. (Davison and Mourad 2018)

A number of publications have pointed recently to the boundless and expanding power of the army in controlling and financially speculating on desert land, in further holding the natural resources, and in tightening their hegemony over the industries.[2] Zeinab Abul-Magd's crucial work (Abul-Magd 2016, 2017) is perhaps amongst the first studies to have pointed to the paramount role of the army's involvement in the current economy and why their activities have been kept opaque. According to Abul-Magd, the armed forces have been financially involved for many decades, contributing an estimated 25 to 40 per cent of Egypt's economy. This includes mega-projects, large factories in the food and beverage industries, and running cafeterias and gas stations. It explains why the army opted for the ouster of Mubarak and his son's clique of crony capitalists, since they constituted a parallel competing elite. Then we are told that the army's business is run through agencies like the National Service Products Organisation (NSPO), which controls some twenty-one major companies, as published on its website, while it preserves an independent budget from the Ministry of Defence (Transparency International 2018: 8). Some of the companies included the industrial, engineering, mining, and services sectors, as well as in food security, water, and fisheries. Furthemore, the army currently plays a paramount role in a number of economic and consumer spheres, transforming the entire country into an endless, expanding, open-air 'camp' by legitimising novel forms of cheap 'slave labour' via the well-established system of conscripts who end up working in egg farms and pasta factories. These finance-oriented 'neo-liberal officers' flourished between the 1990s and the 2000s, by switching the military businesses towards the civilian spheres, to which Abul-Magd dedicated an entire chapter (Abul-Magd 2017: chapter 3). These officers have been regarded as an emerging new class of business managers who seem to be the dominant players in the reconfigured market economy, standing in clear competition with the former neo-liberal Mubarakist tycoons. If one speaks of an open-air camp, then the question of the 'state of exception' (Agamben 1998) remains vital for interpreting the extreme opacity of information and the increasingly precarious state that confronts the citizens in daily life.

But the militarisation of urban life, and the increasing public visibility of the military in everyday matters, takes a myriad of other forms as well. Apart from weapons and military industries, they also operate industrial farms. They distribute rationed food and subsidised bread through a 'smart card' system, allowing five loaves per family member per day (Fick 2015). They own many of the proliferating 'modern' gas stations with small attached supermarkets. The armed forces are today the largest owner of desert land in Egypt, and one of the major players in the construction of the Dubai-inspired new Egyptian capital city in the Eastern Desert. This means that they have become the main speculators in real estate and in the further development of the satellite cities. The military have turned out to be our urban planners, as Graham prophesied. They have gained popularity by building roads and bridges connecting provincial towns and have installed 'modern' payment systems on highways, often staffed by female employees who collect the tickets – a gender-friendly image that is part of the army propaganda. The numerous newly constructed gas stations along these roads also include supermarkets run by the conscripts. The website of the Egyptian Armed Forces/Ministry of Defense (see Egyptian Armed Forces/Ministry of Defense) boasts among its major national projects an extensive list of main axis roads that are either under construction, being improved, being widened, or recently completed: the Cairo–Alexandria desert road, the Cairo–Ismailiyya desert road, the Ismailiyya–Port Said road, the Wady al-Malak road, the Western arc of the regional ring road from the Cairo–Asyut road to Cairo, and the Rawd al Farag–Dabaa Axis. They have also built sewers and power lines and have recently announced their intention to build schools (Gotowicki 1994).

The army's most recent economic hegemony was boosted with some US$20 billion in aid from the Gulf just after 2013 (Gotowicki 1994: 9). The specialists in the field of the military economy point to two main features that can explain how high profits, clearly representing surplus value, can be made in this sector. First, the use of the conscripts' forced labour in these businesses allows the army to offer the cheapest prices, contrasting with the soaring prices in the food market. Second, the expanding system of subcontracting, through which ministers can sign contracts without competitive tendering, increases the risks of corruption and the much-lamented opacity of the transactions (Gotowicki 1994: 13).[3] We are told that the magic term *subcontracting* explains it all. It became effective with the passing of Law 32 in 2014, which 'bans third parties, including even Egypt's Public Prosecutor, from challenging the conditions of public contracts' (Gotowicki 1994: 13). These recent transformations create even more space for patronage and corruption in the business and real-estate world. This brings me to Eric Denis's concluding point in his article on the gated communities (Denis 2006), regarding the articulations between the State and the private neo-liberal business class (while he refers to Timothy Mitchell's analysis of neo-liberalism, which does not necessarily imply the retreat of the State making room for the expansion of the market).

This newly reconfigured articulation taking place today between the business class and the army, precisely through subcontracting, needs further scrutiny, in order to understand the unmaking and remaking of the new alliances in the business world. While a continuity of the army's predominance could be traced from the previous regimes of Sadat and Mubarak, a new class constellation seems to be in the making today, which results in the creation of novel segregations and divisions in the forthcoming cities. For instance, the choice for the location of the new capital on the Cairo–Suez Road, as part of the development of an economic node around the Suez Canal zone, raised eyebrows, since the question of transport was repeatedly not addressed, just as occurred in the planning of the previous satellite cities. Nor does the expansion towards the desert solve the problem of increasingly decaying services and buildings in the centre.

Above all, the military has been able to appropriate huge amounts of real estate, thanks to a law allowing them to obtain any land for commercial purposes. Most significant is the army's visible involvement in gargantuan projects in the desert, where it has developed joint ventures and engaged in lucrative financial speculation. This became all the more evident with *Mada Masr* reports on the Armed Forces Land Projects Agency that, together with Sheikh Zayed of Abu Dhabi, recently took over 16,000 acres and the supervision of the building of the New Capital City (Sawaf 2016). A year earlier Sisi announced the military's involvement in a US$40 billion joint housing project with the Arabtec Company from the Emirates (Saba 2014). Then the *Cairobserver* reported that in 2014 the Defence Ministry signed an agreement with Emaar, the mega-company based in the UAE, to construct a huge Emaar Square that would include the largest shopping centre in uptown Cairo, counterposing to Tahrir Square a neo-liberal market oriented to Dubai. This dream of a market economy is envisaged under an authoritarian military rule in which the army controls vast land markets without any transparency in its transactions ('From Tahrir Square', 2014). Of course, this is not the first time a market economy with neo-liberal dreams has worked hand in hand with authoritarian militarism.

Sisi's grandiose, Napoleonic dream of erecting the New Capital Cairo, a dream that will surpass all records for speed of construction, should be completed in the next five to seven years. The U\$45 billion capital is advertised on its website as an Egyptian Renaissance of a dream, if not as a surreal fantasy world.[4] A series of websites on Vimeo Egypt about the New Capital Cairo[5] sells a futuristic, science-fiction-like, virtual speculation of the new capital, parading mostly modern and Western-looking women, walking in idyllic landscapes. New Capital Cairo should be conceived of as the antithesis of the central old city of the thousand minarets. It will be a gigantic city that will include over a million new homes, 1,950 houses of worship, 660 hospitals and an enormous medical city, a 'knowledge city', a theme park, an expo city, a conference zone, and another gigantic opera house. It will be a 'global', 'modern', and 'smart city' offering a variety of economic activities. Particularly featured are the twenty mega-skyscrapers that will be erected by the Chinese, who seem to hold the monopoly on constructing the central business district (CBD), provoking the critical commentary of urban planners, architects, and journalists on the recurrent theme of the inferiority complex inherent in the Dubai mimicry (Michaelson 2018). New Capital Cairo will evidently be one more huge walled city, in view of the fact that the spokesman of the Administrative Capital for Urban Development (ACUD), a former army general who is supervising the gigantic project, has consistently avoided providing any information to the *Guardian* about affordable housing (Michaelson 2018). ACUD is owned 51 per cent by the military and 49 per cent by the Ministry of Housing, which also owns the vacated old buildings and the architecturally significant *Belle Epoque* ministry buildings in the centre of Downtown. Thus, according to the *Guardian*, an exchange of buildings between the ACUD managers and the Ministry of Housing can realistically be foreseen, evidence of the growing military intervention in civil life.

It is equally fascinating to see how the advertisement of the New Capital Cairo is taking a biblical twist. The magical numbers of seven and twelve keep reappearing in its descriptions. Thus, the new capital is projected to be seven times bigger than Paris and twelve times bigger than Manhattan (Williams 2015). It will be roughly the size of Singapore, housing 5 million residents and providing 2 million jobs (Elba 2015). As if the regime is reinventing history from scratch, it remains firmly oblivious to the criticisms of a number of urban planners (Sims 2014) who have already pointed to the failure of the multiplying and deserted satellite cities in the desert. As Rodrigo José Firmino argued, with a focus on Rio de Janeiro's Smart City, these emerging global 'smart cities' are founded on 'code, automation, data, surveillance, monitoring, control, connection, smart, and things' (Firmino 2016: 43). Such sites are concerned with managing, distributing, manipulating, and regulating an endless, and often an uncontrollable, amount of information. But above all, according to Firmino, we will be witnessing new constellations between technological concentration and territorial sites, leading to further surveillance and control by governments at the expense of individual freedoms. Within these concentrated spaces of information, surveillance and 'dataveillance' will clearly mean more control, walls, and barbed wire around this huge city. New Capital Cairo will be one more laboratory in which to observe the amalgamation of militarised urban life, increasingly surrounded with walled islands of consumer culture and 'smart' and 'informational' spaces, stripped of politics, protesters, street children, street vendors, and, above all, trade unions. With all these securitising measures, January 2011 ought to *never, ever* happen again. If and only if, by mere coincidence, an insurrection would unfortunately recur, the powers that be have clearly sent the message that the foreseen human carnage will be unimaginable.

## Notes

1  Sisi's continuous shifting of symbols and rhetorical usage is fascinating. When Morsi was ousted by the army takeover in 2013, Sisi was often compared to Gamal 'Abdel Nasser; his emphasis on nationalist rhetoric, versus the Muslim Brotherhood's Islamic internationalist networks (presumably terrorist and portrayed as dangerous), was noticeable. When the inauguration of the enlarged 'new Suez Canal' took place in August 2015, Sisi once again played on nationalist sentiments, the more so since the flotilla that inaugurated the ceremony had previously belonged to the Egyptian royal family. It was the same flotilla that carried out the original inauguration of the Suez Canal in 1869 in the presence of Empress Eugénie. The message could be interpreted as a wish to consolidate nationalistic sentiments in order to boost pride for grandiose infrastructure projects, with a reference to colonial/cosmopolitan culture that would appeal to neo-liberal sentiments. This went well together with the fact that French president François Hollande was given the lion's share of attention amongst the international delegates present at the inauguration, marking the historical continuity with France. It is interesting, too, that the 1956 nationalisation of the Suez Canal under Nasser was hardly referred to.
2  Amongst the important works on the military, see Sayigh 2012.
3  Transparency International refers to the work of Robert Springborg on the crucial and expanding phenomenon of the army's subcontracting.
4  http://thecapitalcairo.com/about.html (accessed 14 June 2018).
5  It is worthwhile to watch these series as if they were children's video games. See 'The Capital Cairo' and 'Egypt – the New Capital Cairo', 2015 – two advertisements produced jointly by the Ministry of Housing and the Ministry of Defence and Military Production.

# Conclusion: Making sense of the collage

Has this book convinced the reader that the grand narrative of the large-scale political and social changes in Egypt brought on by the 2011 revolution is mirrored in the smaller story narrating the everyday interactions of a middle-class building? Has the narrative succeeded in connecting the mundane details of daily endurance with the complex forms of military authoritarianism, in which the 'rule of nobody' has become omnipresent in a chaotic daily life, in parallel with a police state? Perhaps the collages of four tales provided a myriad of divided snapshots: scenes of Tahrir Square and its protesters; of violence and the reinvention of public spaces in a moment of insurrection; of phantasmagorias in mimicking mini-Dubai(s) and Singapore; of mushrooming mega shopping malls; of the transforming neighbourhood of Doqi pushing away its middle classes, transmuting the 'popular' street into a site of lucrative commercial activities; of moving to New Cairo and compound life at the far end of an exhausting commute; of evictions in popular neighbourhoods; and finally of the militarisation of urban life. That Cairo is a divided city is indeed no news. This collage's basic dilemma remains: how is it that what 'some' would consider a dystopian urban life is packaged and reimagined by 'others' as utopia?

In a number of Middle Eastern countries such as Algeria and Sudan, following the example of Egypt, it seems that the current politics and the reshaping of urban life have been engineered by the military seizing overt power over civil life. It also seems that explicit military control will continue to increase for some time, as a global world order dictated by Trump's Pax Americana politics in the Middle East.

In view of this overt military rule, one main recurring question I have tried to raise is how to trace the elements of continuity on a micro level, when the urban transmutations in post-January Cairo are so pervasive. Here, referring time and again to the groundbreaking work of Stephen Graham, *Cities under Siege: The New Military Urbanism* (2010), to what extent is the 'new military urbanism' actually new, when all but one of Egypt's presidents since 1952 have been military men? Mohamed Naguib, Gamal Abdel Nasser, Anwar al-Sadat, Hosni Mubarak, and today Abdel Fattah el-Sisi – with the exception of the one-year rule of the Muslim Brotherhood president Mohamed

Morsi in 2012 – all were consecutive army officers. They ruled the country in an unbroken succession for over six decades.

Each president launched grandiose urban schemes and new cities, the wisdom of which is today questioned more than ever. Inspired by Bauhaus architecture, Nasser constructed Nasr City in what was then desert, with the intention of relocating a significant number of government ministries there; today it suffers horrendous traffic jams and unmistakable urban chaos. Sadat started the expansion to the desert with satellite cities; Sadat City became one of the largest first-generation industrial cities (apart from Helwan, which expanded as an industrial area under Nasser), but it did not attract as many residents as expected because of its poor infrastructure. Mubarak promoted the Cairo 2050 plan, which would have led to further evictions in the name of gentrification advantaging the rich. This plan has not progressed since Mubarak's ouster. Sisi's gigantic New Administrative Capital beats all records for size, speed of construction, and the dizzying scale of investment.

Those who argue that continuity prevails over change in today's politics, because of the overt military control, refer to the classic work of Anouar Abdel Malek, *Egypt: Military Society* (1968), which confirms the idea that the country's modernisation has been closely associated with military rule because of its highly centralised administration dating back to pharaonic times. In another work, Abdel Malek (1964) provides a Marxist reading by dissecting both the effectiveness and the failures of the Nasserite military rule. Abdel Malek builds on Karl Wittfogel's concept of 'Oriental despotism' as a consequence of the 'hydraulic bureaucratic state', to explain why change seems to be possible only through a centralised power like the army. In other words, Egypt's 'specificity' in its path of modernisation can only be achieved through a centralised, bureaucratic power like the army.

Egypt's nineteenth-century modernisation, if not Westernisation, took place under a military ruler of Albanian origin who used draconian measures with the peasantry by nationalising the *iltizam* (tax-farmed) land, appropriating it, and levying high taxes on farmers. Mohamed Ali started industrialisation and created the modern army, leading to a modern-day debate among historians on whether he was a moderniser or simply an oriental despot. His scientific innovations in the irrigation system, and his system of financing industry through agriculture, were influenced by the Saint-Simonians. Abdul Karim Rafeq argues that it was the Saint-Simonians who inspired Mohamed Ali to resort to European loans and debts to finance industry, which led eventually to the country's bankruptcy (Rafeq 2005: 242).

Abdel Malek then draws a close analogy between Mohamed Ali's taking control over water, land, and state centralisation with Abdel Nasser taking over the public sector (Abdel Malek 1964: 47). Ironically, if Gamal Mubarak had succeeded his father, Hosni Mubarak, he would have been the first civilian president in the long line of military rulers.

While referring extensively to the work of Abdel Malek, Zeinab Abul-Magd also reveals that in spite of the *longue durée* influence of the army on all aspects of life, a clear 'rupture' has taken shape since the nineties that culminated in the overt military takeover after 2014. For Abul-Magd an obvious break has occurred between the Free Officers who made the revolution in the early fifties and the institutional transformations in the eighties that gave birth to the new class of managers and business 'neo-liberal officers' mentioned in the previous chapter. In this transformation, ideological orientation changed the mindset of the military from being trained for warfare, socialism, and Arab nationalism to a narrower form of patriotism and a business orientation (Abul-Magd 2017: 9). This break explains how neo-liberalism translates into enhanced policing measures that continue to disregard human rights and basic rights of citizenship, along with neglect of the welfare state and celebration of the *laissez-faire* economy. And yet, although they enjoy the entitlements that the State provides, it is not at all clear that these 'neo-liberal' officers truly function according to *laissez-faire* and market policies, as Abul-Magd convincingly argues.

Applying Giorgio Agamben's concept of the 'state of exception' (which he closely associates with the application of emergency law; Agamben 1998) to the Egyptian context, then clearly, according to Nathan Brown (Brown 2017), 'martial law', later renamed 'state of emergency' in Egypt, seems to have been repeatedly applied already under British rule at the beginning of the twentieth century, when the British governor was declared a military governor. This state of affairs was transformed directly into 'emergency law' in 1958 under Nasser. Except for a few short intervals, and with a few variations, it continued under Sadat, then under Mubarak, and today under the military regime (Brown 2017; Auf 2018). However, human rights have deteriorated under the current military rule, as a new law, no. 65, which in fact violates the constitution, was passed in 2016. It grants more powers to the military by allowing military trials for civilians and non-military crimes (Auf 2018). This draconian measure directly concerns the growing policing and controlling of public spaces and of urban life in general, as it was issued after the Rabe'a al-'Adaweyya killings. This law was part of a larger set of newly imposed laws pertaining to the continuing state of emergency, namely, 'the Protest Law (No. 107/2013), Assembly Law (No. 10/1914), Anti-terrorism Law (No. 94/2015), Law Criminalizing Attacks on Freedom of Work and Devastating Establishments (No. 34/2011, commonly called the Strike Law), Weapons and Ammunition Law (No. 394/1954), and Freedom of Worship Law (No. 113/2008). It also includes crimes related to terrorism' (Auf 2018).

It is thus possible to argue that martial and emergency laws have been applied as a continuous mode of rule, normalising the exceptional situation. In fact, the abuse of human rights exemplified in the murder of the young Alexandrian Khaled Said, who was tortured at a police station and whose disfigured face went viral on social media, went in parallel with an increase in the number and forcefulness of human rights and civil society activists challenging the state of emergency. It should be recalled that these very issues were the main triggers of the January 2011 revolution.

To return to the little commonplace story of the Doqi building, if the revolutionary momentum has had an impact on daily life, it was reflected in the novel ways the residents started to communicate among each other to solve the ongoing problems of public utilities and the infrastructure of the building. For even though everyday life became harder and street life even more chaotic, with the invasive cafés and other informal activities, it is precisely because of the absence of the State and of the rule of order that the residents eventually resorted to more effective action with collective and communal work. They simply circumvented the State and avoided the establishment of any legal institution by formalising, for example, a residents' association. The way they learned to negotiate communal problems together amounted to a kind of bricolage. And all the residents remained openly apolitical.

While evictions of the poor from informal settlements will continue – although not without resistance – the Doqi neighbourhood, even though the better-off middle classes regard it as degenerating, is being transformed by the popular life of the street into something else. The charming but disappearing villas and colonial-style houses feed the collective nostalgic feeling of desolation. However, far from dying, the neighbourhood is simply changing hands and pushing the better-off to the segregated compound life.

The death of my neighbour Ali Sharaawi in November 2018 marked the symbolic end of an entire era for the building. The late Ali had invested so much positive energy and effort in the overall upgrading of the building. He cared for details and knew how to communicate with the street and the shopkeepers; above all, he never failed to 'give and take' with the *bawaab* and the garage keeper. Ali was an excellent negotiator who over time developed the art of deflating tensions among neighbours. With his sudden dramatic death, one more old-generation resident has vanished. Ali's mother, who is in her nineties, moved out of the flat in 2019 to be taken care of by Ali's younger brother. According to Y., the *bawaab*, Ali's family wanted to give away Ali's flat to the owner of the building – as it was an extremely cheap fixed-rent contract – provided the family was compensated by a sum of money. However, the owner refused to pay the proposed amount to Ali's family. As a consequence, one more flat was closed, adding to the already large number of deserted flats. If the two parties ever come to an agreement, it will surely be transformed into one more commercial space, as the owner has done with all the other recuperated flats.

# Appendix I: Interview with E. D. 18 November 2018, the Gezira Club, Zamalek Island, Cairo

*E. D. has lived in the building for about twenty years. The interview was conducted in Arabic, but included many French terms and expressions since E. D. is a francophone and earned a PhD in political sociology in France.*

Mona: Were you born in this building?

E. D.: I imagine, yes, I was born in this building; I was born in 'Ali Ibrahim Hospital in Finni Square, in Doqi. My parents were already living in this building and the hospital was not far away. The tradition at that time [she is using the French word *repère*] was to have the delivery in the nearest neighbourhood hospital. My sister was nine years older than me and was born in a hospital in Shubra.

Mona: Did you live all your life in this building?

E. D.: I lived in the building until I was in my first year of secondary school. Then we moved to another house in Sudan Street in the Mohandessin district for only two years. This was until I was in my third secondary year, the baccalaureate. Then my parents moved back to the Doqi building because they realised that they could not afford living in a huge palace, or rather in a large villa. So we returned back during my baccalaureate year, and remained in the building until my third university year.

We purchased the flat after my father passed away in 1996, because a new law was passed that could have evicted us from the building, so we decided that this was the best thing to do. We then sold it two years later.

Mona: Why did you sell the flat later?

E. D.: Because my sister and I both realised that we were not good with renting flats. We sold both houses after my parents passed away to dissolve the inheritance – I had moved to the Aguza district after I was married and my sister realised that she would never live in my parents' flat. We each got our share in the inheritance, which made life easier.

Mona: Until when did you live in the building and when did your family move in?

E. D.: I lived in the building until 1982. My family came into the building in 1961.

Mona: Let me start with memories. How did you experience your youth in the building?

E. D.: I was very happy in my youth in this building, because it entailed an independent, lively, and interactive microcosm. We had friends in other schools in the quarter. I was in the *Lycée* school; my sister was at the French *Bon Pasteur* School; our first-floor neighbour H. was in the English Port Said School, whose mother was of Jewish origin and married to an Egyptian military officer; Laila Bahaa Eddin was also at the *Mère de Dieu* school and her brother was at the Jésuit School. The children of the S. family on the second floor were in the *Daar al-Tarbiyya* School. On the fourth floor above us, A. N.'s children were at Port Said School. These were all different but well-reputed language schools. You cannot imagine how this neighbourhood, or rather how all the neighbours in the building, knew each other, and this can systematically make you become part of a larger web of networks, and circles of friends that have nurtured me from very early times. The circles of the building widened and also became part of various other larger circles of friends and acquaintances from very early times. We went to the same clubs, played tennis together, often arranged to go for swimming classes together; we attended each other's birthdays and had reciprocal friendships.

Then, there was also the generation of my sister, born in the fifties; she is nine years older than me. They were already smoking cigarettes, constantly talking politics, and had certain freedoms in their circles. They had boyfriends and girlfriends in the building. ... I was luckier because I knew what was going on amongst the 'older kids' and I had learned a lot from their boyfriends and girlfriends.

I recall that the son of our neighbour A. N. was the first in the building to have had a girlfriend from the Palestinian Girls' Hostel. 'They were making out in the stairs' [this was said in English] and kissing in the stairs. I recall the mothers in the building complaining at their behaviour and coming out to shout at them at the stairs, arguing that the children would see them and it was a shame. This story remained enshrined in my memory, since I was eleven years old at the time.

.... Now I would like to raise the issue of the multiplicity of historicities (*taadudd al-taarikhiyyaat*).

I loved the building so much in my youth because it symbolised the plurality, and in a way a tolerance, that existed in the society at that time. It was, in fact, a plurality in historicities. If my father, who was a lawyer, Ahmed Bahaa Eddin, who was a prominent journalist, and the military officer who was married to our Jewish-origin neighbour on the first floor, were considered to belong to the Nasserite camp, my next-door neighbours were cousins to the famous upper-class C. A. family, *Tante* W.'s family [all neighbours were addressed as 'aunt' and 'uncle' – *tante* and *oncle* in French – by the youngsters of the building], who was our next-door neighbour, was a staunch anti-Nasserite. This family had a completely different lifestyle; they considered themselves upper-class aristocrats and they looked upon us as the rising 'petit bourgeois'. We [my family], on the other hand, thought that they were decadent. ... [This is of course said in a highly ironic tone.] The husband and the wife had each been married three times. However, they represented good manners and *usuul* [which could be translated as 'etiquette and fine manners']. I recall that they had at that time a villa elsewhere called Gazebo. Just mentioning the name, for the child I was, had a tremendous magical effect on me. This was well before the rich had weekend chalets. My neighbours' lavish and different lifestyle was an eye-opener for me. ... It was the first time I learned that some of the grown-up neighbours had lovers and affairs and they were hiding things from each other [this is said once again with great irony]. ... Their lifestyle was like a dream for us. ... The first time I heard of, or saw, a hashish cigarette was at their place. Men and women socialised through mesmerising '*bal masqué*' parties. It was the first I knew about the existence of dancing parties, and I will never forget that the language circulating was '*les soirées dansantes*' in French. ... The first time I heard about *Mardi gras* and the *bal masqué* was through them. ... I recall very well when my family was invited to our neighbours' party. My father was totally against wearing the large Indian Maharaja hat for the *bal masqué*, and I recall quite well the tremendous fight that resulted between my mother and father when she bought him that Indian hat. He burst into a fit of anger, arguing that he was a respectable man. He felt he was losing face by wearing such a ridiculous hat. These were two different worlds encountering each other on the same floor.

My early sociological instinct and sharp sense of observation, which I developed from childhood, allow me to say that this was another historicity – '*c'était une autre historicité*' for us. My neighbours spoke French amongst themselves. ... Their father, Uncle A., had numerous properties in Doqi and was extremely rich. He never worked, really. However, they thought that my family were parvenus, the rising petite bourgeoisie. My family and my father, on the other hand, were working so hard and tirelessly. ... As a child I used to tell my parents that I wished that Uncle A., our neighbour, would replace my father [once again told with a grain of salt]. I wished that he were my father instead; I envied Uncle A. for he was simply 'doing nothing'. I recall that Uncle A. used to spend his time listening to Umm Kalthoum while sitting on his Bergère-style chair, and he lived in a state of absolute leisure.

He introduced us to top-notch woodwork, fashionable interior decorators, and fancy furniture. ... My family and I thought then that their world was decadent, that it was ending [*c'était un monde décadent, qui finissait*], but there was *usuul* [there were traditions and etiquette]. ... *C'était les nantis* [the wealthy and well-heeled] that Pierre Bourdieu talked about. They did not need to work. They did not have any structure in their lives, nor constraints on their time, which was exactly the opposite of my family.

And we made friendships through them. ... There was a kind of endogamy in the building on the level of friendships and there was a lot of flirting within our generation. ... However, these love stories and flirtations did not reach the stage of marriage. ... These were what one would call first-love experiences. These were happening amongst a number of the youngsters in the building. ...

At the same time, the Bahaa Eddin family were in the pan-Arabism mode of thought, and their house was open. These were still the times in the aftermath of the dissolution of the union between Egypt and Syria. It was thanks to the Bahaa Eddins that I first encountered the late famous poets Nezar Qabbani and Mahmud Darwish. It was something to meet the famous singer/star Nagaat al-Saaghira, the Palestinian writer Samih al-Qassim, in someone's house. ... Imagine the effect it has on you when you are in your first year of secondary school and you meet the late novelist Ihsan 'Abdel Quduus and then you diligently search for his books and purchase them. The Bahaa Eddins represented a kind of Arab salon, open to writers and intellectuals. It was for me another world. ... They were like a dream of an alternative family ... the dream of a family that was nicer than mine. [Once again, narrated with laughter and irony.]

Laila was not my friend, as kids we did not like each other, but we met at the farm of friends of my parents in Bassus (a village in the vicinity of the barrage of al-Kanaater al-Khayriyyah) and at various parties because we had friends in common. But I was a highly achieving, first-in-class student and Laila was not really a good student. It was only when Uncle Ahmed Bahaa told me to come and study with Laila and help her with her homework that we started becoming close friends, in secondary school. I am thankful that Ahmed Bahaa Eddin allowed me to enter his house so that I could study with Laila. For me their flat was a discovery. They were not the typical Egyptian family. For instance, in their daily life, they did not sit or gather in the living room around the television set like most Egyptian families. Instead, each member had his own room and worked on his own. Or they had events and invitations; otherwise, each member of the family had his own space. I recall quite well that they had a maid's room that was later transformed into Zyad's own room after he asked his family for it.

This was one main reason why I insisted in my house, in an enormous fight with my parents, to have the same right, namely, to have my own room – that the maid's room should not remain the maid's room, and she should not stay overnight at our place. This was an enormous change in my mother's *mode de vie*.

The most endearing historicity (*tarikhiyya*) is tolerance and acceptance of others. For example, our next-door neighbours on the left, *Oncle* G. S. and his wife *Tante* M., were Christian. I can say that the case of this family was the start of 'endogamy' (although she uses 'endogamy', it is rather 'intermarriage') in the building: Uncle G. S.'s daughter married Aunt Daisy's brother. This is the first endogamy, as the residents of the third floor married from the second floor. While the cousins did not adhere to the same religion as Aunt Daisy, the wife of Ahmed Bahaa Eddin is Christian. The grandmother of the cousins of Leila and Zyad, who are Christians, married Uncle A., who is Muslim. I recall that this built a 'relativisation' of religion and tolerance in the building.

Here is one more story. I recall that, as a child, I used to sleep in the same room as my grandmother before the reshuffling of our apartment. ... I had to leave the room when our neighbour, *Tante* M., came every afternoon to have coffee with my grandmother. They drank coffee together on almost a daily basis and they shared their fears and hopes. ... By the way, the entire family of *Tante* M. migrated to the US. ... My grandmother and *Tante* M. were *intime* [intimate] friends. They cooked together, they sat long hours together, they shared the *makwagi* [the man who came to iron our clothes], who worked for them both, and they shared the storage rooms and organised practical matters together. It was a genuine and close friendship. By the way, also important to mention, all the family migrated (like a large number of Christians who left the country), with the exception of one son, N., who started renting out his flat to Arabs, while he was living in it. ... Many residents then thought that the building was starting to disintegrate socially and it was no longer up to their standard when the Saudis came.

Then the Bahaa Eddins went to Kuwait in the mid-seventies. ... This was the time of the Open Door Policy when a number of people started making money. My father decided at that time to build a villa in the Mohandessin quarter, in which they stayed for only two years, from 1975 to 1977. But they returned to the building after my sister decided that she did not want to live with them. They instead purchased three flats for us on the Nile.

When we came back to live in the building, my mother changed lifestyle again. We removed the large and imposing dining table, the '*table attitrée*', and the *salon*. She introduced instead a small round table with four chairs and we broke the walls to have an open space. I got the maid's room and we transformed a guest room for my sister, in case she visited us. My grandmother no longer lived with us. My family went through a modernisation when my sister went to France after she got married. This was a general trend at that time. We rearranged the space of the flat and had many fewer maids than before. For example, we brought a large table into the kitchen, around which we gathered like the Bahaa Eddins. These were the happiest

days of my life. I went with Laila and Zyad and a number of neighbours to
the university at the same time. I got to know AUCians [the students from
the American University] through Laila and her friends and Laila got to know
all my friends from Cairo University. From very early a *shilla* [gang] and
groups of friends were created, which were enlarged into various overlapping
circles and *shillas*. These groups opened horizons to discuss politics, read
books, attend events, and socialise together. For example, I had the opportunity
to know the nephew of the poet Salaah Jahiin, and through him I met a
number of friends who are today prominent intellectuals and politicians.
And Laila brought into the group her friends R., K., and M., who were all
connected to the circles of the American University. And we were highly
aware of the strength of our social networks.

   At that time we had a feeling of social distinction. We had cars from the
first day we entered the university, but there was also a mood of *pudisme*
[modesty] – for example, we did not wear the most expensive clothes.

Mona: What do you mean by *pudique*?

E. D.: *Pudique* [modest] in the sense that the seventies witnessed the highest
level of *prétension sociale*, of the '*m'as-tu vu?*' [Have you seen me?] in society,
of the new Open Door Policy wealth arriving. ... I recall that we saw girls
wearing diamond rings at Cairo University and my father was not at all
happy about it, as this was not the case during my sister's time as a student.
All during the seventies, in our building, there was a mood that was against
showing off, which was quite visible in the redeployment of the flats from
extended to nuclear families.

   Until the early eighties the entire building was stable and remained that
way. For nearly twenty years, from the early sixties until the early eighties,
one can say that in these fifteen flats, no resident moved out and no new
residents [*waafiddin guddud*] came in, with the exception of the flat of Uncle
G. S. that was rented out to Saudis when the entire family migrated to the
US. But from 1961 until 1980, no resident rented out his flat. Even when
Laila's family was in Kuwait, they left it empty.

   On the other hand, the Palestinian hostel had always existed, ever since
I became aware of things. I do not recall the building without it. This hostel
always remained a controversial issue in the building. *Tante* Daisy and *Oncle*
Bahaa saw that this was bringing a kind of regional, pan-Arab dimension to
the building, while other residents were quite critical of having female Palestinian residents. I recall that my sister was friends with a large number of
Palestinian girls. Laila had two or three of the Palestinian friends from the
hostel studying with her at AUC. It was the Palestinian girls who taught my
sister to smoke cigarettes. They taught Laila to listen to the records of Bob
Dylan and Joan Baez. Thanks to them, it was the first time that I saw Vietnamese combs manufactured from the remains of the Phantom bombs.

These were still highly charged anti-imperialist moments [said ironically], *'caution nombreuse'* [multiplied endlessly], and it seems that my parents, like the Bahaa Eddins, were caught in this ideological mindset. So *it was the thing* [emphasis here] to have these Vietnamese rings and combs. And it was understood to be a form of resistance. My parents also brought these when they went to Vietnam and brought such presents for a number of girls in the building. ... I also recall writing out the words of Joan Baez's 'Lily Rosemary and the Jack of Hearts' [Bob Dylan's words] and could sing the entire song in English.

I was in my fourth year of primary school. When the [Palestinian] girls travelled to Gaza, they brought us presents, like napkins, embroideries, and plenty of food. There was this mood of solidarity with the girls; the politicised camp of the building liked it a lot. But the other camp was disgusted and thought that the situation was damaging. I recall that the families which had sons, like the family next door and the neighbours on the second floor on the left, all thought that the building was being invaded by girls wearing miniskirts and smoking cigarettes. At that time, the girls and boys stood downstairs and talked for hours. You have to imagine the streets then were empty and dark. The boys used to talk to girls for hours, and for some residents this was a sign of a lack of *waqaar* [respectability] in the building.

Mona: Let us come back to the seventies and early eighties and the impact of the Gulf countries.

E. D.: Did I not tell you that there were people who made money when they went to the *Khaliig* [the Gulf countries]? There was only one family that ended up following the Muslim Brotherhood after some of its members worked in the Gulf in the eighties. Amongst the members of family S. on the first floor there were two sisters who were at the Lycée Français, and suddenly in the eighties they wore the hijab. The two sisters were assistant professors at Cairo University. There were only two families who were not following the typical nuclear family with two children who went to foreign schools – which I would say was the typical Nasserite family. Above all, most of us became assistant professors at the national universities, meaning that we were social achievers. The family that became followers of the Muslim Brotherhood were in a way atypical; they had six children and the girls married at quite an early age. But there was one more atypical family, a neighbour who married two women who shared the same flat, and we called them both 'T. and T.' ('so and so'). Like the Palestinian Hostel, they stirred much discussion amongst neighbours, but no one really disturbed or dis-criminated against them. Having said that, the entire building had not one single *muhagabba* [woman who wore the hijab] in the sixties and seventies. It was a very sixtyish, modern type of building. We had coiffeurs like the famous hairdresser Lambo coming to our house and to dress hair in a large number of flats. Manicurists used to knock at each flat. Almost all the girls wore miniskirts.

To come back to the point that the building symbolised the microcosm of the larger societal transformations: this building underwent a myriad of premises and transformations: Jewish and Christian minorities that entered marriages with Muslims; decadent and yet merry aristocrats who enjoyed private freedom but not political freedom; middle-class Nasserites and pan-Arabists, whose children got positions in the academic sphere. The exception was the one family that became followers of the Muslim Brotherhood, and one can track the controversial attitudes of middle-class Egyptians towards the Palestinians. Then the migration of religious minorities of Christians to the West that dates back a number of decades. The phenomenon of migration to the oil-producing countries and the Open Door Policy and the trend towards further Islamisation of lifestyles. Then the complete transformation that followed, when almost all of the neighbours I knew left the building by the second part of the eighties and nineties.

# Appendix II: Excerpts from interview with Laila al-Raa'i
# 5 May 2019, Zamalek Island, Cairo

*Laila al-Raa'i wanted to be personally named as she was glad to evoke the legacy of her father, the late Ali al-Raa'i, who was a prominent writer, playwright, and critic, and chaired the General Institution for the Theatre, Music and Popular Art. Ali al-Raa'i was Professor of English Literature at 'Ain Shams University.*

Mona: Let's start with the history of Doqi and your relationship to the quarter.

Laila: I recall that, when I was a child, we were living in a building in Doqi just opposite the Orman Gardens – a large and wonderful building with a magnificent entrance hall. However, my parents were not happy at all because the partitions of the flat were lousy. The rooms were not comfortable, even though we were facing the Gardens and had the sun all day. One day, my parents decided to move out. They searched a lot around the area of the Messaha Square in Doqi.

Mona: So they loved Doqi.

Laila: Yes, my family wanted to live always in Doqi, they loved the area. Both my mother and father graduated from the Department of English Literature at Cairo University and both went to England while my father completed a doctorate there. When they returned back my mother became editor-in-chief of the children's magazine *Samiir*, which explains why our house was thriving with journalists, intellectuals, and a large circle of artists dealing with children's books. Cairo University holds a unique history for my family. [Laila's father was a professor at 'Ain Shams University.] ... So my family found an old building in Harun Street ... It was really an old and wonderful building constructed during colonial times ... it dated from the time of the British ... it had a unique style ... with *fer forgé* [wrought iron] stairs, and high ceilings ... There were many spacious rooms. The building had a small entrance that was not as impressive as the former building where they lived ... but it was a huge apartment with beautiful rooms. This was 5 Harun Street. The owner of the house was a 'chic' and fashionable Turkish lady. She had a loud voice and used to shout quite often. But she was extremely kind and had a wonderful character. She was married to the father of the famous actor/singer Samir Sabri. This has to be mentioned because when Samir Sabri came to visit our building, all the admiring girls stood out at the elevator to stare at him.

This Turkish lady warmly welcomed my father, as he was already a known intellectual and a university professor. This played a positive role in the way we were treated in the building and the quarter. I recall that my father told me that her husband asked my father to find a job for Samir Sabri [this is said with a touch of irony] ... My father was then the director of the theatre and music institution and had numerous friends in the milieu of art and culture.

We lived on the first floor while the Turkish lady lived on the top floor. These were really beautiful times. In the back of the building there was something like a courtyard, with a large garage. There were quite a large number of small rooms, similar to the old buildings of Downtown – quite similar to the Yacoubian Building, but instead of being on the rooftop, these were in the courtyard ... For example, there were plenty of rooms for the *bawaab*s and the servants. There was also a very large roof. So all the Nubian servants – and there were quite a large number – lived in these rooms. The Turkish lady issued leases for them, exactly like our leases. Although she gave the impression of being a conceited Turkish lady, in reality she had socialist sentiments for the servants. She cared tremendously for them and sent them to her doctors when they were ailing ... In a nutshell, she was a character. They were not just servants to her. But if you saw her ... she was frightening ... She used to shout so much ... in the end she was truly a good person and she was intelligent ...

Unfortunately, the building was torn down ... some three years ago ... No one could believe that such a wonderful building could have been destroyed. It was a historic building ... surely you must have seen it. It was a remarkable building from the outside. It had a wonderful living room with an English-style chimney. It was simply a marevlous house with old tiles and high ceilings that could have included one extra floor.

My family moved into the building in 1960. They lived in this house for the rest of their lives. My father lived there almost his entire life and passed away in his armchair there. He would never have wanted to leave the house.

Mona: When did your father die?

Laila: He died in 1999. My mother lived in the house until it was torn down. My brother stood by my mother in this highly difficult situation. But there was this contractor who rose from the quarter. He specialised in buying old houses and tearing them down, and then constructing *abraag* (towers) and then selling these. From then on, the landscape or the topography of the quarter of Doqi changed tremendously ... so many houses and buildings were destroyed in this way. But our building was truly quite remarkable and particular ... This contractor started in the quarter with a very small grocery, mostly selling dairy products ... if you recall the times when we could buy milk in glass bottles [which have disappeared today]. Then he kept on expanding until he became extremely rich during the period of the *infitah* [the Open Door Policy launched by former president Sadat in the early seventies] ... until his family became monstrous ... [or 'ferocious' – Laila is using the Arabic word *tawahashu*, 'monstrous') ... Then they started targeting the old constructions, the old villas and houses in the quarter. These became their focus, and they destroyed one villa after the other in the area.

It is such a shame that such a historic building was torn down ... This contractor was like a cat. He kept on closely monitoring our building ... He scrutinised it for many years because he wanted to buy it ... He had started negotiations with the owner of the house a number of years earlier but he failed ... When the owner passed away, he continued talking and bargaining with his son. And the son passed away as well, but the contractor remained resilient. Then, eventually, the residents of the building split up. One half accepted the offer of this contractor while the other half completely refused to give up their flats. Those who agreed to leave were given a truly insignificant amount of money – 300,000 L.E. to vacate.

We refused to leave. Neither our upstairs nor our downstairs neighbours accepted the offer of the contractor ... It was not a question of money then. It was our house ... it was a disgrace to history and our memory. Why should we leave our house? My family went to the *ra'is al-hay* (the head of the neighbourhood/quarter), but nothing worked. Then they went to court and filed endless cases against the contractor, but to no avail. The contractor was able to bribe the *ra'is al-hay*, and in the end, they won, after fierce and endless fighting. The *ra'is al-hay* was quite corrupt and actually he later underwent judicial investigation, but it was too late for us. In the end they won ... Suddenly one day my brother had to take my mother out of the flat because the contractor obtained the licence of eviction ... My mother had to move to another flat in Mohandessin.

Mona: Did you own the flat?

Laila: No, it was the old rent system, but it was our flat ... This happened only some three years ago ... The irony of the story is that he cannot build on it now and it has been turned into a car park ... I am still very angry as I talk to you now ...

When the earthquake occurred in the nineties, experts were brought in, who concluded that our house would stand much better than any of the newly built towers ... it was seriously such a solid construction, apart from being aesthetically unique ...

Mona: How many years did your mother live there?

Laila: My mother lived most of her life there. She is today in her late eighties and she moved out about three years ago ... My brother struggled and struggled for many years and we are still pursuing a court case because we obtained nothing at all after we were evicted ...

Mona: How many flats were there in the building?

Laila: There were two flats on each floor and five floors – ten flats in total. Five families agreed to leave and five refused any negotiations, thus they ended up obtaining no money ... actually they got nothing because they refused the evictions.

Mona: So did the contractor pay the other five the sum of 300,000 pounds?

Laila: No, because there were already quite a number of the residents who had passed away.

There is one more point I want to add. The contractors also sold what one calls the *kharg* ... the 'remains' [the floors, doors, tiles, wood, and glass], and this brought them a lot of money too ... I managed to take away a door of *fer forgé* that I took to my mother's new flat as a remembrance of the place.

Mona: How did the contractor manage to tear down such a historic building?

Laila: Everything is possible ... he really bribed the *baladiyya* (the quarter/ neighbourhood administration) but because he has such a bad reputation and is known in the quarter, he has been stopped recently from undertaking further damages. He could not obtain the licence. So the space where the building stood has been a car park for the past three years ... but he will eventually be able to obtain the licence for construction.

The problem is that the damage is done ... The building was almost more than a century old. It was a crime to tear it down ... I am still shaking with anger as I speak to you ... But the country is as you see ... some can get away with anything because of money.

Mona: It is possible to say that these massive evictions and tearing down of old buildings intensified after the 2011 revolution. Many villas were torn down.

Laila: The problem is that would they have torn down your building, this would have been less of a problem, but this is really a historic building ... one problem was added. A lot of the old residents died and the owner of the house also passed away, so those renting could be easily evicted and got nothing ...

It is such an architectural loss. My brother's concerns were for my mother's survival. I think she has done well so far. She is now in a smaller and more modern building and she is not complaining.

Mona: We move now to your memories in Harun Street.

Laila: In Harun Street, I experienced my childhood, my adolescence, my youth, and university life. It had everything. Our neighbours across the hall were friends and we used to play out in the street together. For example, we went out together to Saudi [today a supermarket, it was then a smaller grocery]. There was a nice Nubian man who sold us ice cream *cassata*. There was the Club of Cairo University opposite our building. We attended so many parties and feasts there; even if we were not formally invited, we were always welcome. My father frequently gave lectures there and my family was known among their circles. What was nice was the hostel of foreign females nearby our house. This was a different institution from the Palestinian women's hostel. Mrs Muntaha al-Atrash, who was related to the famous singer Farid al-Atrash and ran that institution, always brought sweets and presents for my family whenever she returned from Syria. She was a lovely person. We looked forward to her return from abroad because she was so generous with presents. My father was loved by so many people as well as the students of the hostel in the quarter. He dedicated so much of his time for them. By the way, he was not a very smiley person, but a number of people in the neighbourhood loved to talk and sit with him ... They enjoyed his company as he was delightful to talk to.

During the 1967 war, there was a euphoria we experienced together ... We also attended the many events at the Russian Institute and the Goethe Institute ... Most important is my nostalgia for the unique trees of Doqi ... I am nostalgic for our time meditating on the balcony and just listening to music. My father and my family spent almost all our time on the balcony, listening to music ... My father loved singing and he sang to us so many songs of Abdel Wahhab on this balcony. At a certain point, a mat was placed on the balcony, and we all lay on the floor enjoying nature until we fell asleep and my father put us in bed.

My father had an armchair on the balcony. He read, worked, and meditated upon the landscape, which was simply wonderful.

The trees were really unique.

My only consolation today is that the contractor was not able to build on the land, so it is still a car park. One more important point is that the contractor was not able to throw out the Nubians ... at least, it took him a very long time to do so. The courtyard where the Nubians lived was huge and there were plenty of rooms ... The paradox was that they had contracts, so these poor Nubians were the real obstacle for him for a number of years ... The contractor continued to bribe and give money right and left until everyone left ... We were the last ones to leave. Imagine my father's large library that we had to give away ... We gave away the English books to the library of 'Ain Shams University ... so many objects were lost ... an entire life was gone ... We left this house under such harsh conditions ... Today I can no longer pass or walk along Harun Street. I try to avoid it because I still feel very emotional about it. I am drowning in sadness. I avoid the entire quarter because my heart bleeds ... We lived the most beautiful times ... I became attached to the place and find it difficult to detach.

When we moved to Doqi, the lawyer Ahmed al-Khawaga, the journalist Ahmed Bahaa al-Din, and my father all turned out to be neighbours. This created a special atmosphere and a network of friends who were all basically intellectuals ...

When Father travelled overseas and returned, he used to say that he considered his working room as the most beautiful office in the world. It consisted of two vast rooms with a huge library ... It had a character ... It was a house of intellectuals. We were not rich but there was a particular style I cherish.

My father went to auctions and purchased old furniture. There were always intellectuals and singers visiting us ... Once the famous singer Abdel Halim Hafez visited us ... Unfortunately it was all destroyed.

My grandmother's house in Soliman Gohar market, I always thought of as *baladi* [too popular], but there was everything, like good bread and wonderful vegetables and meat ... When we slept there we woke up to the sound of a rooster, which I always found exotic ... My grandmother's house was then taken by my Uncle Saad, who could not afford to buy another flat so he ended up living there. His flat was always full of intellectuals, and every Thursday there was a large dinner. There were constantly prominent intellectuals coming in and out. The entire left was invited there ... The flat had old-fashioned furniture ... My father got engaged to my mother there ... The house is full of memories ... and now my cousin lives there, but she complains that she lives in the midst of memories, and memories can be very exhausting ... I can no longer look at photo albums.

Cairo University. I remember the first day I went to the university. I was enrolled in the Department of Economics. It was a delight to walk through the Orman Gardens. I recall quite clearly that once my mother was driving her Fiat car and she saw me in the street. She waved to me and I walked ahead ... I used to reach the campus exactly at the sound of the clock striking ... The Orman Gardens were wonderful ... There were lovers holding hands and no one bothered them.

Also living in the quarter (near Vini Square) was the family of Lutfi al-Khuli, and his daughter went to school with me ... We were all at the Lycée Français, so our mothers picked us up to take us to school ... In fact, the quarter comprised a lively network of leftist intellectuals who knew each other and frequented the same places.

# References

## Sources in Western languages

Abaza, M. 2006. *Changing Consumer Cultures of Modern Egypt: Cairo's Urban Reshaping*. Leiden and Boston: Brill.

Abaza, M. 2011a. 'The banality of evil: Thinking Hannah Arendt in Cairo'. *Ahram Online*, 15 October. http://english.ahram.org.eg/News/%2024196.aspx. Accessed 22 September 2016.

Abaza, M. 2011b. 'Downtown Cairo imagined: Nostalgia and/or Dubaization?' *Urban Studies*, 48:6 (May), 1075–87. https://doi.org/10.1177/004209801.

Abaza, M. 2012. 'An emerging memorial space? In praise of Mohammed Mahmud Street'. *Jadaliyya*, 10 March. www.jadaliyya.com/pages/index/4625/an-emerging-memorial-space-in-praise-of-mohammed-m. Accessed 25 September 2019.

Abaza, M. 2013a. 'The dramaturgy of a street corner'. *Jadaliyya*, 25 January. www.jadaliyya.com/pages/index/9724/the-dramaturgy-of-a-street-corner. Accessed 25 September 2019.

Abaza, M. 2013b. 'Walls, segregating downtown Cairo, and the Mohammed Mahmud graffiti'. *Theory, Culture & Society*, 30:1, 122–39. https://doi.org/10.1177/0263276412460062.

Abaza, M. 2014. 'Post-January revolution Cairo: Urban wars and the reshaping of public space'. *Theory, Culture & Society*, 31:7–8, 163–83. https://doi.org/10.1177/0263276414549264.

Abaza, M. 2016. 'Violence, dramaturgical repertoires and neo-liberal imaginaries'. *Theory, Culture & Society*, 33:7–8, 111–35. https://doi.org/10.1177/0263276416670729.

Abaza, M. 2017. 'Repetitive repertoires: How writing about Cairene graffiti has turned into a serial monotony'. In K. Avramidis and M. Tsilimpounidi (eds), *Graffiti and Street Art: Reading, Writing and Representing the City*. Oxford: Routledge.

Abdel Malek, A. 1964. 'Nasserism and socialism'. https://socialistregister.com/index.php/srv/article/view/5927/2823. Accessed 15 May 2019.

Abdel Malek, A. 1968. *Egypt: Military Society: The Army Regime, the Left, and Social Change under Nasser*. New York: Random House.

Abdel Rahman, M. 2017. 'Policing neoliberalism in Egypt: The continuing rise of the "securocratic" state'. *Third World Quarterly*, 38:1, 185–202. https://doi.org/10.1080/01436597.2015.1133246.

Abou El-Naga, S. 2015. 'Beyond memory: Exploring nostalgia after the Arab revolutions'. *Ahram Online*, 13 December. http://english.ahram.org.eg/NewsContentP/4/173293/Opinion/Beyond-memory-Exploring-nostalgia-after-the-Arab-r.aspx. Accessed 6 January 2016.

Abul-Magd, Z. 2016. 'The army and the economy in Egypt'. *Midan Masr: An Opinionated Paper*. www.midanmasr.com/en/article.aspx?ArticleID=222. Accessed 12 December 2018.

Abul-Magd, Z. 2017. *Militarizing the Nation: The Army, Business, and Revolution in Egypt.* New York: Columbia University Press.

Abu-Lughod, J. 1965. 'Tale of two cities'. *Comparative Studies in Society and History*, 7:4, 429–57.

Abu-Lughod, J. 1971. *Cairo: 1011 Years of the City Victorious.* Princeton: Princeton University Press.

Adey, P. 2010. 'Vertical security in the megacity: Legibility, mobility, and aerial politics'. *Theory, Culture & Society*, 27, 51–67. https://doi.org/10.1177/0263276410380943.

Agamben. G. 1998. *Homo Sacer: Sovereignty, Power and Bare Life.* Stanford: Stanford University Press.

Alaa El-Din, M. 2015. 'Governor bans tok-toks in 8 Cairo neighbourhoods'. *Ahram Online*, 29 July. http://english.ahram.org.eg/NewsContent/1/64/136500/Egypt/Politics-/Governor-bans-Toktoks-in–Cairo-neighbourhoods.aspx. Accessed 11 December 2018.

Alexander, J. C. 2011. *Performative Revolution in Egypt: An Essay in Cultural Power.* London and New York: Bloomsbury Academic.

Alexandrani, I. 2016. 'Le saccage d'Alexandrie: Le général, le promoteur, et la dupe'. *Orient XII Magazine*, 14 January. https://orientxxi.info/magazine/le-saccage-d-alexandrie,1152. Accessed 12 December 2018.

Alloula, M. 1986. *The Colonial Harem.* Minneapolis and London: University of Minnesota Press.

Amar, P. 2013a. 'Egypt'. In P. Amar and V. Prashad (eds), *Dispatches from the Arab Spring: Understanding the New Middle East.* Minneapolis and London: University of Minnesota Press.

Amar, P. 2013b. *The Security Archipelago: Human-Security States, Sexuality Politics, and the End of Neoliberalism.* Durham: Duke University Press.

Appadurai, A. 1990. 'Disjuncture and difference in the global cultural economy'. *Theory, Culture & Society*, 7:2–3, 295–310. https://doi.org/10.1177/026327690007002017.

Amnesty International. 2011. *We Are Not Dirt: Forced Evictions in Egypt's Informal Settlements.* London: Amnesty International.

Arendt, H. 1963[1965]. *On Revolution.* London: Penguin Books.

Arendt, H. 1969[1970]. *On Violence.* New York: Harcourt.

Aswat Masreya. 2013. 'Court orders Al-Qursaya residents to stay, military to depart'. *Ahram Online*, 22 August. http://english.ahram.org.eg/NewsContent/1/64/79707/Egypt/Politics-/Court-orders-AlQursaya-residents-to-stay,-military.aspx. Accessed 25 September 2019.

Auf, Y. 2018. 'The state of emergency in Egypt: An exception or rule?' Atlantic Council, 2 February. www.atlanticcouncil.org/blogs/menasource/the-state-of-emergency-in-egypt-an-exception-or-rule. Accessed 25 September 2019.

Bamyeh, M. A. 2013. 'Anarchist method, liberal intention, authoritarian lesson: The Arab Spring between three enlightenments'. *Constellations*, 20:2, 188–202. https://doi.org/10.1111/cons.12031.

Barbery, M. 2006. *L'elégance du hérisson.* Paris: Gallimard.

Battesti, V. 2006. 'The Giza Zoo: Reappropriating public spaces, reimagining urban beauty'. In D. Singerman and P. Amar (eds), *Cairo Cosmopolitan: Politics, Culture, and Urban Space in the New Globalized Middle East.* Cairo: American University in Cairo Press.

Bayat, A. 2012. 'Politics in the city-inside-out'. *City & Society*, 24:2, 110–28. https://doi.org/10.1111/j.1548–744X.2012.01071.x.

Bishop, R., G. Clancey, and J. W. Phillips (eds). 2012. *The City as Target*. London: Routledge.

Bourdieu, P. 1998. 'The essence of neoliberalism: Utopia of endless exploitation'. Trans. J. J. Shapiro. *Le Monde diplomatique*. https://mondediplo.com/1998/12/08bourdieu. Accessed 11 December 2018.

Bourdieu, P. 1999. *La misère du monde*. Paris: du Seuil.

Boym, S. 2007. 'Nostalgia and its discontents'. *The Hedgehog Review*, 9:2, 7–18.

Brown, N. J. 2017. 'Egypt is in a state of emergency. Here's what that means for its government'. *The Washington Post*, 13 April. www.washingtonpost.com/news/monkey-cage/wp/2017/04/13/egypt-is-in-a-state-of-emergency-heres-what-that-means-for-its-government/?utm_term=.8f0298fc3534. Accessed 25 September 2019.

Cairobserver. 2011. 'Qursaya Island'. *Cairobserver*, 16 December. https://cairobserver.com/post/14282867951/qursaya-island#.XMdphZMzZp8. Accessed 25 September 2019.

Cairoscene Team. 2018. 'Cairo ranked second worst in the world for "silent killer"'. *Cairo Scene*, 15 March. http://cairoscene.com/Buzz/cairo-second-world-silent-killer-noise-pollution. Accessed 12 December 2018.

CEDEJ. 2018. 'Revue de presse, 10 juin'. Centre d'études et de documentation économiques, juridiques et sociales. http://cedej-eg.org/index.php/2018/06/10/revue-de-presse-ville-mai-2018/. Accessed 12 December 2018.

Challand, B. 2001. 'The counter-power of civil society and the emergence of a new political imaginary in the Arab world'. *Constellations*, 18:3, 271–83. https://doi.org/10.1111/j.1467-8675.2011.00650.x.

Chams El-Dine, C. 2016. 'Egypt from military reform to military sanctuarization'. In H. Albrecht, A. Croissant, and F. H. Lawson (eds), *Armies and Insurgencies in the Arab Spring*. Philadelphia: University of Pennsylvania Press.

Choe, J. 2015. 'Singapore's Zaha-topia'. *Urban Architecture Now*, 31 March. www.urbanarchnow.com/2015/04/dleedon.html. Accessed 10 December 2018.

Colonna, F. 2004. *Récit de la province égyptienne*. Paris: Sindbad Actes Sud.

Conley, V. A. 2012. 'The city as target: Retargeting the city: French intellectuals and city spaces'. In R. Bishop, G. K. Clancey, and J. Phillips (eds), *The City as Target*. London: Routledge.

Comaroff, J. 1985. *Body of Power, Spirit of Resistance: The Culture and History of a South African People*. Chicago: University of Chicago Press.

Cossery, A. 1994. *La maison de la mort certaine*. Paris: Editions Joëlle Losfeld.

Chua, B. H. 2011. 'Singapore as a model: Planning innovations, knowledge experts'. In A. Roy and A. Ong (eds), *Worlding Cities: Asian Experiments and the Art of Being Global*. Hoboken: Blackwell Publishing.

Das, V. 2007. *Life and Words: Violence and the Descent into the Ordinary*. Berkeley: University of California Press.

Davis, M. 2006a. *Planet of Slums*. London: Verso.

Davis, M. 2006b. 'Fear and money in Dubai'. *New Left Review*, 41 (Sept–Oct), 46–68.

Davis, M., and D. B. Monk (eds). 2007. *Evil Paradises: Dreamworlds of Neoliberalism*. New York and London: The New Press.

Davison, J., and M. Mourad. 2018. 'Demolition on the Nile puts squeeze on two Cairo districts'. *Reuters*, 26 September. www.reuters.com/article/us-egypt-cairo/demolition-on-the-nile-puts-squeeze-on-two-cairo-districts-idUSKCN1M619V. Accessed 25 September 2019.

Debord, G. 1956. 'Theory of the *dérive*'. *Situationist International Online*. www.cddc.vt.edu/sionline/si/theory.html. Accessed 10 December 2018.

De Certeau, M., L. Giard, and P. Mayol. 1994. *L'invention du quotidien II: Habiter, cuisiner*. Paris: Gallimard.

Denis, E. 2006. 'Cairo as neo-liberal capital? From walled to gated communities'. In D. Singerman and P. Amar (eds), *Cairo Cosmopolitan: Politics, Culture, and Urban Space in the New Globalized Middle East*. Cairo: American University in Cairo Press.

Diken, B., and C. B. Laustsen. 2002. 'Zones of indistinction: Security, terror, and bare life'. *Space and Culture*, 5:3, 290–307.

Due-Gundersen, N. 2018. 'Private security in Egypt is becoming President Sisi's personal fiefdom'. *TRT World*, 12 October. www.trtworld.com/opinion/private-security-in-egypt-is-becoming-president-sisi-s-personal-fiefdom-20631. Accessed 11 December 2018.

Egypt Solidarity. 2016. 'Alexandria shipyard workers and Cairo bus workers in court 18 and 19 October'. *Egypt Solidarity: An International Initiative against Repression in Egypt*, 17 October. https://egyptsolidarityinitiative.org/2016/10/17/alexandria-shipyard-workers-and-cairo-bus-workers-in-court-18-and-19-october/. Accessed 11 December 2018.

Egypt Today. 2018. 'Egypt completes demolition of 75% of Maspero Triangle slums'. *Egypt Today*, 14 August. www.egypttoday.com/Article/1/55933/Egypt-completes-demolition-of-75-of-Maspero-triangle-slums. Accessed 25 September 2019.

Elamrani, I. 2001. 'Modernism on the Nile: Architect Antoine Selim Nahhas left his mark on Cairo's skyline'. *Cairo Times*, 3–9 May.

Elba, M. 2015. 'Arrested development: The "new capital" in Egypt'. *Journal of Political Inquiry*. http://jpinyu.com/2015/05/04/arrested-development-the-new-capital-in-egypt/. Accessed 22 September 2016.

Elias, N., and J. L. Scotson. 1994. *The Established and the Outsiders: A Sociological Inquiry into Community Problems*. London and Thousand Oaks: Sage Publications.

Elsheshtawy, Y. 2010. *Dubai: Behind an Urban Spectacle*. Planning, History and Environment Series. London and New York: Routledge.

Elsheshtawy, Y. 2014. 'Searching for Nasser Square: An urban center in the heart of Dubai'. *City*, 18:6, 746–59. https://doi.org/10.1080/13604813.2014.962890.

Esterman, I. 2016. 'Is it safe to drink the tap water in Cairo?' *Mada Masr*. www.madamasr.com/sections/environment/it-safe-drink-tap-water-cairo. Accessed 8 July 2016.

Fick, M. 2015. 'Egypt's Sisi scores early success with smart cards for bread subsidies'. *Reuters*, 12 January. www.reuters.com/article/us-egypt-bread/egypts-sisi-scores-early-success-with-smart-cards-for-bread-subsidies-idUSKBN0KL1452015 0112. Accessed 12 December 2018.

Firmino, R. J. 2016. 'Connected and controlled surveillance: Security and cities'. LA+ (Landscape Architecture Plus). *Interdisciplinary Journal of Landscape Architecture*, 3, 42–9.

Foucault, M. 1978. *The History of Sexuality*. Vol. 1. New York: Pantheon Books.

Foucault, M. 2006. *History of Madness*. London and New York: Routledge.

Ghoneim, W. 2018. 'Egypt's revolution, my life, and my broken soul'. *Medium World*. https://medium.com/@ghonim/egypts-revolution-my-life-and-my-broken-soul-91fae189d778. Accessed 17 November 2017.

Gotowicki, S. H. 1994. 'The role of the Egyptian military in domestic society'. Foreign Military Studies Office Publications. https://community.apan.org/wg/tradoc-g2/fmso/m/fmso-monographs/240947. Accessed 12 December 2018.

Graham, S. 2010. *Cities under Siege: The New Military Urbanism*. London: Verso Books.

Graham, S. 2014. 'Super tall and ultra deep: The cultural politics of the elevator'. *Theory, Culture & Society*, 31:7–8, 239–65. https://doi.org/10.1177/0263276414554044.

Greenberg, J. 2011. *After the Revolution: Youth, Democracy, and the Politics of Disappointment in Serbia*. Stanford: Stanford University Press.

Hamdy, R. S., M. M. Abd El-Ghani, T. L. Youssef, and M. El-Sayed. 2007. 'The floristic composition of some historical botanical gardens in the metropolitan of Cairo, Egypt'. *African Journal of Agricultural Research*, 2:11, 610–48.

Hanafi, S. 2012. 'The Arab revolutions: The emergence of a new political subjectivity'. *Contemporary Arab Affairs*, 5:2, 198–213. https://doi.org/10.1080/17550912.2012.6688 303.

Harutyunyan, A. 2012. 'Before and after the event: There was the art work'. Keynote lecture, Photo Cairo 5 Symposium. Cairo, 17 November.

Harvey, D. 2008. 'The right to the city'. *New Left Review*, 53 (Sept–Oct), 23–40.

Hashem, M. 2018. 'Cairo Metro a magnet for people wanting to commit suicide'. *Asharq al-Awsat*, 1 August. https://aawsat.com/english/home/article/1349871/cairo-metro-magnet-people-wanting-commit-suicide. Accessed 23 September 2018.

Hassan, F. 1999. 'Palaces of change'. *Ahram Weekly*, 1–7 July. http://weekly.ahram.org.eg/Archive/1999/436/special.htm. Accessed 15 May 2017.

Heller, A. 2016. *Von der Utopie zur Dystopie: Was können wir uns wünschen?* Vienna and Hamburg: Edition Konturen.

Human Rights Watch. 2011. 'Egypt: Don't cover up military killing of Copt protesters'. Human Rights Watch, 25 October. www.hrw.org/news/2011/10/25/egypt-dont-cover-military-killing-copt-protesters. Accessed 25 September 2019.

Ismail, R. 2018. 'In-depth look at Cairo Metro's fare increase'. *Egypt Today*, 11 May. www.egypttoday.com/Article/2/49814/In-depth-look-at-Cairo-metro-s-fare-increase. Accessed 11 May 2018.

Al-Jaberi, A. 2012. 'Once again, Qursaya residents fight for their land'. *Egypt Independent*, 19 November. www.egyptindependent.com/once-again-qursaya-residents-fight-their-land/. Accessed 25 September 2019.

Jansen, S. 2015. *Yearnings in the Meantime: 'Normal Lives' and the State in a Sarajevo Apartment Complex*. New York and Oxford: Berghahn Books.

al-Jibali, L. 2016. 'Completely horrific and painfully plausible: Muhammad Rabi's *'Utarid'*. *Mada Masr*, 24 June. https://madamasr.com/sections/culture/completely-horrific-and-painfully-plausible-mohamed-rabies-otared. Accessed 11 December 2018.

El Kadi, G. 2000. 'Le Caire: Mobilités résidentielles et fonctionnelles à la lumière des politiques urbaines'. In *Métropoles en Mouvement*. Paris: Anthropos. https://docplayer.fr/70450225-Le-caire-mobilites-residentielles-et-fonctionnelles-a-la-lumiere-des-politiques-urbaines.html. Accessed 12 December 2018. Also at www.documentation.ird.fr/hor/fdi:010023873.

El Kadi, G. 2012. *Le Caire: Centre en mouvement*. Marseille: Institut de recherche pour le développement.

Kanna, A. 2009. 'A tale of two (Asian) cities: Dubai and Singapore before and after the crisis'. Centre for Urban and Global Studies at Trinity College, Inaugural Working Papers Series I:3.

Kanna, A. 2010. 'Flexible citizenship in Dubai: Neo-liberal subjectivity in the emerging city corporation'. *Cultural Anthropology*, 25:1, 100–29. https://doi.org/10.111 1/j.1548–1360.2009.01053.x.

Kanna, A. 2011. *Dubai: The City as Corporation*. Minneapolis: University of Minnesota Press.

Kanna, A. 2012. 'Urban praxis and the Arab Spring: Beyond the pathological city?' *City*, 16:3, 360–8. https://doi.org/10.1080/13604813.2012.687879.

El-Khawaga, D. 2014. 'The Zamalek Metro station: 6 lessons on citizenship'. *Mada Masr*, 9 January. www.madamasr.com/opinion/zamalek-metro-station-6-lessons-citizenship. Accessed 11 December 2018.

King, L. A. 2006. *Zenana: Everyday Peace in a Karachi Apartment Building*. Bloomington: Indiana University Press.

Kingsley, P. 2014. 'How did 37 prisoners come to die at Cairo prison Abu Zaabal?' *Guardian*. www.theguardian.com/world/2014/feb/22/cairo-prison-abu-zabaal-deaths-37-prisoners. Accessed 5 January 2017.

Kuppinger, P. 2004. 'Exclusive greenery: New gated communities in Cairo'. *City & Society*, 16:2, 35–62. https://doi.org/10.1525/city.2004.16.2.35.

Lane, E. W. 2005[1836]. *An Account of the Manners and Customs of the Modern Egyptians*. New York: Cosimo Classics.

Mahrous, D. 2011. 'Why are the snipers targeting the eyes of the revolutionaries?' *Al-Raya*, 3 December. www.raya.com/home/print/f6451603-4dff-4ca1-9c1 0-122741d17432/2f9e75a6-c981-4bf8-9199-7db13ba291aa. Accessed 26 July 2015.

Malsin, J. 2016. 'What the murder of an Italian student says about Egypt's security state'. *Time*, 10 April. http://time.com/4285659/giulio-regeni-italian-student-torture-murder-egypt/. Accessed July 2016.

Mehrez, S. 2008. 'From the *hara* to the *imara*: Emerging urban metaphors in the literary production on contemporary Cairo'. In S. Mehrez, *Egypt's Culture Wars: Politics and Practice*. London and New York: Routledge.

Mehrez, S. (ed.) 2012. *Translating Egypt's Revolution*. Cairo: American University in Cairo Press.

Mermier, F. 2015. *Récits de villes: D'Aden à Beyrouth*. Paris: Actes Sud.

Michaelson, R. 2018. 'Cairo has started to become ugly: Why Egypt is building a new capital city'. *Guardian*, 8 May. www.theguardian.com/cities/2018/may/08/cairo-why-egypt-build-new-capital-city-desert. Accessed 12 December 2018.

Ministry of Agriculture and Land Reclamation. 2009. '*Historical Gardens in Egypt*'. Central Administration for Arboriculture and Environment – Orman Garden, vol. 1.

Mitchell, T. 1991. *Colonizing Egypt*. Berkeley: University of California Press.

Mitchell, T. 2002. 'Dreamland'. In T. Mitchell (ed.), *Rule of Experts: Egypt, Techno-Politics, Modernity*. Berkeley: University of California Press.

Mitchell, T. J. W. 2012. 'Image, space, revolution: The arts of occupation'. *Critical Inquiry*, 39:1, 8–32. https://doi.org/10.1086/668048.

Mumford, L. 2002. 'What is a city?' In R. T. LeGates and F. Stout (eds), *The City Reader*. London: Routledge.

Myntti, C. 1999. *Paris along the Nile*. Cairo: American University in Cairo Press.

Nagati, O., and B. Stryker. 2013. 'Archiving the city in flux'. *Cluster*, 5 December. https://issuu.com/clustercairo/docs/archiving_the_city_in_flux. Accessed 10 December 2018.

Nandy, A. 1983. *The Intimate Enemy: Loss and Recovery of the Self under Colonialism*. Delhi: Oxford University Press.

Nora, P. 1989. 'Between memory and history: les lieux de mémoire'. *Representations*, 26, 7–24. https://doi.org/10.2307/2928520.

Oakford, S. 2014. 'Egypt's expansion of the Suez Canal could ruin the Mediterranean Sea'. *Vice News*, 9 October. https://news.vice.com/en_us/article/yw448x/egypts-expansion-of-the-suez-canal-could-ruin-the-mediterranean-sea. Accessed 12 December 2018.

Oikonomakis, L., and J. E. Roos. 2013. '"Que no nos representan": The crisis of representation and the resonance of the real democracy movement from the Indignados to Occupy'. Paper presented at the Conference on Street Politics in the Age of Austerity: From the Indignados to Occupy. Montreal: University of Montreal, 20–1 February.

Ortner, S. B. 1995. 'Resistance and the problem of ethnographic refusal'. *Comparative Studies in Society and History*, 37:1, 173–93.

Paul, I. A. 2015. 'The revolutionary practice of endurance'. *Jadaliyya*, 25 January. www.jadaliyya.com/pages/index/20636/the-revolutionary-practice-of-endurance. Accessed 22 September 2016.

Perec, G. 2017. *La Vie mode d'emploi*. Paris: Livre de Poche.

Raafat, S. 1999. 'Zamalek Lebon says it all'. *Cairo Times*, 23 December. www.egy.com/zamalek/99-12-23.php. Accessed 8 September 2018.

Rafeq, A. K. 2005. 'A different balance of power: Europe and the Middle East in the eighteenth and nineteenth centuries'. In Y. Choueiri (ed.), *A Companion to the History of the Middle East*. Malden: Blackwell Publishing.

Rennick, S. A. 2018. *Politics and Revolution in Egypt: Rise and Fall of the Youth Activists*. London: Routledge.

Ryder, S., and M. Rizk. 2017. 'When Egypt's World Youth Forum #WeNeedToTalk backfires'. *BBC Trending*, 2 November. www.bbc.com/news/blogs-trending-41842825. Accessed 12 December 2018.

Saba, J. 2014. 'The military and the state: The role of the armed forces in post-30 June Egypt'. *Daily News*, 27 September. https://dailynewsegypt.com/2014/09/27/military-state-role-armed-forces-post-30-june-egypt/. Accessed 12 December 2018.

Said, E. 1979. *Orientalism*. New York: Vintage Books.

Samih, M. 2013. 'Visiting the Orman Garden'. *Al-Ahram Weekly*, 7–13 November. http://weekly.ahram.org.eg/News/4560.aspx. Accessed 11 December 2018.

Sawaf, L. 2016. 'The armed forces and Egypt's land'. *Mada Masr*, 26 April. www.madamasr.com/en/2016/04/26/feature/economy/the-armed-forces-and-%20egypts-land/. Accessed 12 December 2018.

Sayigh, Y. 2012. 'Above the state: The officers' republic in Egypt'. *The Carnegie Papers*, 1–33.

Scott, J. 1985. *Weapons of the Weak: Everyday Forms of Peasant Resistance*. New Haven: Yale University Press.

Séjourné, M. 2009. 'The history of informal settlements'. *Cairo's Informal Areas between Urban Challenges and Hidden Potentials: Facts, Voices, Visions*. www.citiesalliance.org/sites/citiesalliance.org/files/CA_Docs/resources/Cairo%27s%20Informal%20Areas%20Between%20Urban%20Challenges%20and%20Hidden%20Potentials/CairosInformalAreas_fulltext.pdf. Accessed 15 July 2010.

Shakran, K. 2016.'The uneven city: Planning insurgencies in Ramlet Bulaq and Maspero Triangle'. MA thesis, University of California, Irvine. Permalink https://escholarship.org/uc/item/2441k3s4. Accessed 25 September 2019.

Shenker, J. 2011. 'Egyptian student protests hit elite Cairo university'. *Guardian*, 15 September. www.theguardian.com/world/2011/sep/15/egyptian-student-protests-american-university-cairo. Accessed 11 December 2018.

Shukrallah, S., and Y. Shawkat. 2017. 'Analysis: Government policy commodifies housing'. The Built Environment Observatory. http://marsadomran.info/en/policy_analysis/2017/11/1218/. Accessed June 2018.

Simone, A. 2013. 'Cities of uncertainty: Jakarta, the urban majority, and inventive political technologies'. *Theory, Culture & Society*, 30:7–8, 243–63. https://doi.org/10.1177/0263276413501872.

Simone, A. 2015. 'Sociability and endurance in Jakarta'. In H. Frichot, C. Gabrielsson, and J. Metzger (eds), *Deleuze and the City*. Edinburgh: Edinburgh University Press.

Simone, A., and E. Pieterse. 2017. *New Urban Worlds: Inhabiting Dissonant Times*. Cambridge: Polity.

Simone, A., and V. Rao. 2011. 'Securing the majority: Living through uncertainty in Jakarta'. *International Journal of Urban and Regional Research*, 36:2, 1–21. https://doi.org/10.1111/j.1468-2427.2011.01028.x.

Sims, D. 2014. *Egypt's Desert Dreams: Development or Disaster?* Cairo and New York: American University in Cairo Press.

Sims, D., and M. Séjourné. 2000. *Residential Informality in Greater Cairo: Typologies, Representative Areas, Quantification, Valuation, and Causal Factors*. Cairo: ECES.

Sklair, L. 2017. *The Icon Project: Architecture, Cities, and Capitalist Globalization*. Oxford: Oxford University Press.

Taha, A., and C. Combs. 2012. 'Of drama and performance: Transformative discourses of the revolution'. In S. Mehrez (ed.), *Translating Egypt's Revolution: The Language of Tahrir*. Cairo: American University in Cairo Press.

Tarek, S. 2015. 'Suicidal rates increase: Reflection of new realities in Egypt'. *Ahram Online*, 20 January. http://english.ahram.org.eg/%20NewsContent/1/151/120751/Egypt/Features/Suicide-rates-increase-Reflection-of-new-realities.aspx. Accessed 22 September 2016.

Al Tawy, A. 2018. 'Residents of Cairo's Maspero Triangle cling on as demolition looms'. *Ahram Online*, 10 March. http://english.ahram.org.eg/NewsContent/1/64/292339/Egypt/Politics-/Residents-of-Cairos-Maspero-Triangle-cling-on-as-d.aspx. Accessed 25 September 2019.

Temlali, Y. 2008. 'Albert Cossery: De l'usage révolutionnaire de la dérision'. *Babelmed*, 25 June. www.babelmed.net/article/1945-albert-cossery-de-lusage-revolutionnaire-de-la-derision/. Accessed 15 August 2018.

Teo, Y. 2017. 'Singapore sociology, after meritocracy'. *Global Dialogue*, 7:1. http://globaldialogue.isa-sociology.org/singapore-sociology-after-meritocracy/. Accessed 10 December 2018.

Thiele, H. n.d. 'Conversion and new construction of the Goethe Institute in Cairo'. *Al-Habashi*. www.alhabashi.com/?portfolio=conversion-and-new-construction-of-the-goethe-institute-in-cairo. Accessed 11 December 2018.

Thompson, E. P. 1966. *The Making of the English Working Class*. New York: Vintage Books.

Transparency International. 2018. 'The officers' republic: The Egyptian military and abuse of power'. Transparency International: Defence and Security. http://ti-defence.org/publications/the-officers-republic/. Accessed 12 December 2018.

Veblen, T. 1953. *The Theory of the Leisure Class*. New York: New American Library.

Weizman, E. 2005. 'Walking through walls: Soldiers as architects in the Israeli/ Palestinian conflict'. Lecture at the symposium 'Archipelago of exception: Sovereignties of extraterritoriality', 10–11 November 2005. Posted at Public Space, 3 June 2009. www.publicspace.org/multimedia/-/post/walking-through-walls-soldiers-as-architects-in-the-israeli-palestinian-conflict. Accessed 10 December 2018.

Westmoreland, M. R. 2016. 'Street scenes: The politics of revolutionary video in Egypt'. *Visual Anthropology*, 29, 243–62. https://doi.org/10.1080/08949468.2016.1154420.

Williams, A. 2015. 'Ambitious plan unveiled to create new Egyptian capital'. *New Atlas*, 23 March. https://newatlas.com/capital-cairo-egypt-som/36648/. Accessed 31 July 2015.

Youssef, A. 2014. 'Egypt's cinematic gems: Cairo 30'. *Mada Masr*, 13 December. www.madamasr.com/en/2014/12/13/feature/culture/egypts-cinematic-gems-cairo-30/. Accessed 11 December 2018.

Zeinobia. 2018. 'World Suicide Prevention Day: Something to worry about in Egypt'. *Egyptian Chronicles: 7000 Years and Counting*, 10 September. https://egyptianchronicles.blogspot.com/2018/09/world-suicide-prevention-day-more-than.html. Accessed 10 September 2018.

## Sources in Arabic

Abd al-Aziz, B. 2013. *Al-Taabuur*. Cairo: Dar al-Tanweer.

'Abdel Qader, N. 2015. 'Half a million buildings are subject to death elevators'. *Masrawy*, 5 October. www.masrawy.com/News/News_Reports/details/2015/10/5/668366/. Accessed 11 December 2018.

Abu Golayyel, H. 2004. *Lusus mutaqa'idun*. Cairo: Merit Publishing House.

Arab Network for Human Rights. 2018. 'Index of social and workers' protests in June 2018'. The Arab Network for Human Rights, 25 June. www.anhri.info/?p=164. Accessed 12 December 2018.

Al-Aswany, A. 2007. *'Imaarat Ya'qubyan*. Cairo: Madbouly Books.

Bahaa El-Din, L. 2016. 'In Bahaa El-Din's home'. *Akhbar al-Adab*, 20 August. www.masress.com/hawadeth/279791. Accessed 12 December 2018.

EREM News. 2019. 'The Nahda prisoners'. *Erem News*, 21 March. www.eremnews.com/news/arab-world/egypt/1735453. Accessed 25 September 2019.

Fadel, M. 2018. 'Surprises in the "Death Elevator" incident in Banha'. *Al-Masry al-Youm*, 31 January. www.masrawy.com/news/news_regions/details/2018/1/31/1253801/. Accessed 11 December 2018.

Fishere, E. C. 2012. *Baab al-khuruug*. Cairo: Daar al-Shorouk.

al-Gallad, N. 2018. 'After the Banha incident: Six steps when elevators collapse'. *Masrawy*, 31 January. www.masrawy.com/howa_w_hya/relationship/details/2018/1/31/1253323/. Accessed 11 December 2018.

al-Guindi, A. 2018a. 'Final report of "the death elevator of Banha's University Hospital": The company made some illusive maintenance'. *Al-Masry al-Youm*, 13 February. www.almasryalyoum.com/news/details/1258424. Accessed 11 December 2018.

al-Guindi, A. 2018b. 'Surprise in the technical committee's report on "the death elevator" incident'. *Al-Masry al-Youm*, 4 February. www.almasryalyoum.com/news/details/1254440. Accessed 11 December 2018.

Guweida, F. 2017. 'Suuq al-iquaaraat wal, adaalat al-igtimaiyya' (The real-estate market and social equity). *Al-Ahram*, 21 September, p. 13.

Ibrahim, S. 1998. *Dhat*. Cairo: Dar al-Mustaqbal al-Araby.

Kamel, A. 2018. 'After Banha's disaster: An elevator's falling with nine football players in Beni Suef'. *Al-Masry al-Youm*, 3 February. www.masrawy.com/news/news_regions/details/2018/2/3/1255669/. Accessed 11 December 2018.

Khalil, M. M. 2018. 'Acquittal of Banha University hospital'. *Al-Masry al-Youm*, 1 February. www.almasryalyoum.com/news/details/1253418. Accessed 11 December 2018.

Mahfouz, N. 2006. *Al-Qahira al-jadida*. Cairo: Dar El-Shorouk.

Mounir, M. 2018. 'Banha University releases a statement on the elevator incident'. *Watany*, 30 January. www.wataninet.com/2018/01/جامعةبنهاتصدربياناحولحادثمصعدالج/. Accessed 11 December 2018.

Naaji, A. 2014. *Istikhdaam al-Hayaat*. Cairo: Marsoum.

Negm, N. 2012a. 'Mohamed Mahmud, the first day (Al-Tahrir 11/12/2012)'. *Al-Tahrir*, 12 November.

Negm, N. 2012b. 'The second day (bis), 15/11/2012'. *Nashron*, 15 November. www.nashron.com/6793. Accessed 20 November 2014.

Negm, N. 2012c. 'Mohamed Mahmud, the fourth day (bis)'. *Al-Tahrir*, 24 November.

Negm, N. 2012d. 'The third day'. *Al-Tahrir*, 17 November, http://almogaz.com/news/opinion/2012/11/19/585010. Accessed 25 September 2019.

Negm, N. 2013. 'Would Ikhwan go to Tahrir on Mohamed Mahmoud's memorial to dance on the bodies of those who betrayed them?' *Al-Mogaz*, www.christian-dogma.com/t413369. Accessed 4 December 2018.

Rabii', M. 2014. *'Utaarid*. Cairo: Dar al-Tanweer.

al-Sennawi, A. 2015. 'The paradox of the security crisis'. *Al-Shorouk*, 26 August. www.shorouknews.com/columns/view.aspx?cdate=26082015&id=6c47c8e4–3b04–4807-a1db-a76ada88ba35. Accessed 12 December 2018.

Tawfik, A. K. 2008. *Utopia*. Cairo: Merit Publishing House.

Tawfik, M. 2003. *Tifl shaqi ismuhu Antar*. Cairo: Merit Publishing House.

Youssef, A. 2018. 'Considerations in Nahda's dispersal'. *Al-Watan*, 7 February. www.elwatannews.com/news/details/3043114. Accessed 11 December 2018.

## Internet sources

'3 Daqat – Abu Ft. Yousra'. YouTube. www.youtube.com/watch?v=ejvpVhvKesM. Accessed 12 December 2018.

'Albert Cossery: Portrait entre Paris et le Caire'. 1991. YouTube. www.youtube.com/watch?v=ip74Zse1Crg. Accessed 8 December 2018.

'Archive 858, an Archive of Resistance'. *Mosireen*. http://mosireen.org.

'Arkan Real Estate'. www.facebook.com/arkanoctober/photos/rpp.1058981057456289/1600418996645823/?type=3&theater. Accessed January 2018.

'Attorney general orders the imprisonment of the responsible officials in the Banha elevator incident'. 2018. *Al-Masry al-Youm*, 3 February. www.almasryalyoum.com/news/details/1254242. Accessed 11 December 2018.

'AUC students describing their neighborhood: A short series'. 2015. *Cairobserver*, 3 November. http://cairobserver.com/post/132433665694/auc-students-describing-their-neighborhoods-a. Accessed 11 December 2018.

'Between the Sky and Earth' (فيلم بين السماء والارض). www.dailymotion.com/video/x30dfo2. Accessed 10 June 2018.

'Beverly Hills Development'. http://beverlyhills-eg.com/?page_id=9. Accessed 25 September 2019.

'Cairo Festival City Mall'. http://digitaleg.com/Cairo-Festival-City/cairo-festival-city-mall/shopping.html#category. Accessed 13 September 2019.

'The Capital Cairo'. https://vimeo.com/180717384. Accessed 28 September 2018.

D-CAF (Downtown Contemporary Arts Festival). https://d-caf.org/wp-content/uploads/2015/01/Digital-English-Brochure.pdf. Accessed 25 September 2019.

'Details of Warraq riots against campaign to remove squatters'. 2017. *Egypt Today*, 17 July. www.egypttoday.com/Article/1/12136/Details-of-Warraq-riots-against-campaign-to-remove-squatters. Accessed 25 September 2019.

Egyptian Armed Forces/Ministry of Defense. www.mod.gov.eg/ModWebSite/Default.aspx. Accessed 25 September 2019.

'Egyptian revolution of 2011'. Wikipedia. https://en.wikipedia.org/wiki/Egyptian_revolution_of_2011. Accessed 12 December 2018.

'Egypt's army distributes "largest food supplies" in bid to ease economic hardships'. 2016. *Ahram Online*, 1 November. http://english.ahram.org.eg/NewsContent/1/64/247077/Egypt/Politics-/Egypts-army-distributes-largest-food-supplies-in-b.aspx. Accessed 10 December 2018.

'Egypt – the New Capital Cairo'. 2015. https://vimeo.com/129894528. Accessed 28 September 2018.

'*Fawq mustawa al-shubuhaat*' (*Above Reproach*). 2016. YouTube. Episode 1. www.youtube.com/watch?v=eB2k6FT2LfQ&list=PLmucH9T-TQvnxBIr-WsNSKMjDTXpizXbZ. Accessed 23 September 2019.

'From Tahrir Square to Emaar Square'. 2014. *Cairobserver*, 23 February. http://cairobserver.com/post/77533681187/from-tahrir-square-to-emaar-square#.%20WHN1ptLhCM8. Accessed 12 December 2018.

'Goethe-Institut und Deutscher Akademischer Austauschdienst in Kairo'. Bundesamt für Bauwesen und Raumordnung. www.bbr.bund.de/BBR/DE/Bauprojekte/Ausland/KulturundBildungseinrichtungen/GoetheInstitutKairo/gikairo.html. Accessed 11 December 2018.

'Government officials: Phosphate leaks in the Nile River are not going to affect drinking water'. 2015. *Mada Masr*, 22 April. https://madamasr.com/ar/2015/04/22/news/-مجتمع/مسؤولون-حكوميون-تسرب-الفوسفات-في-نهر/. Accessed 10 May 2015.

'HarassMap: Stop sexual harassment, together'. HarassMap. https://harassmap.org/en/. Accessed 12 December 2018.

Al-Ismaelia. n.d. *Buildings We Own*. http://al-ismaelia.com/buildings. Accessed 18 May 2016.

'al-Kahuul'. 2013. YouTube. www.youtube.com/watch?v=pSabZiMoXD8&feature=youtu.be. Accessed 12 December 2018.

Majid al-Futtuaim. www.majidalfuttaim.com/en/who-we-are. Accessed 17 September 2019.

'Maspero Demonstrations'. Wikipedia. https://en.wikipedia.org/wiki/Maspero_demonstrations. Accessed 25 September 2019.

'Masr Bitnadikom – Hesham Abbas'. YouTube. www.youtube.com/watch?v=HcF0XJNRuo. Accessed 12 December 2018.

'Metro is not a suicidal destination'. 2018. *Egypt Today*, 4 September. www.egypttoday.com/Article/1/57109/Metro-is-not-a-suicidal-destination-Official. Accessed 4 September 2018.

'Mohamed Mahmoud Street's incidents'. Wikizero. www.wikizero.com/ar/أحداث_محمد_محمود. Accessed 5 December 2018.

Mohamed Ramzy 'Omar. www.ramzyomar.com. Accessed 18 May 2017.

'More than 150 given 2 to 5 years in prison for protesting Egypt–Saudi islands deal'. 2016. *Ahram Online*, 14 May. http://english.ahram.org.eg/NewsContent/1/64/216807/ Egypt/Politics-/More-than–given–to–years-in-prison-for-protesti.aspx. Accessed 12 December 2018.

'New Cairo Campus'. American University in Cairo. www.aucegypt.edu/about/ visitor-information/new-cairo-campus. Accessed 15 May 2017.

'Oriana Villas'. YouTube. www.youtube.com/watch?v=knISXPhNv1U (English: www. youtube.com/watch?v=uyX9mOSoluk). Accessed 13 September 2019.

'Ramadan series feature violence, psychological problems, negative portrayals of women: Egypt's Women's Council'. 2016. *Ahram Online*, 27 June. http://english. ahram.org.eg/News/231951.aspx. Accessed 11 December 2018.

'Regent's Park'. www.facebook.com/regentsparknewcairo/photos/a.112925532066520. 1073741827.112912532067820/2265213553504373/?type=3&theater. Accessed 25 September 2019.

'Sniper targeting eyes'. YouTube. www.youtube.com/watch?v=YZ5bgruvanM. Accessed 11 September 2019.

'Taj City'. 2015. www.tajcity.com/?source¼Eg&adsId¼4107. Accessed 15 August 2015.

'Testimonies of Mohamed Mahmud bear witness Mohamed Mahmud. Lest we never forget'. Al-Nadeem Centre. www.alnadeem.org/en/file/209/download?token=RMe. Accessed 15 September 2017.

'Traffic diverted in Zamalek in preparation for 3rd Metro line construction'. 2017. *Egypt Independent*, 26 July. www.egyptindependent.com/zamalek-traffic-diverted/. Accessed 11 December 2018.

'Vintage photo of the palace of H. H. Prince Hussein Kamel – later Sultan of Egypt & Sudan – currently the Orman Garden at Giza, Egypt, 1895 (demolished in 1955)'. Flickr. www.flickr.com/photos/kelisli/31205626203. Accessed 10 October 2018.

'World Youth Forum – the official song'. YouTube. www.youtube.com/watch?v=hPo HPBkp1VM. Accessed 12 December 2018.

# Index

Note: 'n.' after a page reference indicates the number of a note on that page; page numbers in *italic* refer to illustrations